Gender and Educational Achievement

Gender inequalities in education – in terms of systematic variations in access to educational institutions, in competencies, school grades and educational certificates along the axis of gender – have changed considerably over the course of the 20th century. Although this does not apply to all stages and areas of the educational career, it is particularly obvious when looking at upper secondary education. Before the major boost of educational expansion in the 1960s, women's participation in upper secondary general education, and their chances of successfully finishing this educational pathway, have been lower than men's. However, towards the end of the 20th century, women were outperforming men in many European countries and beyond.

The international contributions to this book attempt to shed light on the mechanisms behind gender inequalities and the changes made to reduce this inequality. Topics explored by the contributors include gender in science education in the UK; women's education in Luxembourg in the 19th and 20th century; the 'gender gap' debates and their rhetoric in the UK and Finland; sociological perspectives on the gender-equality discourse in Finland; changing gender differences in West Germany in the 20th century; the interplay of subjective well-being and educational attainment in Switzerland; and a psychological perspective on gender identities, gender-related perceptions, students' motivation, intelligence, personality and the interaction between student and teacher gender.

This book was originally published as a special issue of *Educational Research.*

Andreas Hadjar is Professor of Sociology of Education at the University of Luxembourg. His research interests centre on sociology of education, inequalities (class, gender and ethnicity), political sociology (particularly participation, social values and attitudes), well-being, methods of empirical research and international comparisons. His research and publications focus on education systems, inequalities, attitudes and values, well-being, school alienation and methods of social science research.

Sabine Krolak-Schwerdt is Professor of Educational Measurement at the University of Luxembourg. Her research topics include statistical and research methods, educational psychology and social cognition. She is a member of the advisory board of the *Journal of Educational Research Online* and an editorial consultant for journals including *Psychometrika*, the *American Educational Research Journal*, the *British Journal of Mathematical and Statistical Psychology*, the *Journal of Classification* and grant agencies including the German Research Foundation, Swiss National Science Foundation and the German Federal Ministry of Education and Research.

Karin Priem is Professor of History of Education at the University of Luxembourg. She has been president of the German History of Education Association (2007–2011), is a member of the international advisory board of the *Revue Suisse des Sciences de l'Éducation*, and is Secretary of the International Standing Conference for the History of Education. She is co-editor of two book series and her research focuses on the history of educational theories and concepts, the social, visual and material history of education and the history of entrepreneurship and education.

Sabine Glock is a member of the School of Education at the Bergische Universität Wuppertal, Germany. She studied Psychology and holds a PhD from the University of Saarland, Saarbrücken, Germany. Her research focuses on teachers' decision making and how the ethnic background of students influences teachers' academic achievement judgments or classroom management strategies. Her main research interest is implicit cognition, in particular implicit teacher attitudes toward ethnic minority students.

Gender and Educational Achievement

Edited by
**Andreas Hadjar, Sabine Krolak-Schwerdt,
Karin Priem and Sabine Glock**

Routledge
Taylor & Francis Group

LONDON AND NEW YORK

Evidence for
Excellence in
Education

First published 2016 by Routledge

2 Park Square, Milton Park, Abingdon, Oxfordshire OX14 4RN
711 Third Avenue, New York, NY 10017

Routledge is an imprint of the Taylor & Francis Group, an informa business

First issued in paperback 2018

British Library Cataloguing in Publication Data
A catalogue record for this book is available from the British Library

ISBN 13: 978-1-138-65505-8 (hbk)
ISBN 13: 978-1-138-39200-7 (pbk)

Typeset in Times New Roman
by RefineCatch Limited, Bungay, Suffolk

Publisher's Note
The publisher accepts responsibility for any inconsistencies that may have
arisen during the conversion of this book from journal articles to book chapters,
namely the possible inclusion of journal terminology.

Disclaimer
Every effort has been made to contact copyright holders for their permission to
reprint material in this book. The publishers would be grateful to hear from any
copyright holder who is not here acknowledged and will undertake to rectify
any errors or omissions in future editions of this book.

Contents

Citation Information

The chapters in this book were originally published in *Educational Research*, volume 56, issue 2 (June 2014). When citing this material, please use the original page numbering for each article, as follows:

Editorial

Gender and educational achievement
Andreas Hadjar, Sabine Krolak-Schwerdt, Karin Priem and Sabine Glock
Educational Research, volume 56, issue 2 (June 2014) pp. 117–125

Chapter 1

Females in science: a contradictory concept?
Ruth Watts
Educational Research, volume 56, issue 2 (June 2014) pp. 126–136

Chapter 2

The construction of 'female citizens': a socio-historical analysis of girls' education in Luxembourg
Catherina Schreiber
Educational Research, volume 56, issue 2 (June 2014) pp. 137–154

Chapter 3

How gender became sex: mapping the gendered effects of sex-group categorisation onto pedagogy, policy and practice
Gabrielle Ivinson
Educational Research, volume 56, issue 2 (June 2014) pp. 155–170

Chapter 4

Troubling discourses on gender and education
Elina Lahelma
Educational Research, volume 56, issue 2 (June 2014) pp. 171–183

Chapter 5

Reversal of gender differences in educational attainment: an historical analysis of the West German case
Rolf Becker
Educational Research, volume 56, issue 2 (June 2014) pp. 184–201

For any permission-related enquiries please visit:
http://www.tandfonline.com/page/help/permissions

Notes on Contributors

Rolf Becker is Professor (Chair: Sociology of Education) and Director of the Department of Sociology of Education at the University of Bern, Switzerland. His research interests include educational sociology, analysis of social structures, and labour market and mobility research.

Christine Eckert is a Researcher in the Department of Educational Psychology at the University of Heidelberg, Germany. Her research interests include the improvement of university teaching, self-regulation of university processes and gender differences in educational success.

Sabine Glock is a member of the School of Education at the Bergische Universität Wuppertal, Germany. She studied Psychology and holds a PhD from the University of Saarland, Saarbrücken, Germany. Her research focuses on teachers' decision making and how the ethnic background of students influences teachers' academic achievement judgments or classroom management strategies. Her main research interest is implicit cognition, in particular implicit teacher attitudes toward ethnic minority students.

Samuel Greiff is Professor of Educational Assessment at the University of Luxembourg. His research interests include educational assessment, problem solving, and multivariate statistics and structural equation modelling.

Andreas Hadjar is Professor of Sociology of Education at the University of Luxembourg. His research interests center on sociology of education, inequalities (class, gender and ethnicity), political sociology (particularly participation, social values and attitudes), well-being, methods of empirical research and international comparisons. His research and publications focus on education systems, inequalities, attitudes and values, well-being, school alienation and methods of social science research.

Bettina Hannover is Professor in the Division of School and Teaching Research, Department of Education and Psychology, at the Freie Universität Berlin, Germany. Her works combines the pursuit of basic and applied issues from social and educational psychology, in order to gain a better understanding of self and identity related processes.

Jarkko Hautamäki is a Professor Emeritus at the Centre for Educational Assessment at the University of Helsinki, Finland. He researches educational assessment, primary education teaching methods, developmental psychology and early childhood education.

Anke Heyder is a Research Associate of the Department of Education and Psychology at the Freie Universität Berlin, Germany. Her research focuses include teacher education, gender stereotypes, and gender differences in educational attainment and engagement.

Gabrielle Ivinson is Professor of Education at the School of Education, University of Aberdeen, UK. Her recent projects involve working with a range of artists to co-produce art forms and artefacts to enable young people to communicate with persons in authority by drawing on the affective power of art to move.

Ursula Kessels is Professor of Educational Research/Heterogeneity and Education at the Freie Universität Berlin, Germany. Based on her background in educational and social psychology, her research interests regarding heterogeneity include stereotypes, self-concept and identity, motivation, attitudes and how all these factors interact for explaining gender and/or ethnic differences in academic outcomes.

Katarina Krkovic is a Research Associate in Clinical Psychology and Psychotherapy at the University of Hamburg, Germany. Her research interests include the roles of teacher and student gender in student-teacher interaction.

Sabine Krolak-Schwerdt is Professor of Educational Measurement at the University of Luxembourg. Her research topics include statistical and research methods, educational psychology and social cognition. She is a member of the advisory board of the *Journal of Educational Research Online* and an editorial consultant for journals including *Psychometrika*, the *American Educational Research Journal*, the *British Journal of Mathematical and Statistical Psychology*, the *Journal of Classification* and grant agencies including the German Research Foundation, Swiss National Science Foundation and the German Federal Ministry of Education and Research.

Sirkku Kupiainen is a Researcher in the Centre for Educational Assessment at the University of Helsinki, Finland. Her expertise lies in educational assessment, educational evaluation and education policy.

Elina Lahelma is Professor of Education at the University of Helsinki, Finland. The focus of her research is in the fields of sociology of education, gender studies in education and ethnographic methodology.

Martin Latsch is a Research Associate in the Department of Child and Adolescent Psychiatry and Psychotherapy at the Otto-von-Guericke University Magdeburg, Germany. His research in the Department of Education and Psychology at the Freie Universität Berlin, Germany focused on gender-related disparities in educational attainment.

Karin Priem is Professor of History of Education at the University of Luxembourg. She has been president of the German History of Education Association (2007–2011), is a member of the international advisory board of the *Revue Suisse des Sciences de l'Éducation*, and is Secretary of the International Standing Conference for the History of Education. She is co-editor of two book series and her research focuses on the history of educational theories and concepts, the social, visual and material history of education and the history of entrepreneurship and education.

Robin Samuel is a Professor at the University of Luxembourg and an Honorary Fellow at the University of Edinburgh, UK. His research addresses youth lifestyles, migration and transitions; social stratification and well-being; the role of cognitive and non-cognitive characteristics for social mobility; and the application of Bayesian statistics to fallacies.

Catherina Schreiber is a Postdoctoral Researcher at the Institute for Applied Educational Sciences at the University of Luxembourg. Her research deals with the development of the Luxembourgish curriculum.

Birgit Spinath is Professor of Educational Psychology at the University of Heidelberg, Germany. Her research interests include motivational conditions for learning and performance, self-regulation in educational processes, teacher education and the university research field as a labour market.

Ricarda Steinmayr is Chair of Educational Psychology at the Technische Universität Dortmund, Germany. Her research interests include determinants of school performance, gender differences in educational achievement, motivational conditions for learning and performance, and emotional intelligence and knowledge.

Mari-Pauliina Vainikainen is Project Manager at the Centre for Educational Assessment at the University of Helsinki, Finland. She is interested in the development of learning to learn skills – cognitive competencies and learning-related attitudes – in primary school, and the role of group processes in explaining differences in the development of pupils' learning-related attitudes.

Ruth Watts is Emeritus Professor of History of Education at the University of Birmingham, UK. Her research interests are in the history of education and gender and she has published much on these, her latest being *Women in Science: A Social and Cultural History* (Routledge, 2007).

Gender differences in educational attainment

In many countries, gender differences in educational success are part of long standing political, public and scientific debates about education. Whereas, for example, at the end of the nineteenth century and in the 1960s, the educational disadvantages of women (but also their difference) were central to debates about gender, by the end of the 20th century attention had turned to boys, their difference from girls and their lack of educational success. However, though the focus of the gender difference debate changed very much in some respects, in other ways there is a common thread. Before educational expansion in Europe, girls attained lower educational levels than boys. Upper secondary schooling and tertiary education were male-dominated. After the 1960s, girls benefited greatly from the educational expansion. Although their superior performances in some school subjects (e.g. languages) is not at all new, there has been an increase in the opportunities for transition and successful completion of upper secondary education. In many countries, girls are now more likely than boys to transition to upper secondary schools (Hannum and Buchmann 2005; Hadjar and Berger 2011). However, the actual transition rates to tertiary education for women being eligible to enter Higher Education institutions are still lower than those of men, and there is still a rather persistent gender separation in the choice of study subjects and vocational options.

This special issue focuses on current educational inequalities but also brings fresh insights by looking back in time to trace continuities and discontinuities, employing a historical perspective. It centres, however, on the current debate on the underperformance of boys in comparison with girls. This is often regarded as a European phenomenon, but is also visible outside Europe (Hannum and Buchmann 2005). While focusing on gender and educational achievement, we employ a broader definition of achievement that covers all aspects of educational success – including educational transitions and school grades. Although school grades and transitions are linked to achievement and ability, they are indicative of a type of success in school that does not necessarily equate to aptitude and is, therefore, inextricably constrained by assessment processes. For the individual school students, it can be argued that such aspects of educational success are, in reality, even more important than actual ability, since school grades are usually 'what counts' for the greater part of a continuing educational career, school pathways and the labour market.

The main aims of the special issue are to theorise gender inequalities from different disciplinary perspectives and to bring together different methodological approaches. This also involves consideration of practical implications for improving boys' and girls' school outcomes. Within the scientific debate about gender differences in educational success, several aspects are discussed that include long-term perspectives on gender debates about differences of educational careers, school student characteristics as well as institutional settings and the role of the teacher. The special issue comprises a collection of papers that explore different aspects of the topic and deal with gender differences in educational success from a range of disciplinary perspectives, including historical, socio-logical and psychological approaches.

What is known about gender differences in educational success?

From the perspective of gender differences in education today, patterns of gender inequalities that are specific to a certain stage within the educational career need to be considered. A recent meta-analysis of empirical studies from Germany and Switzerland (Blossfeld et al. 2009; Hadjar 2011) indicates certain distinctions: there are no gender 'differences' as such in attendance at pre-schooling, as girls and boys frequent pre-school institutions to the same extent. What can be recognised at this early stage, though, are gender-typical behavioural and interest patterns in terms of expressions of gendered socialisation. Boys, more often than girls, start primary school late after being diagnosed with learning difficulties. In primary school, gender differences in competenc-es develop, with girls scoring more highly in reading and boys outperforming girls in mathematics and sciences. In highly stratified education systems with early selection into different school tracks that lead to different educational certificates like the compul-sory school leaving certificate, intermediate school leaving certificate or A level certifi-cate (being linked to very different career and life chances, as is the case in Germany, Luxembourg, Switzerland), the likelihood of boys being placed in a lower secondary school track is greater than for girls (Caro et al. 2009; Klapproth et al. 2013). Addition-ally, boys drop out of school more often. Results of a Swiss study (Hadjar and Lupatsch 2010; Hadjar et al. 2012) – based on a random school sample – shows that the school grades of girls are significantly better than those of boys in language subjects (German, French, English) and Music. In terms of other subjects, there are no gender differences in educational success to be noted. No gender differences favouring boys were found. A study conducted in Luxembourg revealed a higher tendency for boys to be placed more often than girls on lower secondary school tracks (Klapproth et al. 2013). However, these differences diminished when academic achievement was controlled for – suggest-ing no gender differences in tracking decisions when boys academically perform as well as girls (Klapproth et al. 2013). Nonetheless, there is a clear gender gap in school marks: girls typically outperform boys. In the Programme for International Student Assessment (PISA; OECD 2013) competence tests, the superior performance of girls in languages is much greater than that of boys in mathematics. In many countries, more women than men start studying at Higher Education institutions. However, the transition rates to Higher Education – i.e. the percentage of people being eligible to access Higher Education who actually start Higher Education studies – are still higher for men. In aca-demia, the tendency of the'leaky pipeline' (Leemann, Dubach, and Boes 2010) is still visible: with every step in the academic hierarchy, the overrepresentation of men increases – with only a small percentage of women being full professors at the highest academic level.

There are several theoretical and empirical explanations for the different kinds of gender inequality in education. In terms of the long-term underperformance and under-representation of women and the evolution of that situation, an explanation centres around educational investments and educational motivations. Following human capital theory (G.S. Becker 1964), investments in women's education only pay off when women are able to convert their education into income and status at the labour market. From this perspective, the main factors behind the traditional pattern of lower educational participation in the case of women had been their higher affiliation to the household and to child-rearing activities, as well as their lower opportunities in the labour market. The increasing educational participation of women was strongly linked to the changing gender images and the higher labour force participation of women – partly caused by a stronger demand for labour in service professions. Female life-prospects and life plans altered very much during the last decades, occasioned by a modernisation of life plans – in particular, the decreasing social and economic significance of marriage and the increasing importance of labour force participation for earning a living among women – and also the institutional change of the educational and social systems that make education more attractive both to women and men (Breen et al. 2010). The increase in educational returns for women is the major mechanism behind the increasing educational motivation of women, their higher participation in upper secondary schooling and their increasing participation in higher education (Buchmann, DiPrete, and McDaniel 2008; DiPrete and Buchmann 2006; Buchmann and DiPrete 2006). Therefore, it can be argued that the change in the educational aspirations of girls and the anticipated greater opportunities for women in the labour market (particularly regarding public services) are the main causes of the increase in the educational success of girls (c.f. R. Becker and Müller 2011). However, there are still persistent patterns in respect of vocational choice and choice of study. Gendered interests and life plans – being related to socialised gender stereotypes – still reinforce work force separation in terms of women more often becoming nurses, teachers or engaging in other service professions, and men being more likely to choose professions that are characterised by higher authority, prestige and status.

Within the scientific debate surrounding boys who fail at school, several aspects have been discussed, focusing on school students and their characteristics, as well as motivational, attitudinal and behavioural issues. Boys lack intrinsic motivation, have less of an interest in school and are more likely to feel alienated at school. Boys also achieve lower scores with regard to their subjective well-being at school. In addition, there are gender differences in behaviours that are relevant to educational success.

Most approaches highlight different *behavioural patterns* at school: A behavioural cause of the lower educational achievement of boys is linked to non-conformity and antisocial behaviour in the school environment. Findings indicate behaviour-specific gender gaps: boys indulge more often in more offensive behaviour, such as disturbances during lessons and violence; and they conform less (Eagly and Chrvala 1986). Boys also respond more often to failing experiences and frustration by aggressive and violent behaviour (Hannover 2004). This is associated with lower educational success, as it implies disruptive behaviour that diverts boys from successful learning and may be sanctioned by teachers (Salisbury and Jackson 1996; Francis, Skelton, and Read 2010). Furthermore, Weinert and Helmke (1997) described boys as having "lazybones syndrome". It has been suggested that boys frequently make less effort and have less of a sense of duty than girls. Furthermore, leisure-time behaviours outside school are also of importance: boys are less school-oriented than girls, and are more oriented towards leisure time. One frequently cited cause of boys' relative lack of success at school is media consumption. Boys spend more of their leisure time than girls in front of the computer playing games and watching films that are not appropriate for their age (Mössle et al. 2010). This may draw some of their attention away from learning, as well as diverting some of their cognitive abilities that they need for school-related activities.

It is helpful to consider school delinquency as rooted in two cognitive representations: school alienation and non-egalitarian gender role orientations. According to findings of Hadjar et al. (2012), boys are more alienated from school and adhere to more traditional gender images than girls. Both higher school alienation and higher preference for non-egalitarian gender roles go along with a higher school delinquency and, finally, lead to a lower educational success. According to the Stage-Environment-Fit Theory of Eccles and Midgley (1989), the gender difference in *school alienation* is due to several mechanisms: on the one hand, girls' needs seem to be better fulfilled by school; and on the other hand, girls can adapt much better to the expectations of school (Hascher and Hagenauer 2010). Referring to the theory of subculture (Cohen 1955), it can be argued that school alienation is a kind of reaction of boys whose needs are not fulfilled at school. School alienation is an expression of resistance to school in the sense of Willis (1977), who identified the opposition of working-class boys to school, its authoritative structures and its middle-class culture: working-class boys joined motorcycle gangs and left school to enter the labour market earlier than others. A main consequence of school alienation on the behavioural level is a lack of participation in learning activities and a lack of conformity to school rules, namely higher deviance (Murdock 1999). This even-tually leads to lower school success and might even result in school dropout (Vallerand, Fortier, and Guay 1997). The increasing emotional and physical distance from school and the decreasing identification of the school students means a lack of resources to cope with experiences of failing in school (Hascher and Hagenauer 2010).

The *traditional image of male identity*, which includes dominant, 'go-getter' or even deviant roles, is incompatible with contemporary schools. Non-egalitarian boys cannot gain approval by being good at school, but must instead express a dislike of school around their peer groups. Characteristics such as conformity, cooperation and submis-sion, that might be important for educational success, are devalued as 'female', and so is educational success in some socialisation environments (Frosh, Phoenix, and Pattman 2002). In the British discourse on failing boys, traditional gender-role patterns are addressed as a 'laddish construction' (Francis, Skelton, and Read 2010). The laddish attitude is anti-academic: hard work and school achievement are devalued. The school culture and the 'laddish culture' are, in this sense, antagonistic. 'Laddish attitudes' lead to a disassociation or disintegration from school, are expressed in deviant behaviours and are, therefore, negatively associated with educational success. In particular, some scholars (Willis 1977; Martino 1999) highlight that this 'laddish' construction of masculinity implies a devaluation of schoolwork, diligence and application as feminine; especially among working-class boys. School alienation is expected to be highly gender-specific.

Moving the focus from school students to *teachers*, female teachers have been at the centre of the debate regarding boys who fail at school from the beginning. The idea put forward, for example, by Diefenbach and Klein (2002) is that female teachers interpret and respond to boys' behaviour at school in a different way than male teachers. The dif-ferent socialisation experiences of female teachers and boys may result in a lack of understanding and therefore in conscious or unconscious discrimination. From this point of view, the feminisation of the profession of the (primary) school teacher (which in German-speaking countries already has been at stake during the nineteenth century and, then, was put on the political agenda of male teacher unions to fight the promotion of female teachers by feminist movements) has been expected to lead to a feminine school culture that may be a main cause of the lack of success experienced by boys. However, recent studies do not support this idea: on the individual level, the gender of the teacher has been shown not to have an influence on boys' educational success, and the argu-mentation of the feminisation of schooling does not explain the gender gap with regard to educational success (Francis, Skelton, and Read 2010; Neugebauer, Helbig, and

Landmann 2010). On the other hand, it may be useful to consider the stereotypes held by both male and female teachers about boys and girls (when related to potential interests and abilities in different school subjects) which may serve as "anchors" for evaluations of school students' performances. The stereotypical assumptions that boys do not perform well in languages and that girls are not good at mathematics may influence the grades given out by teachers (Ziegler, Kuhn, and Heller 1998; Hörstermann, Krolak-Schwerdt, and Fischbach 2010). Moreover, other student-related stereotypes might be even more negative and pronounced for boys (Glock and Krolak-Schwerdt 2013). For instance, race has been shown to influence teachers' assessment judgements (e.g. McCombs and Gay 1988). Students may experience a double disadvantage when they are male (Parks and Kennedy 2007). Quantitative results of a Swiss study (Hadjar and Lupatsch 2011) also indicate that female teachers do not discriminate against boys. The gender of the teacher turns out to be of some (minor) importance for the interest levels of boys and girls: for example, boys being instructed by a male German teacher are slightly more interested in this ("feminine") subject than boys with a female German teacher. This speaks for the need of more heterogeneity among the teachers and not for gender-homogeneous teaching.

This special Issue on gender and achievement

In order to capture some of the breadth of the issues discussed above, the papers in this special issue are organised along three axes. From historical and philosophical perspectives, the first axis addresses questions such as how gender as an educational issue and related potential inequalities and (socially constructed) differences became manifest historically, and a theoretical reflection on the debate is provided. Along the second axis, these reflections are followed by sociological perspectives, consisting of papers with a general focus on educational inequalities from a longitudinal perspective, and also comprising papers that provide insights into empirical findings and the debate on gender inequalities in terms of specific countries. The last axis, on psychological perspectives, deals with factors such as identity, students' motivation, personality and intelligence. Again, the main objectives of this special issue include an exploration of gender variations in educational success from a cross-cultural and historical perspective, as well as the search for possible causes of the underperformance of boys. Aspects being discussed include school student characteristics as well as institutional settings and the role of the teachers. In summary, the following areas are central to the special issue:

- New historical perspectives on gender issues of education (gender and education in the sciences, education and citizenship), and biases of gender and sex as categories of research
- Gender and motivation for high achievement at school
- Traditional gender patterns and school achievement
- The teaching profession and the school achievement of boys and girls.

Next, we outline the papers in more detail.

Firstly, *Ruth Watts (University of Birmingham)* explores gender in science education in the UK and the US during the 19th and 20th centuries. In her studies of historical sources, she identifies a substantial gender gap within the sciences. Science, which was, and still is, perceived as a male or masculine domain followed gender-oriented patterns itself in its different disciplines that were organised in a gendered hierarchical, status-oriented order. Female domains of science were mainly biology, hygiene and medicine as they could be easily associated with professions in welfare, gynaecology and childcare or the domestic sphere. As a result, women in the sciences were channelled into less prestigious areas. *Catherina Schreiber (University of Luxembourg)* examines female citizenship in the Grand Duchy of Luxembourg at the end of the 19th and beginning 20th centuries. She analyses the wide spread narrative of women as a homogeneous category and group of citizens, usually explained by their 'nature', which she found contrasted by stratifying, class- and gender-related patterns as well as rural and urban schemes of femininity and masculinity in the education system and society in general. Hence female citizenship historically has taken diverse patterns and biographies. Its homogenisation by nature surely must be seen as a rhetorical political strategy to tie women to domestic domains. *Gabrielle Ivinson (Aberdeen University)* detects educational gender-gap discussions as a problematic rhetoric of quantification, which reduces gender to the two sex groups and related genetic or biological classifications. Ivinson argues that social and societal variables therefore slip out of the focus of research and simplify related educational issues.

Elina Lahelma (University of Helsinki) reviews the 'gender equality discourse' and the 'boy discourse', using examples from Finland in her discussion paper. Her main conclusions are that there have been no sustainable reforms drawing on either of these discourses and that both the interests of boys and of girls are often seen as antagonistic issues. As a solution, she recommends the concept of gender awareness that includes a consciousness of how differences, inequalities and 'otherness' are treated and often confirmed in educational practices, as well as the belief that these practices can be changed. Focusing on the case of West Germany, *Rolf Becker (University of Bern)* attempts to determine what processes have led to the reversal of gender differences in educational attainment in the post-1945 period. He relates the changing gender inequalities in particular to the increasing educational motivation of women – since their opportunities for realising their educational investments in status and income on the labour market have improved. His quantitative results regarding the educational attainment and social mobility of successive cohorts support this argument. The interplay between educational attainment and subjective well-being is analysed in the contribution of *Robin Samuel (University of Basel/Cambridge University)*. Subjective well-being appears to be a major source, but also a consequence of educational success. This relation is gendered – as conceptual consideration and empirical evidence suggest. The main conclusions derived from the quantitative results presented in the paper are that females seem to benefit more in terms of well-being, while males seem to be less affected by failure, and that women are more able to use subjective well-being as a personal resource.

From a psychological perspective, it is argued that reasons for the underrepresentation of female students in mathematics and science and for male students' lower school engagement might be gender identity and gender-related social perception. *Ursula Kessels, Anke Heyder, Martin Latsch, and Bettina Hannover (Free University Berlin)* combine these assumptions on gendered interests as identity-regulation model. Students seem to adjust their academic engagement according to their gender identity. Male students perceive school engagement as feminine, whereas female students acknowledge mathematics and science as a male domain. Particularly, male students' perception of school as feminine and their self-perception as masculine might contribute to the lower education success of male students. In order to reduce those gender identity differences, the authors propose strategies aimed at changing those gender-related social perceptions. Applying an individual differences approach, *Birgit Spinath, Christine Eckert*

(University of Heidelberg), and Ricarda Steinmayr (University of Dortmund) focus on the role of students' motivation, intelligence, and personality as possible moderators of gender differences in educational success. Girls achieve higher scores in verbal intelligence, show more self-discipline and are more agreeable than boys – all factors contributing to a higher adaptation to school environment. The reviewed empirical findings, however, reveal that those factors only partially account for gender differences. Although there is a relationship, individual differences cannot be suggested to causally explain gender differences due to absent experimental approaches. The authors conclude that changing the school environment might be a useful strategy to reduce gender differences. Although some empirical findings did not provide support for the assumption that teacher gender is a source of gender differences, teachers have been shown to prefer students of same gender. *Katarina Krkovic, Samuel Greiff (University of Luxembourg), Sirkku Kupiainen, Mari-Pauliina Vainikainen, and Jarkko Hautamäki (University of Helsinki)* present a Finnish study investigating whether the interaction between student and teacher gender contribute to biases in ability judgments. Male teachers do not judge the academic performance of male students more favourably than that of girls, and female teachers do not show a preference for evaluating female students' performance more favourably than those of boys. Independent of teacher gender, female students' potential success and first language performance was evaluated more favourably than those of male students, even when objective performance was controlled for. The authors conclude that although Finnish teachers might be aware of gender-biases they cannot fully disengage from gender-related influences.

In sum, all these different accounts show that it is worthwhile and necessary to take a closer look and to refrain from simplistic generalisations in regard to gender differences in academic achievement. Gender variations and their causes are multifaceted. In this special issue, historical perspectives, institutional and social structural factors as well as psychological factors are considered to compose a more holistic picture. Surely, it is the interplay of institutional settings, societal climate, individual motivation patterns, gender role orientations, parental resources and decisions as well as school structure and teacher evaluations and decisions that contribute to the genesis of gender inequalities. Gender differences in education are (and always were) a social problem as they exist along with disadvantages within the labour market and, finally, reduced life chances. Thus, the main and most general deduction from this special issue for policy makers is to provide both boys and girls with environments that support well-being, motivation and, thus, academic achievement.

Andreas Hadjar, Sabine Krolak-Schwerdt, Karin Priem and Sabine Glock
University of Luxembourg

References

Becker, G. S. 1964. *Human Capital*. New York: Columbia University Press.
Becker, R., and W. Müller. 2011. "Bildungsungleichheiten Nach Geschlecht Und Herkunft Im Wandel [Educational Inequalities Due to Gender and Origin are Changing]." In *Geschlechtsbezogene Bildungsungleichheiten*, edited by A. Hadjar, 55–75. Wiesbaden: VS Verlag.
Blossfeld, H., W. Bos, B. Hannover, D. Lenzen, D. Müller-Böling, M. Prenzel, and L. Wössmann, eds. 2009. *Geschlechterdifferenzen Im Bildungssystem. Jahresgutachten 2009* [Gender Differences in Educational Systems]. Wiesbaden: VS Verlag.

Breen, R., R. Luijkx, W. Muller, and R. Pollak. 2010. "Long-term Trends in Educational Inequality in Europe: Class Inequalities and Gender Differences." *European Sociological Review* 26: 31–48. doi:10.1093/esr/jcp001.

Buchmann, C., and T. A. DiPrete. 2006. "The Growing Female Advantage in College Completion: The Role of Family Background and Academic Achievement." *Annual Review of Sociology* 34: 515–541. doi:10.1177/000312240607100401.

Buchmann, C., T. A. DiPrete, and A. McDaniel. 2008. "Gender Inequalities in Education." *Annual Review of Sociology* 34: 319–337. doi:10.1146/annurev.soc.34.040507.134719.

Caro, D. H., J. Lenkeit, R. Lehmann, and K. Schwippert. 2009. "The Role of Academic Achievement Growth in School Track Recommendations." *Studies in Educational Evaluation* 35: 183–192. doi:10.1016/j.stueduc.2009.12.002.

Cohen, A. K. 1955. "A General Theory of Subcultures." In *The Subcultures Reader*, edited by K. Gelder and S. Thornton, 50–59. London: Routledge.

DiPrete, T. A., and C. Buchmann. 2006. "Gender-specific Trends in the Value of Education and the Emerging Gender Gap in College Completion." *Demography* 43: 1–24. doi:10.1353/dem.2006.0003.

Diefenbach, H., and M. Klein. 2002. "'Bringing Boys Back in': Soziale Ungleichheit Zwischen Den Geschlechtern Im Bildungssystem Zugunsten Von Jungen Am Beispiel Der Sekundarschulabschlüsse ['Bringing Boys Back in': Social Inequality Between the Sexes in the Educational System to the Disadvantaged]." *Zeitschrift Für Pädagogik* 48: 938–958. doi:10.1007/978-3-531-92779-4_14.

Eagly, A. H., and C. Chrvala. 1986. "Sex Differences in Conformity: Status and Gender-role Interpretations." *Psychology of Women Quarterly* 10: 938–958. doi:10.1111/j.1471-6402.1986.tb00747.x.

Eccles, J., and C. Midgley. 1989. "Stage-environment Fit." In *Research on Motivation in Education*, edited by C. Ames and R. Ames, 139–186. San Diego, CA: Academic Press.

Francis, B., C. Skelton, and B. Read. 2010. "The Simultaneous Production of Educational Achievement and Popularity: How do Some Pupils Accomplish It?" *British Educational Research Journal* 36: 317–340. doi:10.1080/01411920902919265.

Frosh, S., A. Phoenix, and R. Pattman. 2002. *Young Masculinities: Understanding Boys in Contemporary Society*. London: Palgrave.

Glock, S., and S. Krolak-Schwerdt. 2013. "Does Nationality Matter? The Impact of Stereotypical Expectations on Student Teachers' Judgments." *Social Psychology of Education* 16: 111–127. doi:10.1007/s11218-012-9197-z.

Hadjar, A. 2011. "Einleitung." In *Geschlechtsspezifische Bildungsungleichheiten* [Gender Inequalities in Education], edited by A. Hadjar, 7–19. Wiesbaden: VS Verlag.

Hadjar, A., and J. Berger. 2011. "Geschlechtsspezifische Bildungsungleichheiten in Europa [Gender Differences in Education in Europe]." In *Geschlechtsspezifische Bildungsungleichheiten* [Gender Inequalities in Education], edited by A. Hadjar, 23–54. Wiesbaden: VS Verlag für Sozialwissenschaften.

Hadjar, A., E. Grünewald-Huber, S. Gysin, J. Lupatsch, and D. Braun. 2012. "Traditionelle Geschlechterrollen Und Der Geringere Schulerfolg Der Jungen. Quantitative Und Qualitative Befunde Aus Einer Schulstudie Im Kanton Bern (Schweiz) [Traditional Gender Roles and the Lower Educational Attainment of Boys. Quantitative and Qualitative Findings from a School Study in the Kanton Bern (Switzerland)]." *Schweizerische Zeitschrift Für Soziologie* 38: 375–400.

Hadjar, A., and J. Lupatsch. 2010. "Der Schul(miss)erfolg Der Jungen. Die Bedeutung Von Sozialen Ressourcen, Schulentfremdung Und Geschlechterrollen [The Lower Educational Success of Boys. The Impact of Social Resources, School Alienation and Gender Role Patterns]." *Kölner Zeitschrift Für Soziologie Und Sozialpsychologie* 62: 599–622. doi:10.1007/s11577-010-0116-z.

Hadjar, A., and J. Lupatsch. 2011. "Geschlechterunterschiede Im Schulerfolg. Spielt Die Lehrperson Eine Rolle? [Gender Differences in Educational Success. Does the Teacher Matter?]." *Zeitschrift Für Soziologie Der Erziehung Und Sozialisation* 31: 79–94.

Hannover, B. 2004. "Gender Revisited." *Zeitschrift Für Erziehungswissenschaft* 7: 81–99.

Hannum, E., and C. Buchmann. 2005. "Global Educational Expansion and Socio-economic Development: An Assessment of Findings from the Social Sciences." *World Development* 33: 333–354.

Hascher, T., and G. Hagenauer. 2010. "Alienation from School." *International Journal of Educational Research* 49: 220–232. doi:10.1016/j.ijer.2011.03.002.

Hörstermann, T., S. Krolak-Schwerdt, and A. Fischbach. 2010. "Die Kognitive Repräsentation Von Schülertypen Bei Angehenden Lehrkräften. Eine Typologische Analyse [The Cognitive Representation of Student-types in Future Teachers. A Typological Analysis]." *Schweizerische Zeitschrift Für Bildungswissenschaften* 32: 143–158.

Klapproth, F., S. Krolak-Schwerdt, S. Glock, R. Martin, and M. Böhmer. 2013. "Prädiktoren Der Sekundarschulempfehlung in Luxemburg: Ergebnisse Einer Large-Scale-Untersuchung [Predictors of the Luxembourgish Secondary School Recommendations: Findings from a Large Scale Study]." *Zeitschrift Für Erziehungswissenschaft* 16: 335–379. doi:10.1007/s11218-012-9197-z.

Leemann, R., P. Dubach, and S. Boes. 2010. "The Leaky Pipeline in the Swiss University System: Identifying Gender Barriers in Postgraduate Education and Networks Using Longitudinal Data." *Swiss Journal of Sociology* 36: 299–323.

Martino, W. 1999. "'Cool Boys', 'Party Animals', 'Squids' and 'Poofters': Interrogating the Dynamics and Politics of Adolescent Masculinities in School." *British Journal of Sociology of Education* 20: 240–263. doi:10.1080/01425699995434.

McCombs, Regina C., and Judith Gay. 1988. "Effects of Race, Class, and IQ Information on Judgments of Parochial Grade School Teachers." *The Journal of Social Psychology* 128: 647–652. doi:10.1080/00224545.1988.9922918.

Mössle, T., M. Kleimann, F. Rehbein, and C. Pfeiffer. 2010. "Media Use and School Achievement: Boys at Risk?" *British Journal of Developmental Psychology* 28: 699–725.

Murdock, T. B. 1999. "The Social Context of Risk: Status and Motivational Predictors of Alienation in Middle School." *Journal of Educational Psychology* 91: 62–75. doi:10.1037/0022-0663.91.1.62.

Neugebauer, M., M. Helbig, and A. Landmann. 2010. "Unmasking the Myth of the Same-sex Teacher Advantage." *European Sociological Review* 27: 669–689. doi:10.1093/esr/jcq038.

OECD. 2013. *PISA 2012 Results: What Students Know and can do – Student Performance in Mathematics, Reading and Science*. Paris: OECD Publishing. http://dx.doi.org/10.1787/9789264201118-en.

Parks, F. R., and J. H. Kennedy. 2007. "The Impact of Race, Physical Attractiveness, and Gender on Education Majors' and Teachers' Perceptions of Student Competence." *Journal of Black Studies* 37: 936–943. doi:10.1177/0021934705285955.

Salisbury, J., and D. Jackson. 1996. *Challenging Macho Values: Practical Ways of Working with Adolescent Boys*. London: Falmer Press.

Vallerand, R. J., M. S. Fortier, and F. Guay. 1997. "Self-determination and Persistence in a Real-Life Setting: Toward a Motivational Model of High School Dropout." *Journal of Personality and Social Psychology* 72: 1161–1176. doi:10.1037/0022-3514.72.5.1161.

Weinert, F. E., and A. Helmke. 1997. *Entwicklung Im Grundschulalter*. Weinheim: Psychologie Verlags Union.

Willis, P. E. 1977. *Learning to Labour: How Working Class Kids get Working Class Jobs*. Aldershot: Coger.

Ziegler, A., C. Kuhn, and K. Heller. 1998. "Implizite Theorien Von Gymnasialen Mathematik- Und Physiklehrkräften Zu Geschlechtsbezogener Begabung Und Motivation [Implicit Theories of Gender-specific Giftedness and Motivation of Mathematics and Physics Teachers from the German Gymnasium]." *Psychologische Beiträge* 40: 271–287.

The authors would like to note that the following article has since been published in English:

Hadjar, A., Backes, S., Gysin, S. (2015). School Alienation, Patriarchal Gender-Role Orientations and the Lower Educational Success of Boys. A Mixed-method Study. *Masculinities and Social Change*, 4 (1), 85–116. doi: 10.4471/MCS.2015.61.

Females in science: a contradictory concept?

Ruth Watts

School of Education, University of Birmingham, Birmingham, UK

Background: the belief that women and science, including mathematics and medicine, are incompatible has had a long and complex history and still often works to exclude women from and/or marginalise them in science.

Purpose: this article will seek to explore gender and educational achievement through investigating how such gendered presumptions have persisted at various levels of science, despite perceptions of science itself changing over time and scientific studies expanding, differentiating and becoming professionalized. In particular, after a brief discussion of the historical debates on the provenance and lasting recurrence of gendered assumptions in science, it will try to discover how these prejudices affected the education of girls and women in England from c.1910 to c. 1939 and then, to widen the picture, make some comparison with the USA in the same period, although, necessarily in an article of this length, this analysis will be somewhat cursory. It will then bring the history up-to-date by examining the situation in England today.

Sources of evidence: the article will proceed by using extensive local sources in case study research on Birmingham, by then the second largest English city. The comparisons with the situation in the USA in the same period and the examination of the present situation will be based largely on secondary sources.

Main argument: factors of location, family background, supportive networks and greater educational, political and employment rights will be shown to have allowed some women to break through the barriers that hindered many from accessing or rising in science. Thus, it will be seen through the Birmingham example that there was a growing yet limited field of scientific practice for women, ordered by a gendered philosophy which routed them into specific areas. This picture was further permeated by class, wealth, identity, contacts, networks and location albeit this was modified by the scholarship system. Comparisons with the USA show that similar factors were present there, albeit in a different context. Twenty-first century sources indicate that on the one hand there is still gendered access and progress for females in science in England yet, on the other hand, there have been, and are at present, a number of initiatives seeking to overcome this.

Conclusion: Even today, therefore, whatever sciences females do is affected by underlying gendered assumptions and structural power relationships which need to be understood.

Introduction

The belief that women and science, including mathematics and medicine, are incompatible has had a long and complex history. Science, a field of knowledge so important in our modern world, has generally been perceived as 'masculine' and women have been excluded or pushed to the periphery despite changing perceptions of science and its expansion, differentiation and professionalization. Even where a woman won renown in science, this rarely allowed her progress into the scientific world in the same way as men or opened doors to other women; it might, indeed, cause a negative reaction. This article will briefly discuss historical debates on the provenance and lasting recurrence of such assumptions and then how they affected the education of girls and women in England from c.1910 to c. 1939, a particularly interesting period when, despite the growth of scientific studies at all levels of education, gendered attitudes increasingly excluded girls from the physical sciences and higher mathematics and pushed them, insofar as they did science at all, towards the biological sciences and even more so, towards domestic science. To assess how this happened, it will be necessary to understand how gender inequalities in work and education were made manifest and to look at structural power relationships, while also ensuring that science is not defined only from a masculine point of view (Kenway and Willis 1995; Kourany 2002). The situation in Birmingham will be examined to investigate how women fared in science and medicine in the second largest English city in this period. Using a wealth of local sources, changes in schooling, further and higher education for women and in scientific fields themselves will be investigated to explore how far different sciences were opening up to females and how far they remained much influenced by contemporary, albeit changing, gendered theories and assumptions. To widen the picture, some comparison with the situation in the USA in this period will be made, although only general trends in this huge and diverse country can be noted here. Finally there will be a brief examination of the present situation in England to see how far this past history is still affecting access to and progress in science for girls and women today and to note some initiatives which seek to rectify the situation.

It is necessary to define first, however, how the ever changing concepts of 'science', 'gender' and 'education' are used here. 'Science' is taken to include all subjects based on objective knowledge of physical matters including medicine, mathematics and technology. Without ignoring the biology of sex, 'gender', is seen as largely culturally determined, changing according to place, time and situation (Maynard 1997; Wallach Scott 1999). Interrelating with this are factors such as class, 'race' and religion which together can dramatically affect access to knowledge. 'Education', is accepted as the development of mental or physical potential rather than just schooling, systematic instruction, or training, thus helping understanding of how people of both sexes often made educational progress despite disadvantages and lack of access to prime educational routes.

Science in the twentieth century: a gendered subject?

In the last decade in Britain there has been some agitation over girls' high performance rate in public examinations and boys corresponding seeming under-achievement in a way that was rarely shown when girls were struggling for equal education (Hinsliff 2004a). This is the case, despite the still very unequal pay and career prospects of men and women and continuing lack of encouragement to schoolgirls to try non-traditional work for women. In the USA rumours that the Ivy League universities were so worried by similar trends suggested that they were manipulating their admissions procedures against women (Hinsliff 2004b). Yet, simultaneously, alarm is shown by governments about the shortage of scientists and engineers and by feminists about a scientific world which appears to exclude women and minorities from an effective voice (Rosser 2000).

Since females appear to have gained a more equal education, it is necessary to examine why they still have to negotiate barriers with regard to the sciences, now prestigious subjects in the curriculum and certainly ones which attract the largest funding. In the past, pupils social class or gender has determined access to different subjects as much as ability. In England, certainly, the study of classics, the hallmark of being a 'gentleman', were reserved largely for males of the upper, middle and professional classes. Yet even as some women were gradually winning the right to be taught Latin at least, and secondary and university education was opening up to them, science, hitherto promoted only by progressive educationalists, was slowly growing in prestige. In the twentieth century, with the huge advances in science and proliferation of its forms, it was, albeit by uneven and sometimes rather wandering steps, eventually to become a dominant part of the curriculum. Yet even as it opened up to girls it often was confined to botany or biology – increasingly declining in status relative to physics and chemistry – as better suiting the 'feminine' intellect. Domestic science was the only option offered to some girls. This gendered outlook, however, also opened up opportunities to females in some areas, notably medicine (see Tolley 2003; Watts 2007, 145–154, 172–173, 176–92).

Gender and science in history

Why women's access to science, particularly its higher reaches, has been so circumscribed has been keenly debated in the last thirty years by both women scientists and historians (especially in the USA) who soon realised that the ambivalent juxtaposition of 'woman' and 'scientist' had a provenance of over 400 years. From this emerged concepts of masculinity and other deeply embedded gendered associations in the very language of science which have deeply affected the practice of it despite its ostensible upholding of critical, rational thinking. Many feminist scientists have argued passionately that feminists should investigate science because scientific research was controlled by those with political power and had been used so often to justify patriarchy as well as class and 'race' inequalities.[1]

The continually expanding growth of biographical material on women in science has shown both the actual diverse contribution of women to science and the constraints which have impeded this, the careful ways marginalised women have had to negotiate their way and the veil history has often drawn over their achievements. Studies exploring how the generality of women found avenues into science have opened up how scientific 'truth' is actually reached and the need to realise the significance of understanding how anyone's progress is affected by place, time, religion and circumstance and that science is and has always been informed by class, racial and gender biases (Watts 2007, 11–14, 209).

This has a strong impact on all educational experiences and institutions (e.g. Kelly 1987; Smail 2000).

Female access to science in the early twentieth century

From the late nineteenth century women appeared to be achieving greater equality politically, professionally and employment–wise. Even so, although or because science was increasing in variety and importance and expanding as a profession, despite some exceptional successes, fewer women proportionately broke the institutional barriers of science by 1939 than 1919. This was despite some recognition in the western world that reputed sexual differences in intelligence, even in mathematics and sciences, were due neither to physiological nor 'innate power of intellect', but because of lack of education and opportunity (Mozans 1991, 131–134).

Yet, women's access to science and medicine in Britain, even if growing, was patchy and often restricted in reality, despite the opening up of most university degrees to women. In medical education, in particular, women had many difficulties of access nearly everywhere (even in the flagship USA; see for example Morantz–Sanchez 1999). Old gendered assumptions were refreshed by new scientific knowledge and ideas, including Darwinism, new psychological theories and medical debates on reproduction, interrelated with a strong drive to ensure medical professionalism built upon strict and scientific qualifications which kept down those assumed to be incapable of achieving them (Watts, 2007, 134–183; Dyhouse, 1976; Rowold, 1996).

At the end of the nineteenth century worry about the lack of science and technical education in English and Welsh schools compared to France and Germany had led to parliamentary enquiries and subsequent regulations which created a growth in the teaching of science at all levels. After 1910 the best higher elementary and central schools had four year courses in practical science and from 1914 science lessons were compulsory in all state supported schools. When the new School Certificate examination was introduced for sixteen year olds in 1917, one of its five compulsory subjects had to be from the science and maths group, although this meant that the majority of pupils took maths. Courses in science were even becoming the norm in public schools, but Oxbridge gave most university awards based on the classics (Gordon 2002).

Science, therefore, was growing in importance, but access to it was uneven both in amount and content. Working class children were largely taught science at a practical not theoretical level and most left school at fourteen. Grammar and public schools might have better facilities, but science was not yet the high status subject for the ablest in most prestigious schools. Furthermore, it became increasingly established that physics and chemistry were too difficult or unsuitable for girls and if they were taught to them they should have a domestic bias. Botany was assumed to appeal more to girls and was certainly cheaper to teach. The very title of the 1923 Consultative Committee of the Differentiation of the Curriculum for Boys and Girls in Secondary Schools, illustrated general beliefs in some natural differences inherent in the two sexes. These were given seeming scientific credibility by eugenicist meanderings and psychological thinking such as that of the American, Granville Stanley Hall and further exacerbated in Britain by post-war and economic worries incorporating a desire to fit girls for their maternal role. Domestic science was urged instead of the other sciences for girls, especially for those lower in the social scale. Consequently, by the late 1920s girls' lack of time on maths led to such poor results that girls were assumed to lack both ability and interest. In technical education too, girls mostly were limited to domestic studies. While boys increasingly faced a range of sciences, in secondary schools girls spent more time on aesthetic and practical subjects, important in themselves but disadvantaging girls in science and mathematics. Although secondary teachers themselves gradually turned against these domestic schemes, the imbalance had been established and few girls took physics from 1925 to 1938, thus ensuring there were hardly any future teachers in this (Hunt 1991, 22–38, 116–132; Bishop 1994, 193).

In England and Wales, as in the USA, the emphasis on domestic science for girls offered a minority of women professional and academic opportunities, but also channelled girls and women into areas not widely accepted as 'science', reinforcing the idea that 'real' science was not for girls. This development was also class-based to some degree, partly because many applied sciences were associated with crafts and manual occupations and thus less esteemed by the more affluent. Furthermore, domestic science rhetoric was associated with that of social Darwinism and eugenicist ideas which portrayed women as inferior (Tolley 2003, 148–176; Hearnshaw 1929, 376–378, 455–457; Oakley 1929, 489–509; Dyhouse 1976, 41–58). Even in medicine, where women were slowly but increasingly emerging as professional practitioners at different levels, there were reversals. From the 1920s to the 1970s many places put quotas on women's admission to medicine and opportunities were largely gender stereotyped (Watts 2007, 167–172).

A case study: developments in female education and science in Birmingham from *c.*1910 to *c.*1939

To explore how this manifested itself in Birmingham, it is necessary to understand first the educational structure. Since 1902 the Education Committee of the Local Council (Local Educational Authority or LEA) had responsibility for all elementary (essentially working class), education, and the right to establish secondary schooling[2] an alternative kind of education for a different social class. From 1926 the LEA developed further the upper classes in elementary schools and built senior elementary schools so that there was separate provision for over 11s. It also funded or aided a small but growing number of secondary grammar schools, some single sex and others with boys' and girls' departments. In addition it was responsible for an array of technical, commercial and arts education which took place in a variety of day and evening schools and technical (from 1927 further education), colleges.[3]

In addition, there were also the endowed King Edward VI schools in Birmingham, comprising by 1911 a high school apiece for boys and girls, three grammar schools for boys and two for girls (Hutton 1952, 52ff, 188). They received scholarship pupils from the elementary schools and also had foundation free places for pupils already within the schools.[4] All the secondary schools were fee-paying and admission to them (apart from the two King Edward VI High Schools), was by entrance exam from 1923. Independent schools included the Edgbaston High School for Girls. The Education committee also granted scholarships to secondary schools as it did to the University of Birmingham, opened 1900.[5]

The science on offer in these institutions varied extensively according to age, class, gender and the predilections of different headteachers. In the elementary schools, observation lessons and nature study constituted science. In the upper classes from the age of fourteen boys took chemistry and physics while girls did hygiene and nature study,[6] but the financial stringencies of the 1930s stymied plans of expansion in all schools.[7]

Thousands of pupils, especially boys, went on to do further education in the technical colleges, albeit many of them part-time and taking industrial and vocational courses. A wide range of science and engineering courses were offered, especially at the Birmingham Central Technical College (BCTC). From 1927, it even regularly had students (mostly part-timers) gaining University of London degrees. Students could also win scholarships to Birmingham University.[8] Yet few women attended these colleges and those who did largely attended domestic science courses (which progressively promoted health), and, increasingly, commercial courses.[9] As late as 1943–4, apart from a few in metallurgy and electrical engineering, women only appeared in any number or showed high achievement in pharmacy and biology which included botany, zoology and physiology.[10] In fact, Birmingham had long led the way in appointing women pharmacists.[11]

It appears that the science taught in the girls' secondary schools was most likely to focus on biology and hygiene with some elementary physics and chemistry.[12] The general prejudice against girls taking 'boys' science' was apparent in both the lack of facilities for them and the agitation caused when girls sought wider opportunities (Schwarz 2000, 263). The two élite girls' high schools, following their early and unusual progress in science for girls, were much better (Watts 1998; Whitcut 1976). Many girls from King Edward's High won university honours in maths and the sciences (Vardy 1928, 79, 118–142), while Edgbaston High's falling science reputation recovered after 1931, although lack of money precluded better facilities as yet. Even so, many ex-students obtained science degrees, particularly in medical subjects, despite their cost (Whitcut 1976, 116–120).

Nationally, the numbers of male science graduates began to rise gradually after 1926, but not at Birmingham University. The number of women science students actually halved, fewer gaining Local Education Authority (LEA) scholarships or taking physical sciences than boys and very few taking engineering. Such choices anticipated the type of science employment available to them - a variety of medical jobs and teaching holding the greatest possibilities.[13] Even in these men could earn more and did not have to leave work if they got married as women did.[14]

There were opportunities for women to work in science in Birmingham, however. Apart from some good, even lucrative openings in low status domestic science,[15] there were others in medicine, although they were largely gender stereotyped. This was exemplified particularly in the local school medical services run by the Local Education Authority, responsible ultimately to the Board of Education to fulfil the demands of the increasing legislation on the medical care of children including prevention and treatment of infectious diseases and various childhood ailments. The whole expanding system was run by the Hygiene Sub-committee of the Birmingham LEA[16] who appointed school medical officers (SMOs), many of whom were women doctors, especially from 1931.[17] They carried out empirical research; promoted the teaching of cookery and hygiene in schools as a health measure;[18] and generally enabled a more scientific to the management of public health.[19] Similarly the Special Schools sub-committee appointed female doctors. Both these committees unusually contained a number of women and many of these were from well-known Quaker and Unitarian families who promoted women's opportunities.[20] The hygiene sub-committee was also proud of its innovative Child Guidance Clinic established in 1932, staffed by female psychologists and others.[21] This illustration of women bringing together scientific medical and educational practice and research exemplified how, from low-skilled dental assistants and hair nurses to highly skilled nurses and then female doctors and the occasional female dental surgeon, opportunities were opening up for girls to use scientific qualifications.[22]

There were also an unusual number of other female doctors Birmingham in those hostile times, not least a few women hospital doctors chiefly working in obstetrics, gynaecology and childcare, medical areas deemed most suitable for women.[23] One of them, Hilda Shufflebotham/Lloyd/Rose[24] was an ex-student of both King Edwards High and the University of Birmingham, and gained many firsts for women in medicine, including becoming a president of one of the medical Royal Colleges. Made a Dame in 1951, Hilda was a surgeon at the Women's Hospital for many years and on the medical faculty of the University, eventually becoming its first woman professor (Vardy, 1928, 125–131).[25]

Even so, it would be foolish to forget that women doctors were a small minority or that the range of job prospects related to science in medicine and education were largely confined to specific fields – a factor limiting the motivation to do relevant sciences in both Britain and the USA (Rossiter 1982, 315; Dyhouse 1998; Bindman, Brading, and Tansey 1993, 11).

Some general comparisons of the situation of females in science in the USA in the first decades of the twentieth century

Comparisons with the USA are interesting. In 1900 American middle class girls were doing well in the physical sciences and mathematics and generally far more of them entered higher education than in Britain and continental Europe. Such advances had been hard fought for, however, and the ensuing backlash after about 1910 was exacerbated by other factors such as many women's preference for natural history and women's promotion of home economics as a 'female science'. Focussing on the drawbacks of women not studying the more prestigious physical sciences undermines the valuable scientific work done in home economics towards reforming both the physical and social environment and buys into an elitist, masculinist and hierarchical view of the sciences. Nevertheless, in reality it helped make the systematic positive discrimination towards men in the award of grants, employment and promotions in the sciences seem justified despite the achievements or outstanding ability of some women. The structural organisation of science itself ensured male backing was crucial for a woman to succeed, but, despite the success of a few, generally by the 1940s sexual segregation in science disabled many women's progress and class and racial attitudes added to this (Watts 2007, 149–154, 172–173; Harding 1993).

This scenario was echoed - usually in more dramatic numerical terms - throughout the western world. Research has shown that family contacts, especially in academia, cultural capital (particularly where education was valued highly), suitable education and academic support were all significant factors in women's success as were supportive mentors later. Yet even high-flying scientific women faced much struggle and often did not receive the remunerative, employment or recognition awards they deserved (Tolley, 2003, 138; Stolte-Heiskanen 1991). Further very significant difficulties occur because of class and 'race' (Harding 1993).

The situation for females in science in the twenty-first century

Despite the growth of numbers of girls and women in secondary, further and higher education in the second half of the twentieth century, accompanied by wider professional opportunities for women and many demonstrations of the ability of girls and women in science, by the early twenty-first century only limited progress has been made (Watts 2007, 200–203). Early gendered choices in studies and children's play imply that societal assumptions are quickly absorbed. Depressingly, a range of studies in Britain show that, in coeducational secondary schools especially, boys quickly dominate science classes and girls are demotivated without teachers either realising or necessarily caring (e.g. Henry 2001, 13; Smail 2000). In 2011 49 percent of Britain's co-educational schools had no female students taking A-level physics, and, although numbers were higher in girls' only schools, generally, from all schools only 17 percent of girls took physics at undergraduate level and vastly fewer became academic scientists of any kind even in biology, where female graduates predominate. Women outnumber men only as laboratory technicians. Some enterprising schools and projects, however, have shown that nerdy and dull stereotypes of the physical sciences and their students can be successfully challenged by encouragement and positive role models of women in science (Day 2012, 14–15).

Some people still assert that women simply cannot undertake 'pure' science at the highest level,[26] yet initiatives such as the partnership of UNESCO and L'Oréal since 1998 has been enabling outstanding women scientific researchers worldwide to develop their work.[27] In Britain Woman in Science and Engineering (WISE) has done much to stimulate organisations 'to inspire women and girls to pursue science, technology, engineering and mathematics (STEM) as pathways to exciting and fulfilling careers'.[28] Its statistics show that girls are now as likely as boys to study STEM subjects at the the General Certificate of Secondary Education (GCSE) exam but fewer girls than boys go on to A level science[29] (although those who do achieve more highly than boys), and very few into apprenticeships. Far fewer women than men are in the STEM workforce or management, particularly at top levels. Both participation and achievement in STEM subjects still tends to differentiate according to the old gender stereotypes but such imbalances are much less severe at post-graduate level.[30]

Some scientists and educators are realising the need to understand the historical basis of the current situation as is exemplified in the new Women in Science Research Network (WISRNet), which aims, among other objectives, to alert policy makers to the detriment to the country caused by women's underrepresentation in science at all levels and to promote science to girls at school, overcoming perceived prejudices and highlighting a wide range of women in science in history.[31]

Conclusion

This paper has attempted to give some historical perspective on gender issues and developments in science education in a period when the latter was growing in status as a subject in English and Welsh education. The example of Birmingham shows a growing yet limited field of scientific practice for women, ordered by a gendered philosophy which routed them into specific areas (not necessarily female ones – there were more male gynaecologists and obstetricians than female, for example), but into ones 'suitable' for women. The whole picture was further permeated by class, wealth and identity, albeit this was modified by the scholarship system. Gendered access to science could be seen in the subjects taught and taken at school, college and higher education - the importance of the curriculum and who has access to any part of it never to be underestimated. In this period grammar (selective, state funded) and independent (fee-paying) schools alike generally still emphasised the classics, or at least Latin, as the pinnacle of élite education so that female high educational achievers may not have felt deprived of subjects which were increasingly becoming powerful pathways to knowledge and employment. In the present century, females have often achieved access to the physical sciences now that males are entering computer and engineering sciences.

Nevertheless, the Birmingham example shows that there were growing opportunities for females especially in medicine, pharmacy and public health at various levels. The Birmingham example also demonstrates the significance of location and of having women in powerful positions to effect change. Girls and women's scientific opportunities have been greatly influenced not only by their identity, their contacts and networks, but even more so by the underlying gendered assumptions which have so long kept them on the periphery of science. Similarly, structural power relationships have also helped stop women realising their potential. Understanding such factors is therefore vitally important if we are to explain the differences in gender achievement in science.

Notes

1. Watts 2007, 4–11, 206–209. For a more detailed discussion and for an extensive bibliography referring to the chief texts on this.
2. 'Secondary' education, first so-called in the early twentieth century, mostly began at about 11 years.
3. *Report of the Birmingham Education Committee (BEC) for the year ended November 9, 1903*, 11–12; *Report BEC for the period of six years ended March 31, 1930*, 95–9, 110–16.
4. *Report BEC 1906*, 40–46, 60; *Minutes BEC 1913*, 302–305, 692–693.
5. *Report BEC for the period of six years ended March, 31 1930*, 96–101; *Minutes* and *Reports* passim.
6. *Minutes BEC 1914*, 284–5; *1917*, 14, 67; *Report BEC 1914–1924*, 36.
7. *Minutes* BEC Jan. 31, 1930, 75, 81–83, 90–106; *Minutes* passim; e.g. Janet Whitcut *1976*, 114, 119.
8. *Minutes BEC 1930*, 139, 164; *1932*, 205, 353; *1933*, 239–243; 399; *1934*, 19, 409; *1936*, 19, 71; *1937*, 20; *1938*, 20, 420; *1939*, 20–1; *Birmingham Central Technical College (BCTC) Annual Report*, 1943–1944, 2.
9. *Minutes BEC 1939*, 20–2, 55; *BCTC*, 1943–1944, 15–16.
10. *BCTC* 1943–1944, 2–4, 8–14.
11. *Birmingham Medical Review (BMR)*, 1931, 142. See also *Minutes BEC* 1943, 389; 1944, 394; 1945, 290.
12. *Report(s) BEC*, passim; Margaret Worsley 2004.
13. Schwarz 2000, 254–65; *Minutes BEC 1930*, 451–2; 1931, 393–4; 1932, 348–9; 1933, 368; 1934, 374; 1935, 217, 380; 1936, 108, 424–5; 1937, 406, 441; 1938, 422; 1940, 387; 1941, 379, 410; 1942, 371; 1943, 386, 421; 1944, 358–9; 1945, 410.
14. *Minutes BEC 1930*, 426; 1932, 78, 188; 1936, 20; 1938, 354; 1939, 87, 114, 233, 334, 388, 416; 1940, 261, 337, 346; 1941, 80, 109, 299; 1942, 22, 71, 231; 1944, 356, 390, 394; 1945, 290.
15. *Minutes BEC 1939*, 398.
16. *Birmingham Medical Review* (BMR), 1935, 33–5; 1938 *Annual Report of the School Medical Officer* (hereafter *Report BEC*) year ending Dec. 31, 1937, 3–4, 19–21.
17. *Minutes BEC 1939*; *Report BEC 1938*, 4; 1941; 1940, 4.
18. *Minutes BEC 1938*; *Report BEC 1937*, 6–9; 1939, 1938, 7–13.
19. *Minutes BEC 1938*; *Report BEC 1937*, 18–20, 38.
20. *Minutes BEC 1938*; *Report BEC 1937*, 4; *Special Schools Annual Report BEC 1937*, 39. See membership of committees at the beginning of each year's *Minutes*.
21. *Minutes BEC 1931*, 59–60, 96; 1934, 427–9; 1938, *Report of the Medical Director of the Child Guidance Clinic*, 1–6; 1937, 30–2, 79; 1941, 313; 1943, 351; 1944, 332, 366–7.
22. *Minutes BEC 1930–1945* passim and especially 1938, 354; 1939, 241; 1945, 368; 1939, 241–2; 1940; *Report BEC 1940, 5*.
23. *BMR 1930–1945*, passim.
24. She married twice.
25. *Dean's Register 1*, 180; *BMR*, 1930–1936 passim; 1930–1946 passim for examples of a medical community supportive of women.
26. Baron-Cohen 2005. See Rossiter 2012 for the best up-to-date view of the situation in the USA.
27. http://www.womeninscience.co.uk/; Vivienne Parry 2006; Wendy Smith, Labs' labour lost as women stay away, *Guardian Unlimited*: http://education.guardian.co.uk/gendergap/story/0.672520,00.html [accessed 26/11/2006].
28. http://www.wisecampaign.org.uk/.
29. The General Certificate of Secondary Education (commonly called GCSE) is generally taken in a number of subjects by students in secondary education aged 14–16; the General Certificate of Education Advanced Level (commonly termed A level) is taken by students (usually at 18) when completing secondary or pre-university education.
30. http://www.wisecampaign.org.uk/ - Sue Botcherby & Lisa Buckner, Women in Science, Technology, Engineering and Mathematics: from Classroom to Boardroom. UK Statistics 2012.
31. http://womeninscience.net/new-home-page/

Internet

http://education.guardian.co.uk/gendergap/story/0..672520,00.html [accessed 26/11/2006] *Guardian* Unlimited. Smith, Wendy. "Labs' labour lost as women stay away."

http://www.wisecampaign.org.uk/ including Botcherby, Sue, and Lisa Buckner. "Women in Science, Technology, Engineering and Mathematics: from Classroom to Boardroom. UK Statistics 2012."

http://www.womeninscience.co.uk/

http://womeninscience.net/new-home-page/

References

Archives

Birmingham City Library: City of Birmingham Education Committee Reports and Minutes including Annual Report of the School Medical Officer and Report of the Medical Director of the Child Guidance Clinic.

University of Birmingham, Cadbury Research Library, University of Birmingham *Dean's Register* 1.

Secondary material

Baron-Cohen, Simon. 2005. "The Truth About Science and Sex." *The Guardian*, 27 January, 6.

Bindman, Lynn, Alison Brading, and Tilli Tansey, eds. 1993. *Women Physiologists*. London: Portland Press.

Bishop, George. 1994. *Eight Hundred Years of Physics Teaching*. Basingstoke: Fisher Miller Publishing.

Day, Elizabeth. 2012. "Girls Just Wanna Have Fun ... with Particle Theory." *The Observer, New Review*, 30 December, 14–15.

Dyhouse, Carol. 1976. "Social Darwinistic Ideas and the Development of Women's Education in England, 1880–1920. *History of Education* 5 (1): 41–58.

Dyhouse, Carol. 1998. "Women Students and the London Medical Schools, 1914–39: The Anatomy of a Masculine Culture." *Gender and History* 10 (1): 110–132.

Gordon, Peter. 2002. "Curriculum." In *A Century of Education*, edited by Richard Aldrich, 187–192. London: Routledge/Falmer.

Harding, Sandra, ed. 1993. *Racial Economy of Science: Towards a Democratic Future*. Bloomington and Indianapolis, IN: Indiana University Press.

Hearnshaw, J. F. C. 1929. *The Centenary History of King's College, London, 1828–1928*, 489–509. Appendix A by Hilda Oakley. London: George G Harrap & Company Ltd.

Henry, Julie. 2001. "Girls Hit by Negative Forces in the Lab." *Times Educational Supplement*, 12 January, 13.

Hinsliff, Gaby. 2004a. "So It's a Woman's World." *The Observer*, 15 August, 3.

Hinsliff, Gaby. 2004b. "Women's Rights – Beyond the Fringe." *Guardian*, 27 October.

Hunt, Felicity. 1991. *Gender & Policy in English Education 1902–1944*. Hemel Hempstead: Harvester Wheatsheaf.

Hutton, T. W. 1952. *King Edward's School Birmingham 1552–1952*. Oxford: Blackwells.

Kenway, Jane, and Sue Willis, eds. 1995. *Critical Visions: Rewriting the Future of Work, Schooling and Gender*. Canberra: Department of Employment, Education and Training.

Kelly, Alison, ed. 1987. *Science for Girls*. Milton Keynes: Open University Press.

Maynard, Mary, ed. 1997. *Science and the Construction of Women*. London: University College London Press.

Morantz-Sanchez, Regina. 1999. *Conduct Unbecoming a Woman: Medicine on Trial in Turn-of-the-century Brooklyn*. Oxford, New York: Oxford University Press.

Mozans, H. J. 1991. *Women in Science*. London: University of Notre Dame Press.

Parry, Vivienne. 2006. "Experimenting with Change." *The Times,* Body and Soul, 11 March, 4–5.

Rosser, Sue V. 2000. *Women, Science and Society*. New York: Teachers College Press.

Rossiter, Margaret. 1982. *Women Scientists in America*. Vol 1. *Struggles and Strategies to 1940*. Baltimore, MD, The John Hopkins Press.

Rossiter, Margaret. 2012. *Women Scientists in America*. Vol. 3. *Forging a New World Since 1972*. Baltimore, MD: The John Hopkins Press.

Rowold, Katherine. 1996. *Gender and Science. Late Nineteenth-century Debates on the Female Mind and Body*. Bristol: Thoemmes Press.

Schwarz, Leonard. 2000. "In an Unyielding Hinterland. The Student Body 1900–45." In *The First Civic University: Birmingham 1880–1980. An Introductory History*, edited by Ives, Eric, Diane Drummond, and Leonard Schwarz, 237–270. Birmingham: University of Birmingham Press.

Smail, Barbara. 2000. "Has the Mountain Moved? The Girls into Science and Technology Project." In *Whatever Happened to Equal Opportunities in Schools?* edited by Kate Myers, 143–155. Buckingham: Open University Press.

Stolte-Heiskanen, Veronica, ed. 1991. *Women in Science: Token Women or Gender Equality?* Oxford: Berg (International Social Science Council in conjunction with UNESCO).

Tolley, Kim. 2003. *The Science Education of American Girls: A Historical Perspective*. London/New York: Routledge Falmer.

Vardy, Winifred I. (Mrs E. W. Candler). 1928. *King Edward VI High School for Girls Birmingham 1883–1925*. London: Ernest Benn.

Wallach Scott Joan. 1999. *Gender and the Politics of History*. New York: Columbia University Press.

Watts, Ruth. 1998. "From Lady Teacher to Professional: A Case Study of Some of the First Headteachers of Girls' Secondary Schools in England." *Educational Management and Administration* 26 (4): 339–351.

Watts, Ruth. 2007. *Women in Science. A Social and Cultural History*. London, New York: Routledge.

Whitcut, Janet. 1976. *Edgbaston High School 1876–1976*. Published by the Governing Body.

Worsley, Margaret. 2004. *A History of Roman Catholic Education in Birmingham*. Unpublished PhD: University of Birmingham.

The construction of 'female citizens': a socio-historical analysis of girls' education in Luxembourg

Catherina Schreiber

Institute of Education & Society, University of Luxembourg, Luxembourg

Background: This paper will empirically investigate female education in Luxembourg from a historical perspective. A special focus will be laid on the question of how women in Luxembourgian society were constructed as female 'citizens', even though they were, rather, considered as a homogeneous category limited to a private sphere separated from the male citizens.

Purpose: The primary purpose of this article is to reveal the narrative of a homogeneous femininity separated from a male sphere associated with citizenship, and the impact this division had on education. Secondly, through the example of Luxembourg, it will show how this narrative served to maintain traditional role allocations, while at the same time linking them to rhetorics of progress – for example, by adding a political dimension to the former 'private sphere'. Thirdly, this article will demonstrate the heterogeneity which shaped female education, despite the rhetorical homogenization, showing how social and local/regional differences were as influential in determining female education as gender differences.

Design and methods: This historical study is based on a longitudinal analysis (contained within a bigger project) of the Luxembourgian curriculum in the nineteenth and twentieth centuries. The source corpus of this project includes 12,000 historical documents related to curricular negotiations in Luxembourg, which were analysed in a combined quantitative–qualitative analysis.

Findings: The analysis demonstrated that public and professional discussions about female education undertook a rhetorical homogenization of women and their education, and that this served to conserve existing gender differences in the school system. By strategies of rhetorical scientification and politicization of domestic tasks, traditional role allocations were ascribed a political dimension and interpreted as progressive. However, though claiming universality, the plurality of concepts proves that this homogenization did not reflect reality. The pedagogical concept of 'the female education' shows only a few rudimentary features, mainly based on the introduction of obligatory handcraft and domestic education. A social differentiation was already given by the structure of the school system, which – given that there were no secondary schools for girls – meant education in Catholic private schools in the first place.

Conclusions: The findings reveal that, by assuming a homogeneous concept of femininity, numerous codifications of female education – unlike those often perceived in literature and public discourse – were not necessarily understood as 'modernizing', but rather as conserving female role allocations. The results, however, suggest that female education was far more heterogeneous than rhetorically assumed in the educational debates, and that rather than gender differences, social and regional differences prevailed in determining schooling.

Background

Following policy and curriculum emphasis, citizenship education has become one of the most burgeoning areas of educational research in recent years. Within this, the conceptualizations of 'diversity' and 'pluralism' sometimes appear to imply a previously existing concept of 'homogenous' citizenship education that is not historically evidenced. This perspective on citizenship education may result principally from the typical contemporary understanding of citizenship education as the education of the democratic citizen via specific school subjects, or within clearly defined extracurricular educational practices which are created with this specific aim in mind.

It is certainly the case that concepts of citizenship education have been remarkably limited in content for a long time. Through mainly essentialist theories of biological/ psychological differences, women were systematically excluded from the education of 'good citizens' through using the criteria 'female' to construct a category of 'woman' separated from notions of the male citizen. In these theories, women were described as an inherent homogeneous category – despite their individual differences in social status and biographical experiences (Arnot 1997, 283).

The concept of the citizen hence fulfilled a triple function of distinction (Appelt 1999, 15): it dissociated the citizen from the authorities (upward distinction), from foreigners (outward distinction), and even from a private sphere that seemed to be dedicated to the women (inward distinction) – a setting that makes the citizen the 'androcentric core of occidental political theory' (13).

The public images around the turn of the twentieth century (as seen in Figure 1) show this perceived homogeneity of femininity as separate from what was considered 'normal' education, visually mostly represented by domestic education and handcraft – a stereotype that also shaped research on female education.

The education system also mirrors this distinction between the male (i.e. public) and female (i.e. private) spheres. Indeed, Luxembourg shared this narrative until 1968 by excluding explicit civic instruction in numerous schools for girls, while ascribing the function of social and moral education to domestic and religious subjects (cf. Schreiber 2012).

This perception helps to explain why issues of female citizenship education were largely neglected in international research. While Anglo-American research in the context of the feminist movement during the 1990s (*Engendering democracy*) drew increasing attention to *gendered citizenry* (Phillips 1991; Kelly 1993), most European research focused on issues of equal treatment and opportunities. Thus, gender differences in citizenship education were not perceived as central to research and the historiography of education was no exception to this.

Using the example of Luxembourg, an analysis of the public discourses in the nineteenth and twentieth century indicates that female education was nevertheless perceived as education for their societal rights, duties and responsibilities, and thus as civic education. Drawing on both recent historiography of education and a broad notion of citizenship education of nineteenth-century concepts (in Luxembourg, for instance, see ChD 1912, 45; Schreiber 2012, 6f.), this article therefore presumes a broader notion of citizenship education, interpreting the whole curriculum as being conducive to the construction of citizens. In this conception, every kind of schooling in all school subjects, and

Figure 1.   Luxembourgian postcards showing female education.
Note: From the *Ecole Ménagère* Luxembourg, Photohèque Luxembourg, card no. 013474
© Photohèque Luxembourg. Permission for reproduction granted.

towards every child implicitly and explicitly, contributes to the construction of nation-
state citizenry. To what extent this citizenship education differs from school to school,
class to class or between genders can be revealed by a curricular comparison.

However, the definition of citizenship education used in this article differs from both
historical and contemporary concepts in one crucial point: it departs from a notion of
the citizen linked to specific values, particularly indicating political beliefs and participation. Such abstraction is of special importance for the time before female suffrage
enabled political participation for women. Hereafter, female education shall be analysed
as a form of citizen construction using the hitherto unexplored empirical example of
Luxembourg as a case study.

The article focuses on three aspects of curricular development:

- The strained relationship between the rhetorical homogenization of women and
  the inconsistency of the debates about the societal functions of women and their
  appropriate education.
- The implementation of such discursive concepts by reforms of female education.
- The resulting differences within female education.

These three fields shall serve as the basis to verify the thesis of the paper: that the education of girls – in the sense of the education of female citizens – had to follow the
same cultural and social differentiations as the education of boys in Luxembourg,
despite the fact that in discussions about the curriculum, girls' education has always
been designed as a homogenous category, based on female nature and in combination
with the tasks of women in society. The thesis furthermore states that social and

regional differences carried much more weight in the design/organization of the curriculum than gender-specific ones. These differences are based on two curricular lines of conflict: on the one hand, there was the demand for further development in the education of girls from higher or middle-class families – orientating itself towards male education and therefore including, for example, the discussion on lessons in Latin and several scientific subjects; on the other hand, there was the demand for an education in practical things, above all through lessons on housekeeping. Overall, one has to distinguish between the education of girls with the purpose of preparing them for their later role in a household and in family life, and the education as training for a later occupation.

The first part of the paper addresses the structure of the girls' school system and pays special attention to differences regarding access to the school system, maintaining bodies, and school profiles both between girls' and boys' schools and within female education. The second part investigates the debates over female role allocations in the Luxembourgian society and their effects on female education, followed by a contextualizing analysis of the curricular differences by comparing two phases of different degrees of institutionalization.

The structure of female education since the mid-nineteenth century

In nineteenth-century Luxembourg, school for most students meant six to seven years of primary school. Even before primary schooling was made mandatory in 1881, the number of children attending primary schools was relatively high – 20,698 in 1842, rising to 28,275 in 1881 (STATEC 1990, 201). Although an increasing number of students went to the *Fortbildungsschule* (continuing school) or the *Oberprimärschule* (upper primary school) – two kinds of post-primary schools requiring two more years – this in combination only adds up to 15–26% of all students who left primary school. Only 3% of students attended secondary school.

In the mid-nineteenth century, schooling largely took place on a co-educational basis, apparently attributable to the necessity of including girls into existent structures of schooling (see Figure 2). During the second half of the century, the developmental trend continuously shifted in support of gender-separated classes. From 1908 to the late 1960s, co-educational classes totalled about a third of all primary school classes. Although this trend was on the decrease after 1945, it was not until 1975 that mixed primary classes reached the percentage they held in 1842 (85%).[1]

Considerably greater differences are apparent in the upper primary schools and continuing schools following primary school. The first upper primary school for boys opened its doors in Luxembourg in 1860; two years later, the first upper primary school for girls followed. Unlike the boys' schools, upper primary schools for girls were denominationally (that is: Catholic) affiliated. Furthermore, unlike boys,[2] girls were not affected by any codification of compulsory school attendance beyond primary schools (Mémorial du Grand-Duché de Luxembourg 1881, 369f.) until the School Law of 1912. Until the first decade of the twentieth century, significantly fewer upper primary classes and continuing classes existed for women (STATEC 1990, 201a; Figure 3). Things changed in the course of the *Landwuôl* policies (well-being of the countryside). Already in 1888 the journal *Luxemburger Bauernfreund* had demanded a better education of girls from peasant families in order to impart to them the 'cultivation of the right religiosity, female needlework and the motherly education of the girls' and a 'solid formal education' (*solide Schulbildung*) (*Der Luxemburger Bauernfreund* 1888, 50 f.). Special

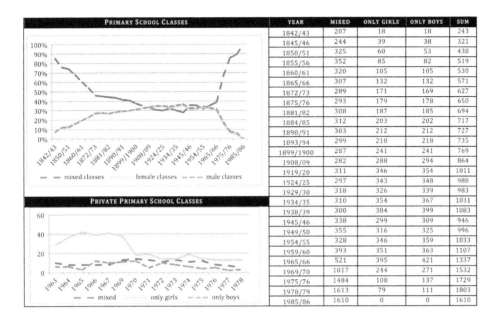

YEAR	MIXED	ONLY GIRLS	ONLY BOYS	SUM
1842/43	207	18	18	243
1845/46	244	39	38	321
1850/51	325	60	53	438
1855/56	352	85	82	519
1860/61	320	105	105	530
1865/66	307	132	132	571
1872/73	289	171	169	627
1875/76	293	179	178	650
1881/82	308	187	185	694
1884/85	312	203	202	717
1890/91	303	212	212	727
1893/94	299	218	218	735
1899/1900	287	241	241	769
1908/09	282	288	294	864
1919/20	311	346	354	1011
1924/25	297	343	348	988
1929/30	318	326	339	983
1934/35	310	354	367	1031
1938/39	300	384	399	1083
1945/46	338	299	309	946
1949/50	355	316	325	996
1954/55	328	346	359	1033
1959/60	393	351	363	1107
1965/66	521	395	421	1337
1969/70	1017	244	271	1532
1975/76	1484	108	137	1729
1978/79	1613	79	111	1803
1985/86	1610	0	0	1610

Figure 2. Mixed and gender-separated primary school classes.
Note: Graphical presentation by the author, based on data of STATEC (1990).

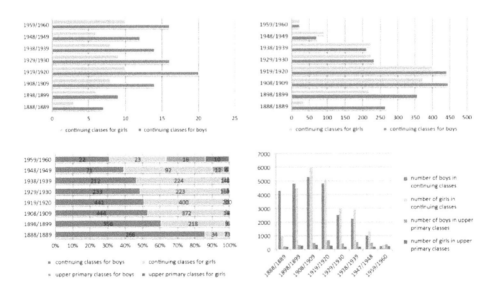

Figure 3. Continuing classes for girls and boys.
Note: Graphical presentation by the author, based on data of STATEC (1990).

demands were first and foremost the erection of domestic science schools (or housewifery schools and Sunday or evening schools) for girls who had completed their primary education. Such sewing and domestic science schools had existed in Luxembourg since 1850; in 11 towns there were additional agricultural residential schools for domestic sciences led by nuns, with the aim of facilitating school attendance for girls from rural areas (Kellen 1930). At the beginning of the twentieth century, their education in primary schools was particularly promoted in upper primary schools, offering them an alternative to the attendance of the recently founded female secondary schools, which most rural families could not afford anyway. These means – such as the mobile agricultural school for domestic education (Cariers 1932), which visited every village for four to five months – were also intended to counteract the effects of the increasing rural depopulation brought about by the industrialization process. Nevertheless it can be observed that, although the number of girls attending the continuing schools was higher than the number of boys attending, it was considerably lower in the upper primary schools. This shows that (with regard to the secondary schools) the majority of women only claimed the minimum of further education for themselves after primary school.

In addition, other forms of extracurricular vocational training, for example in craft occupations, were closed off to girls for the most part. Moreover, continuing schools could serve as a kind of full-time school or professional training/vocational training for the girls, especially as access to secondary education was impossible for a large part of the female population, even after the establishment of the Lycée de jeunes filles (cf. Schreiber 2012).

Until 1968, secondary education for girls meant education in separate schools. Girls from more affluent urban families received their initial education at Catholic private schools and girls' boarding schools in neighbouring countries, or else in 'one of those Belgian or Rhenish monasteries, from which the young girls return with a middling varnish of Bildung' (Weber-Brugmann 1912, 379).[3] In a way, this functioned as an appropriate replacement for the 'sophisticated' education of boys from upper-class families: the main elements included religious instruction and a visit abroad, comparable to the one that men had during their higher education studies. The aim of this education was ironically commented on by Emma Weber-Brugmann: 'And it is so very convenient to go with the great flow, that will so surely and naturally enter in the stagnant lake of snugly satisfied small-township' (1912, 379).[4] The private school Ste. Sophie, which was affiliated with the Congrégation Notre-Dame, was here of particular importance.

The first initiative to found a denominationally unaffiliated secondary school for girls was initiated by the aforementioned *Verein für die Interessen der Frau* (Association for Women's Interests), whose declared aim – to raise the educational level of women – had initially been pursued via courses in aesthetics, literature, French and practical trainings in accountancy, nursing care and housekeeping/budget management. While arguing for the desperate situation of Protestant and Jewish girls who were not able to access any instruction beyond primary school (Götzinger 1997, 69f.), both the personal and topical directionality of the association show it to be rather an initiative for girls of the petite bourgeoisie, whilst Ste. Sophie until the 1930s remained considered as the school of the 'upper and middle ten to twenty thousands' (Das tote Viertel, *Tageblatt*, November 8 1931, 1). After the headmasters of the boys' secondary schools had fiercely protested against a state-run foundation (Rapports de MM. les Directeurs, cited in AN-Lux IP 593), the new Lycée de jeunes filles was initially built up under private funding in 1909. This Lycée, followed by another one in Esch in 1910, was made up of an inferior grade (three years) and a superior grade, which again was divided into three sections: a commercial one with two additional years of study, and a modern languages and a Latin section, both including four more years of study (Lycée de jeunes filles Luxembourg 1912, 6–14). Although the new Lycée was intended to be an accommodative school offering a whole range of possible careers, attendance seemed most likely for children from more affluent urban families, as can be seen in the design of the three sections. In particular, the applied arts were at the core of the curriculum, supplemented by commercial subjects, while the language sections were regarded as vocational training and supposed to prepare for further studies or the profession of a teacher (1912, 6–14). The rural population, on the contrary, was not meant to benefit from the new Lycée (Tockert 1924). This can predominantly be traced back to their distance to the towns of Esch and Luxembourg, as well as the long duration of school attendance (six years instead of two years at the upper primary school) (*Petition der Einwohner der Stadt Esch* 1910, ANLux IP 593.) Beyond that, statistics indicate that only a few female students initially finished with exams qualifying them for university entrance. Only six female students took the final exams in 1916, and it was not until 1934 that this number reached a double-digit (Lycée de jeunes filles Luxembourg 1959, 82). Though the numbers of male and female students receiving secondary education have converged during the second half of the twentieth century, they still reveal evident disparities regarding the number of examinees (Figure 4). The female examinees of the final only reached a number comparable to the male ones as recently as in the late 1970s (STATEC 1990, 203a).

The role of women in Luxembourg's society

Both supporters and opponents of reforms of female education developed their arguments along two major themes:

(1) The 'nature of women' (Zahn 1909, ANLux IP 593): This was used by opponents of reform as an argument for women not being suited to higher education, or rather, not requiring it because of their true duties. Supporters of further reforms, however, held women to be particularly suited to some educational goals, due to their sensibility or their aesthetic sense. This thinking about 'natural' differences between man and woman can also be found in discussions

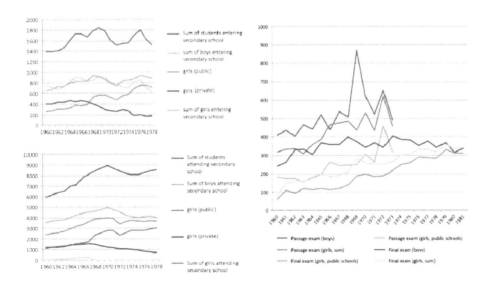

Figure 4. Gender differences in school and exam attendance in secondary school.
Note: Graphical presentation by the author, based on data from STATEC (1990).

27

on whether girls can be taught by men: 'courage, rectitude, strength, honesty in business etc. in boys can be developed better by a man just as girls can be taught kindness, tact, selflessness etc. best by a woman' (*Die Luxemburger Frau*, 21 August 1920, 1).[5]

(2) The needs of both state and society: While the opponents of female secondary schools, for instance, were apprehensive of what was perceived as unhealthful gender rivalry for jobs, supporters of such a reform either expected women to gain better skills for household and familial education, or better conditions for working women. Both are combined in the Luxembourgian *Schulbote* of 1909, affirming the importance of citizenship education for women '(a) in cases they would have to shift for themselves, (b) in regard to their influence in the family, making women aware of the several tolls taken by the state for different reasons' (*Der Luxemberger Schulbote* 1909, 450).[6]

Both areas – nature and societal functions of women – became inseparably linked by no later than the interwar period. Until the First World War, conceptualizing the role of women as housewives, and mothers as 'a law of nature and a necessity of social life'[7] was a dominant pattern (Conférence des professeurs d'Echternach 1909, ANLux IP 593). The Counsellor of the Government especially emphasized the clearly defined field of female responsibility: 'In civilization, the woman has her part, not as citizen, but as companion of the man, as wife and especially as mother'[8] (*Rapport sur la question de l'éducation de la femme*, January 10, 1910, ANLux IP 593.). Yet this statement still liberated the female duties in home and family from a purely private notion, ascribing to them political and social functions.

Things changed fundamentally with industrialization. In agricultural Luxembourg, women took an active part in farming; unmarried Luxembourgian women, due to the increasing urban orientation, either entered a primary teaching profession or earned their living as maid servants in Luxembourg City, Brussels or even Paris – an experience which, coincidently, has been described as an educational experience (Kmec 2010).

The transition to wage-dependent industrial work brought an increasing number of female workers. However, most professions remained closed to women, not only because a secondary education did not exist, but also because only few alternative non-school training situations were open to women. The same holds true for all appointments within civil and public services such as the mail service, to which women were only admitted after the end of the 1920s (Jones 1997, 226).

Around 1908, mass education associations (*Volksbildungsvereine*) were founded, whose influence on the perceptions of women and their role in society should not be underestimated. Within a short period of time, numerous women's associations formed. The Verein für die Interessen der Frau, the most renowned association besides the Catholic Luxemburger Katholischen Frauenbund (Luxembourg Catholic Women's League), played an important role as provider of the first private non-confessional secondary school for girls and organizer of public courses from 1909. Coincidentally, the *Landwuôl* movement began paying more attention to women in its combat against the *Landflucht* (rural depopulation). However, the activities of the *Landwuôl* movement served mainly to consolidate women's domestic and needlework abilities, and the first publications for rural schools additionally supported this (e.g. Huss 1900).

Discussions crucially shifted with the First World War, when debates about the societal role of women became increasingly institutionalized both politically and in the media.

In 1919, the *Luxemburger Wort* published a special enclosure, the *Luxemburger Frau*. This was followed in 1927 by the *Action féminine*, the journal of the eponymous national women's association, and then by *Die Luxemburgerin* in 1933. Propagating a traditional perception of women, the *Luxemburger Frau* was of special importance not only because it attracted the majority of female readers, but because it successfully managed to intertwine rhetorically the political and the private sphere. A specific female sense of self-sacrifice (*Opfersinn*) served as argument, which having at first been associated with familiar and household tasks, was subsequently projected to the political sphere (Besch 2009, 21).

The First World War changed the estimation of female education as a correcting measure needed to compensate a perceived common deficit of civic sentiment (Cravatte 1921, ANLux IP 2054), and which should be counteracted by specifically educating future mothers. The teachers and the ministry particularly stressed the importance of female patriotism and women's housekeeping for the national economy (C.Z. 1939), thereby assigning 'public' functions to tasks that had so far been considered 'female' and 'private'. However, the women's journals and feminist associations used exactly the same strategies, successfully managing to combine the political and the private sphere rhetorically. Even the *Luxemburger Frau* ascribed to women a more developed affinity to their country:

> Luxembourg's women and girls probably experience the patriotic excitement of these days still more than the native male world. The whole depth of their mind resonates with it. They feel – as it were out of a motherly instinct – the value of patriotic allegiance. (*Luxemburger Frau*, April 23 1919)[9]

Harnessing such national argumentation, the early feminist movement in particular supported its arguments for higher secondary education by reasoning about international educational differences instead of gender relations. They felt that Luxembourgian girls should not be condemned to 'notorious inferiority to women of other nations' (*Luxemburger Zeitung*, October 14, 1906).

Each of these perceptions of women held all-embracing aspirations, yet it is clear there were manifold perceptions – a multiplicity that first of all can be ascribed to societal and cultural differences within the Luxembourgian population and mirrored in the structural organization of female education.[10] Seen from the structural analysis, two phases seem to be of special epistemological interest:

- The last two decades of the nineteenth century, when numerous new girls' classes emerged without the syllabi being officially codified; and
- the institutionalization of female education between 1909 and 1916. Of special interest are the ways, in which the curricula were standardized and which particularities *within* female education and *between* female and male education were laid down by law.

Differentiated education without a compulsory syllabus

The curricular contents of female education are similarly varied. This is due to the fact that only few generally valid regulations of the curriculum took place in the field of female education in the nineteenth and early twentieth century. Here, primary schools exemplify the contradictory nature of female education in that education took place co-educationally in some classes. However, a distinction between boys' and girls' education in one-class, two-form and three-form entry schools was made (Mémorial du Grand-Duché de Luxembourg 1914, 385ff.).

Moreover, the primary school syllabus of 1901 distinguishes between uptown (*Oberstadt*) and suburban boys' and girls' education (see Table 1), as can be seen in the example of the programme for the fifth grade.

As well as depicting differences in the curricular content for boys and girls, Table 1 also evidences societal differences, showing foremost in the disparities in French education and in history and geography lessons.

As would seem natural, private female education was least regulated, as best exemplified in the Catholic private school Ste. Sophie. Here, the curriculum, even after aligning to the public syllabus for girls' secondary schools (1911), encompassed lessons in German, French and English language and literature, Greek authors, as well as maths education, history, physics, chemistry, natural sciences, cosmography and public law (*Programme des Cours Ste. Sophie*, ANLux IP 593). Moreover, specific lessons for societal education, such as *heures de politesse* (politeness lessons) and conversation lessons were taught and graded (Neyens 1987, 14f.).

However, the majority of girls only attended obligatory education, namely primary school and up to two more years in continuing schools and upper primary schools. Looking at their respective programs, girls' classes seem to have copied their respective male counterparts.

Admittedly, the lessons in languages, natural sciences and above all in drawing were reduced to allow the inclusion of needlework and domestic education, which mediates the notion of a consistent concept of female education. Yet, the local variations between the upper primary school programs turned out to be more distinct than between the respective local boys' and girls' schools. Apparently, even adjacent girls' schools (like the schools in the towns of Remich and Grevenmacher) mainly chose the local boys' schools as the prevailing model. The content tables indicated in the programs were virtually congruent with their equivalent for boys, and for large parts even took over the exact wording (a notable exemption was maths education, which shows that women were not intended to be educated for public processes and transactions). Furthermore, issues like 'state funds, shared and stocks' (*Staatspapiere, Aktien* and *Renten*) or 'saving

Table 1. Schedule of primary schools in Luxembourg City in hours per week.

| | Uptown | | Suburbs | |
	Boys	Girls	Boys	Girls
Catechism	2	2	2	2
Bible	2	2	2	2
German	6	6	6	5
French	10	8	5	4
Arithmetic	6	6	3	3
Geography			1	1
History			1	1
Calligraphy	2	2	1	1
Singing	1	1	1	1
Physical education	1	1	1	1
Needlework		2		2

Source: Commune de Luxembourg 1901, 26f.

banks and insurance companies' remained limited to boys' education (*School Pro-grammes*, ANLux IP 593).

Needlework exercises, by the same token, were used to distinguish the public upper primary school from the private ones. Unlike needlework in the Catholic private schools, it here was regarded as practical and useful:

> In some schools the little farmer's daughter is taught white stitch, filet knitting, net stitch and crocheting before she is able to knit a well formed simple sock, [...] on the contrary, an aversion to such simple and ordinary work awakens. [...] Soon, the little farmer's daughter, educated by the embroidery frame, holds standing by the stove to be too ordinary and low. [...] The old mother is forced to carry the weight of housekeeping on her weak shoulders and often has to stand by and watch her pampered little daughter [...] squandering the mother's fruits of sweat. (*Der Luxemberger Schulbote* 1863, 60f.)[11]

Prescribed exercises here consist of simple knitting, darning and mending, as well as the sewing of simple clothes.[12]

The institutionalization of female education

These differences were not withdrawn with the institutionalization of female education via codified syllabi and public schools, as can be seen by comparing the repartition of teaching lessons in upper primary schools to that of the new secondary school (Mémorial du Grand-Duché de Luxembourg 1916, 1097ff.).[13] While time for needlework was gained at the expense of lessons in mathematics, natural sciences and drawing in upper primary schools, secondary schools mostly reduced language education for the same purpose.

The inferior grades of the Lycée show similar differences. Basically, women had the same division of lessons as the boys' schools, i.e. fewer lessons were held in French and in physical education. Clear differences, however, show in language education. The differences can be explained by the declared aim to prepare the young girls for their future duties by practical-oriented instruction, which can be linked to the concern not to facilitate access to academic careers or 'liberal' professions for too many women. While

Table 2. Comparison between two upper primary schools in the communities of Remich and Grevenmacher: distribution of teaching time in hours per week.

	Girls: Remich 1891	Boys: Remich 1891	Girls: Grevenmacher 1891	Boys: Grevenmacher 1891
Religion	2	2	3	3
German	5	6	5	4
French	6	7	6	6
Arithmetic	5	4	4	5
History/ Geography	2 (1 each)	3	2 (1 each)	2
Sciences	1	1	1	2
Accountancy	1	1	1	1
Domestic education / Needlework	4	0	5	0
Drawing	1	3	1	5
Calligraphy	1	2	1	1
Singing	2	1	1	1

boys were taught seven hours of Latin in the inferior cycle, girls were initially only taught four hours in English; it was only once girls were in the upper cycle of the Latin section that they received lessons in ancient languages. What had been indicated previously in primary schools by the limitations of French lessons, here manifests itself in their reduction and the substitution of English for Latin. The reduction of Latin lessons was greatly excoriated by the instigators of the Lycée, and was perceived as a retrograde step until Latin and the natural sciences started to be taught more extensively in the run-up to communization in 1911 (Weber-Brugmann 1912, 382). In some ways, communization brought about a certain convergence of the different schools' programs. In the end, the Lycée did not implement the specialization of the boys' secondary schools. While the curricula of the sections differ considerably in the late inferior and the complete superior cycle, female secondary education remained fairly stable.

However, a comparison of the ancient language sections reveals only marginal differences, as instruction was hardly modified for the modern language section, while the commercial section was supplemented by further optional subjects. Furthermore, distinct differences can be seen between the industrial and commercial sections for boys and the commercial section for girls: German language is taught to a lesser extent, while maths education is not even mentioned (only *arithmetique commerciale* is given as an optional subject) and economic subjects are also missing – a clear indicator of the social and artistic directionality of the female commercial section that is also apparent in optional subjects like 'First aid in case of emergencies, artificial drawing, modelling, manual dexterity education and needlework' (Lycée de jeunes filles 1912, 9f., 27f.). A Luxembourgian particularity can be seen in the subject 'Notions of physical, intellectual and moral education' (*Notion d'éducation physique, intellectuelle et morale*), which was meant to prepare for family education and typical female professions in education.

Table 3. Distribution of teaching time (in hours per week) in upper primary schools and the lycée.

Secondary school, 3rd year	Girls	Boys, Latin-Greek section	Boys, Latin section	Boys, Commercial section
Religious education	2	2	2	2
German	4	3	3	5
French	6	6	6	6
Latin	0	7	7	0
Greek	0	4	0	0
English	4	0	4	3
Commercial arithmetic	0	0	0	3
Math	2	2	2	4
Sciences	1	1	1	0
Domestic education	1	0	0	0
Drawing	2	2	1	4
History	1	2	2	2
Geography	1	1	1	1
Physics /chemistry	1	0	0	2
Law	0	0	0	1
Accountancy	2	0	0	3
Stenography	0	0	0	2
Singing	1	0	0	0
Physical education	1	2	2	0
Needlework	2	0	0	0

Daughters of better situated urban families, who were not expected to share their education with rural or working-class children, were offered a new opportunity through these new female secondary schools. This is most apparent in the objectives of the Lycée de jeunes filles' school programme, which clearly grouped students according to their social background. Subjects like educational theory, physiological chemistry, food chemistry, hygiene, social training (*soziale Schulung*) and an introduction to welfare institutions were rather intended for 'young girls from higher and good middle-class families',[14] while the 'young girl from the middle classes' was expected to follow a practical path by studying needlework, domestic education and an 'introduction into the female professions'. Additionally, the girls of the middle classes should primarily acquaint themselves with the rules of etiquette and *bon ton*. Yet, these were the only target groups mentioned in the programme of the new Lycée. Even though the feminist movement had promoted this school as opening new intellectual possibilities, the pronounced intention was to keep *minderwertige Schülerinnen* (schoolgirls of minor value) away from a scientific career (Lycée de jeunes filles 1912, 12). As such, the negotiations in the run-up to communization already show an elitist orientation with the intention to 'not increase the proletariate' (Heuert 1909, ANLux IP 593).

During this time, an alleged curricular homogenization was achieved by making domestic education obligatory in all school branches. Such subjects, seemingly aimed exclusively at the private sphere, bore societal and political dimensions as well. Domestic education was also considered to be 'the most successful way to combat pauperism, immorality and alcoholism' (*Luxemburger Frau*, March 24 1929).[15] Even the preparation of the girls for familial education seemed to have a political dimension, since it appeared that a perceived adolescent deficit in civic sentiment would not be overcome by education in school (Cravatte 1921, ANLux IP 2054).

The Luxembourgian Ministry and the teachers ascribed a political dimension of national scope both to familial educational work and housekeeping tasks:

> She [the girl] easily understands that her future educational work will be crucial for the whole country, but she also has to become aware of the benefits of her good housekeeping for the country, as the major part of the national wealth passes through the hands of the women, and she has to become a conscientious caretaker. (C.Z. 1939)[16]

Since 1912, needlework and domestic education have been compulsory subjects for girls, at the expense of lessons in local studies (*Heimatkunde*), drawing and physical education. The curricular contents clearly display the aim of 'educating the housewife'. Apart from knowledge in hygiene and nutrition, lessons in cleanliness and neatness were most notably scheduled (*Arrêté du 25 mars* 1914, Mémorial du Grand-Duché de Luxembourg 1914, 345f., 370). Other issues besides moral education for 'domestic virtues' were practical matters, such as 'thriftiness and keeping a household account book' (*Arrêté du 25 mars* 1914, Mémorial du Grand-Duché de Luxembourg 1914, 345f., 370). While domestic education had been provided at upper primary schools for girls ever since their creation, domestic education was then introduced in secondary education after communization – a move perceived as retrograde by the initiators of the Lycée:

> In doing so, one was perhaps eager to safeguard the allegedly endangered femininity. Or maybe it was only due to the fact that there are so many bachelors seated in the Luxembourgian ministry, who imagine 'theoretically learned dusting' to be the most certain way to become a 'good housewife'? (Weber-Brugmann 1912, 382)[17]

Nevertheless, upper primary schools focussed more strongly on practical domestic education, not least by erecting school kitchens, gardens and sewing rooms. Beyond that, domestic education was intertwined with other subjects: in particular, lessons in drawing were (unlike the technical emphasis in boys' education) entirely oriented towards the needs of needlework exercises (Mémorial du Grand-Duché de Luxembourg 1916, 1097, 1120). The same holds true for the natural sciences designed to support domestic education: the prescribed topics were related to hygiene and nurture, horticulture and dairy farming (Lycée de jeunes filles 1912, 23, 26f.; *Der Luxemberger Schulbote* 1912, 375ff.), while the Lycée also dealt with the chemical composition of food (Lycée de jeunes filles, 1912 23, 26f.).

Though the lack of a proper scientific education had been one of the major criticisms towards denominationally bound education (Reports of the *commission d'instruction* 1904, 1909, AnLux IP 593), and had been named one of the reasons for the foundation of the Lycée, it was still the case that mathematical and scientific topics were dealt with differently in female and male education in public schools, e.g. natural science in girls' schools was clearly limited to 'practical exercises of domestic economy: domicile and household utensils; alimentation; clothes and laundry; firing and light',[18] topics that also gained belated importance in the upper primary schools after 1939. As of the second gymnasial grade, topics like savings, banks, health and accident insurances were added, while 'stocks, shares and bonds' remained limited to boys' education (Mémorial du Grand-Duché de Luxembourg 1916, 1111). Geometry, too, with its topics like 'measuring and calculating living areas', remained clearly limited to the domestic sphere. This differed greatly from the boys' schools, where 'levelling instruments, cubing of masonries' formed part of the curriculum. Curricula for the natural sciences in secondary schools read similarly, as instruction in physics and chemistry was still dominated by topics like 'Heating, combustible materials [...] studies about [...] chemical materials to be found in everyday housework and in hygiene' or even 'practical exercises for bleaching', revealing a striking scientification of domestic work (Huss 1900).[19]

Educating female citizens: resumé and prospects

The above-mentioned analysis proves that Luxembourg was not exempt from the narrative model depicted at the start of this article. Although it appeared that topics of female education for societal and political functions would gain greater influence in public and professional discourse, Luxembourg's conceptual debates nevertheless did not differentiate regarding perceptions of women and their role in society. Hence, it expressed the very same outlined homogenization of women separated from men.

Many statements from both official bodies and the feminist movement reveal the strategies with which women were assigned a 'societal role', while still inseparably linking these new societal functions to traditional role allocations. This was apparent, for instance: (1) by assigning 'public' functions to tasks that had been previously considered 'female' and 'private'; (2) through strategies of 'scientificating' domesticity; and (3) by constructing female morality in a dichotomy to male politicality, and enforcing role allocations via focussing on 'the concrete experience' as dominant starting point in female education (in contrast to the paradigm of *Bildung* in male secondary education).

It was exactly the rhetorical homogenization of a special girls' education that conserved existing gender differences in the school system. The homogenizing portrayal of female education fundamentally relied on traditional role allocations aimed at preserving the role of women as housewives and mothers. The structure of female education and the numerous codifications that sometimes reacted to private initiatives reveal that the foundations of specific girls' schools – unlike those often perceived in literature and public discourse – were not necessarily understood as 'modernizing', but more as conserving female role allocations, namely via introducing domestic education or stating a specific moral dimension. Also, it shows that female education was (unlike boys' education) not shaped by an ideal of preparing for specific professions.

It is not by coincidence that these measures concur with a politicization of the private sphere by women's associations and journals. In fact, the political initiatives of the feminist movement repeat and reinforce the basic allocation schemes. Education is assigned the role of mediating female students' acceptance of their future 'selfless' role in society. Compared to findings of neighbouring countries, this is not surprising. Both in Germany and in France, the institution of marriage as the real destiny of women was not openly questioned (Albisetti 2007; Clark 1984, 80). Instead, as in Luxembourg, the traditional role allocations were ascribed a political dimension and interpreted as progressive. The structure of female education mirrors the separation of male and female spheres, and goes beyond that by ranking masculinity beyond femininity in terms of access to education.

However, the plurality of concepts – though claiming universality – proves this homogenization did not reflect reality. The pedagogical concept of 'the female education' as a separate category did not exclude intersectional differentiation, although it does show a few rudimentary features, mainly based on the introduction of obligatory handcraft and domestic education. However, social and regional differences were still the prevailing concepts determining schooling, rather than gender differences. A social differentiation is already given by the structure of the school system, which given that there were no secondary schools for girls, meant education in Catholic private schools in the first instance. This remained persistent after the foundation of the Lycées de jeunes filles, which aimed at exclusiveness and were restricted to Luxembourg's major cities.

Admittedly, there was a conjunctive element to the institutionalization of public female education and its compulsory syllabi, foremost the introduction of domestic education and handcraft/needlework in all branches of female education. Yet the term 'domestic education' neither describes the same content from a temporal perspective nor allows a social or regional comparison between schools, as can already be seen in the linguistic distinction between practical domestic education as taught in upper primary schools, and 'theoretical domestic education' in secondary schools. *De facto*, the range of domestic topics spans from the 'education for the future agricultural house-wife' to artistic handcraft in the Catholic private schools, and 'education for charity' of urban girls in the secondary schools to suppression of alcoholism, 'health care' and 'practical cooking' in the upper primary schools.

Similar unifying tendencies are shown in the reduction of the languages spoken by the elite, which meant scientific (Latin) and public service languages (French), and the reduction of science and math lessons. Yet it should be emphasized again that social and regional differences were the prevailing ones. As such, the curricular negotiations on female education in Luxembourg enforce a gender-separated and socially differentiated future citizen.

Notes

1. One reason for this increasing separation is revealed by the mid-nineteenth century primary school evaluation, for example, in Echternach. The commission attested to a remarkably high level of performance in the girls' classes, but also criticised the poor performance of the boys. The commission recommended structural alterations and, in particular, a strict separation of boys and girls.

2. Since 1892, boys were obliged to attend a post-primary school for at least one more year after primary education.

3. *'In einem dieser belgischen oder rheinländischen Klöster, die so billig sind, und von wo die jungen Mädchen mit einem ganz netten Firnis von Bildung wiederkommen'.*

4. *'Und es ist sehr bequem mit dem großen Strom zu schwimmen, der so sicher und selbstverständlich in den stagnierenden See behaglich zufriedenen Kleinstädtertums mündet'.*

5. *'Mut, Geradheit, Stärke, Ehrlichkeit im Geschäft usw. Kann besser in den Knaben durch den Mann entwickelt werden, wie Liebenswürdigkeit, Takt, Selbstlosigkeit usw. Den Mädchen am besten durch eine Frau beigebracht werden'.*

6. *'a) weil die Frau nicht selten auf sich selbst angewiesen ist, b) weil sie wegen ihres großen Einflusses in der Familie wissen soll, wofür und wie der Staat Opfer fordert'.*

7. *'... loi de nature et une nécessité de la vie sociale'.*

8. *'Dans la civilisation la femme y a sa part, non pas comme citoyenne, mais comme compagne de l'homme, comme épouse et notamment comme mère'.*

9. *'Die Luxemburger Frauen und Mädchen erleben in diesen Tagen die patriotische Begeisterung vielleicht noch tiefer als die einheimische Männerwelt. Bei der Frau schwingt [...] die ganze Tiefe des Gemütes mit. Sie fühlen – wie aus einem mütterlichen Instinkt heraus – den Wert der vaterländischen Anhänglichkeit'.*

10. This parallels international findings: According to Albisetti, the largest differences in the German feminist movement were between women from the middle classes and the women from the lower classes (Albisetti 2007, 190).

11. *'In mancher Schule lernt das Bauerntöchterlein das Weißsticken, Filetstricken, Häkeln, ehe es im Stande ist, einen einfachen Strumpf in guter Form zu stricken, [...] dagegen erwacht in ihm eine förmliche Abneigung gegen die einfachen und gemeinen Arbeiten [...]. Das an der Stickrahme erzogene Bauerntöchterlein hält es bald für zu gemein und zu niedrig, am Herde zu stehen [...] Die alte Mutter ist genötigt, die ganze Last der Haushaltung auf ihren schwachen Schultern zu tragen und muß es oft mitansehen, wie das verzärtelte Töchterlein [...] die Früchte ihres Schweißes vertändelt oder vergeudet'.*

12. The comparison is based on all programmes of upper primary schools in 1890 (ANLux IP 1598).

13. The comparison of the secondary schools is based on all school programmes of the secondary schools in 1911.

14. *'... junge Mädchen aus höhern oder gutbürgerlichen Kreisen'.*

15. *'... die erfolgreichste Bekämpfung des Pauperismus, der Unsittlichkeit, des Alkoholismus'.*

16. *'Daß seine spätere Erziehungsarbeit für das Land entscheidend ist, leuchtet ihm leicht ein, es muß sich aber auch dessen bewußt werden, daß es durch eine gute Haushaltsführung dem Lande nützen kann, daß der größte Teil des Volksvermögens durch Frauenhände geht, und es ein gewissenhafter Verwalter werden muss'.*

17. *'Vielleicht suchte man dadurch die angeblich gefährdete Weiblichkeit[...] zu retten. Oder ist vielleicht nur der Umstand schuld daran, daß am Luxemburger Ministertisch [...] so viele Junggesellen sitzen, denen ‚theoretisch gelerntes Staubwischen' [...] als der sicherste Weg zur ‚guten Hausfrau' vorschwebt?'*

18. *'... praktische Aufgaben aus der Hauswirtschaft: Wohnung und Hausgeräte; Nahrung, Kleidung und Wäsche; Feuerung und Licht'.*

19. Such scientification strategies as the legitimation of traditional role allocations can also be found in other European countries, e.g. in Sweden.

References

Albisetti, James. 2007. *Mädchen- und Frauenbildung im 19. Jahrhundert.* Bad Heilbrunn: Klinkhardt.

Appelt, Erna. 1999. *Geschlecht, Staatsbürgerschaft, Nation. Politische Konstruktionen des Geschlechterverhältnisses in Europa.* Frankfurt am Main: Campus.

Archives Nationales de Luxembourg, Portfolio of the Instruction Publique (IP), Files no. ANLux IP 593, ANLux IP 2054. Luxembourg.

Arnot, Madeleine. 1997. "Gendered Citizenry: New Feminist Perspectives on Education and Citizenship." *Britih Educational Research Journal* 23 (3): 275–295.

Besch, Nadine. 2009. "Das Frauenbild in der Zeitungsbeilage 'Luxemburger Frau' (1919–1940)." Master thesis, University of Luxembourg.

Cariers, Pierre. 1932. *Landwirtschaftliche Wanderhaushaltungsschule.* Luxemburg.

Chambre des Députés (ChD). 1912. *La Loi du 10 Août 1912 sur L'enseignement Primaire. Documents et Discussions Parlementaires 1906–1912.* Luxemburg: ChD.

Clark, Linda. 1984. *Schooling the Daughters of Marianne: Textbooks and the Socialization of Girls in Modern French Primary Schools.* New York: SUNY.

Commune de Luxembourg. 1901. *Lehrplan für die Primärschulen der Stadt Luxemburg.* Luxembourg: Community Council.

C. Z. 1939. "Nationale Mädchenerziehung." *Schulfreund. Bulletin de l'Union catholique des institu teurs et institutrices du Grand-Duché de Luxembourg* 1: n.p.

Das tote Viertel. Escher Tageblatt vom 8. September 1931, 1.

Der Luxemburger Schulbote - Le Courrier des Écoles dans le Grand-Duché de Luxembourg. Ene Zeitschrift Zunächst für die Schullehrer des Großherzogtums Luxemburg Bestimmt. Luxemburg: V. Bück. (vols. 20/1863; 66/1909; 69/1912).

Der Luxemburger Bauernfreund: Kalender für Acker- und Gartenbau für das Jahr. 1888. Luxemburg: Acker- und Gartenbau-Verein des Grossherzogtums Luxemburg.

Die Luxemburger Frau. Wochenbeilage des Luxemburger Wort. (23 April 1919; 20 August 1920; 24. March 1929).

Götzinger, Germaine. 1997. "Der Verein für die Interessen der Frau' oder bürgerliche Frauenbewegung in Luxemburg." In *Wenn nun wir Frauen auch das Wort ergreifen.... 1880–1950: Frauen in Luxemburg,* edited by Germaine Götzinger, Antoinette Lorang, and Renée Wagener, 63–79. Luxembourg: Publications nationales.

Huss, Mathias. 1900. *Der Wissensschatz der Künftigen Hausfrau: eine Einführung in das Rationelle Verständnis der Hauswirtschaftlichen Verrichtungen für den Schul- und Hausgebrauch.* Luxemburg: M. Huss.

Jones, Ginette. 1997. "Die Entstehung der Sozialversicherung und ihre Bedeutung für die Situation der Frauen." In *Wenn nun wir Frauen auch das Wort Ergreifen.... 1880–1950: Frauen in Luxemburg,* edited by Germaine Götzinger, Antoinette Lorang, and Renée Wagener, 223–238. Luxembourg: Publications nationales.

Kellen, Tony. 1930. "Aus dem Geistesleben in Luxemburg, Teil V: Unser Bildungswesen." *Luxemburger Illustrierte* 12: 14–22.

Kelly, Elinor. 1993. "Gender Issues in Education for Citizenship." In *Cross Curricular Context: Themes and Dimensions in Secondary School,* edited by Gajendra Verma and Peter Pumfrey, 144–158. London: Falmer.

Kmec, Sonja. 2010. "Da Léiers de e Bësschen Franséisch an d'Welt Kennen: sur les traces d'une Domestique Luxembourgeoise à Bruxelles et Paris." In *Aufbrüche und Vermittlungen. Beiträge zur Luxemburger und Europäischer Literatur- und Kulturgeschichte,* edited by Claude Conter and Nicole Sahl, 63–83. Bielefeld: Aisthesis.

Lycée de jeunes filles Luxembourg. 1912. *Programme publié a la Clôture de l'année scolaire 1911–1912.* Luxembourg: Lycée de jeunes filles.

Lycée de jeunes filles Luxembourg. 1959. *Cinquantième Anniversaire de la fondation du Lycée de jeunes filles.* Luxembourg: Lycée de jeunes filles.

Mémorial du Grand-Duché de Luxembourg. 1881. Memorial A, no. 32. www.legilux.public.lu (accessed 19 October 2010).

Mémorial du Grand-Duché de Luxembourg. 1914. Memorial A, no. 20. www.legilux.public.lu (accessed 19 October 2010).

Mémorial du Grand-Duché de Luxembourg. 1916. Memorial A, no. 76. www.legilux.public.lu (accessed 19 October 2010).

Neyens, Jeanne. 1987. "Mädchen, Schlagt die Augen Nieder! Erinnerungen an Sainte-Sophie vor dem Zweiten Weltkrieg." *Ons Stad* 25: 14–16.

Phillips, Anne. 1991. *Engendering Democracy.* Cambridge: Polity Press.

Schreiber, Catherina. 2012. "Comme Compagne de l'Homme, comme Épouse et Notamment comme mère: Staatsbürgerinnenerziehung in Luxemburg Zwischen Rhetorischer Homogenität und Curricularer Heterogenität." *Hémecht. Revue d'Histoire Luxembourgeoise* 3: 5–21.

Service Central de la Statistique et des études Cconomiques (STATEC). 1990. *Statistiques historiques 1839–1989. Annuaire statistique*. Luxembourg: STATEC.

Tockert, Joseph. 1924. "Die Gründung des Mädchenlyzeums in Luxemburg." *Les Cahiers luxembourgeois* 7: 543–550.

Weber-Brugmann, Emma. 1912. "Luxemburger Mädchenschulwesen." *Frauenbildung* 8/9: 379–383.

How gender became sex: mapping the gendered effects of sex-group categorisation onto pedagogy, policy and practice

Gabrielle Ivinson

School of Education, Aberdeen University, Aberdeen, UK

Background: The paper plots some shifts in educational policy between 1988 and 2009 in England that launched the rhetoric of a 'gender gap' as a key political and social concern. The rhetoric was fuelled by a rise in the importance of quantification in technologies of accountability and global comparisons of achievement. A focus on boys and attainment emerged, along with new requirements for measuring educational achievement in the context of debates about standards and the growing marketisation of education following the 1988 Educational Reform Act (ERA) in England and Wales.

Purpose: Theoretically, the paper explores the effect of 'gender gap' rhetoric on pedagogy. The arguments about pedagogy presented here are based on the premise that *sex-group* is different from *gender*. Sex-group is a form of labelling and categorising persons as either male or female with reference to a biological classification that focuses on genitalia and reproductive organs. The emergence of 'gender gap' rhetoric is investigated within a temporal perspective, through an overview of guidance to teachers about pedagogy published between 1932 and 2007. This temporal lens becomes a heuristic for presenting the main point of the paper, which is that technologies of measurement construct reified representations of the learner. This is used to demonstrate how gender, as a sociocultural and political phenomenon, morphed into sex-group, a biological categorisation, and how this has had unintended effects of pedagogy.

Sources of evidence: Analysis of three landmark educational documents focuses on changes in representations of society, the learner and pedagogy. The documents are the Hadow Report (1931), the Plowden Report (1967) and a guidance document for teachers called 'Confident, Capable and Creative: supporting boys' achievements' (Department for Children, Schools and Families 2007, http://www.foundation-years.org.uk/wp-content/uploads/2011/10/Confident_Capable_Boys.pdf).

Main argument: Analysis demonstrates the way that technologies of measurement construct reified or 'ideal' representations of the learner and how technologies used for measuring sex-group difference have changed across time. Shifts in representations of the learner, from the 'bone child' to the 'gene child' and eventually to the 'masculine child' were detected. These shifts represent a gradual decline in the emphasis on pedagogy as nurture, towards a heightened focus on the supposedly innate characteristics of individuals, in line with neoliberalism.

Conclusions: The discussion points to some of the unintended effects on pedagogy and practice that take place when gender becomes sex. If teachers are constantly presented with the message that boys and girls learn differently due to innate genetic make-up, they may assume that whatever pedagogic strategies they employ, these will be ineffective in the face of what some educational consultants tell them are boys' and girls' innate genetic features. In effect, teachers are being told that biology controls learning and that social and cultural contexts, and thus their own classroom environments, cannot counter the forces of nature. Some methodological implications of studying gender as opposed to sex-group are discussed. The conclusion advocates a shift back to the study of gender as a historical, sociocultural phenomenon.

Introduction: locating the gender gap rhetoric

The social representation of 'gender' remains an insidious and ubiquitous phenomenon that is not easy to capture and categorise. Gender, according to a sociocultural perspective (Ivinson and Murphy 2007; Rogoff 1995, 2003; Murphy and Gipps 1996), is part of the historical, cultural, political and social fabric of life and so is complexly related to persons. In England, the undiminishing political appetite for measuring attainment has brought sex-group to the fore, through a focus on 'numbers' and quantitative methods of analysis (Ball 2012; Goldstein 2001; Lingard and Ozga 2007). In the UK, statistical techniques have been utilised in the creation of educational markets (e.g. Department for Education 2013). As part of this, schools are required to report and publicise educational achievement data by sex-group. Accordingly, the considerable scholarship on how *gender* influences education achievement, that burgeoned during the 1980s (Arnot, David, and Weiner 1999) has been forgotten and sex-group categories are increasingly used as a proxy for gender. The predominance of the application of statistical technologies in the measurement of educational achievement can be seen to relate to globalisation and the rise of neoliberalism.

The global rescaling of educational politics and policies has ushered in specific technologies of visibility and accountability (Ball 2012; Foucault 1972; Miller and Rose 2008; Rose 1999). The measures used to analyse educational achievement privilege numbers (Lingard and Rawolle 2011) and specifically standard test scores such as Programme for International Students Assessment (PISA) and Trends in International Mathematics and Science Study (TIMSS) that supposedly create a level playing field to allow international comparisons of educational achievement to be made objectively. However, these quantitative data analyses control for, or factor out, social and cultural issues (Gipps and Goldstein 1983; Goldstein 2001; Thomas and Mortimore 1996) as, 'noise' and 'mess', either through the way tests are designed as supposedly neutral (Gipps and Murphy 1994) or by using other measures to factor out national, local and personal cultures (Lingard and Ozga 2007; Tikly 2001).

The section that follows plots some shifts in educational policy between 1988 and 2009 in England that launched the rhetoric of a 'gender gap' as a key political and social concern (Arnot, David, and Weiner 1999; Younger, Warrington, and Williams 1999). Next, a brief historical overview of guidance to teachers published in 1932, 1967 and 2007 is presented, placing 'gender gap' rhetoric within a temporal perspective. Analysis of three educational documents suggests how technologies used to measure sex-group difference have changed across time. This temporal lens becomes a heuristic for presenting the main point of the paper, which is that technologies of measurement construct reified representations of the learner. The documentary analysis traces how the pedagogic guidance given to teachers changed between the 1930s and 2007. The discussion points to some of the unintended effects on pedagogy and practice that take place when 'gender' becomes 'sex'. Some methodological implications of studying gender as opposed to sex-group are discussed. The conclusion advocates a shift back to the study of gender as a historical, sociocultural phenomenon.

The emergence of 'gender gap' rhetoric in the UK

This section considers the relationship that politics and policy-making has with education assessment in England and how a dominant narrative contrasting boys' so called
'underachievement' with girls' 'educational success' has emerged. The UK comprises
the four jurisdictions of Northern Ireland, Scotland, England and Wales. Each jurisdiction has a separate education system covering policy and administration; these are
becoming increasingly distinct as devolved control within each jurisdiction increases.
The focus on so-called 'gender gaps' has influenced educational policy and practice in
each jurisdiction in different ways, while the public perception of the 'problem' has
been driven by reports in the national press and media, providing a widespread perception that boys were losing out to girls. The focus on boys emerged along with new
requirements for measuring educational achievement. These arose in the context of
debates about standards following the 1988 Educational Reform Act (ERA) in England
and Wales.

The Educational Reform Act encouraged local educational markets to be created
(Whitty 2002). The political motivation to create markets was based on the idea that if
schools were in competition with each other, teachers would be motivated to teach better and so produce better examination results year on year. Educational markets rely on
the public (in this case, parents) having access to data by which they can compare the
relative performance of schools in their locale. Politicians assumed that parents would
choose to send their children to the school(s) that produced the highest rates of examination success.

Schools were required to measure achievement against targets at key stages identified at ages 7, 11 and 14 using the government's national curriculum tests (which
became known as 'SATs') in English, Mathematics and Science. Data gathered from
these tests were published in league tables, which identified schools according to performance measured by national curriculum levels, GCSE (General Certificate of Secondary
Education, taken at age 16 years) grades and A (advanced) level examinations (taken at
age 18 years) results. Schools were obliged to make performance data available to parents in 1992 (Goldstein 2001) and this data had to be aggregated by sex-group. Data
made visible the differential performance of boys and girls by subject and by year
group. Data demonstrated that girls had been improving their performance in the 'traditional male' subjects such as mathematics, science and technology, year on year. While
boys were said to have been losing ground to girls in these subjects, data also demonstrated that the gap between boys' and girls' performance in English and modern languages was widening rather than narrowing (Gipps and Murphy 1994). Boys became
identified as the losers within co-educational provision which, some believed was deteri-
orating (although these findings have been contested. e.g. Gorard 2000; Skelton 2001;
Elwood and Gipps 1999; Murphy and Whitelegg 2006). However, when sex-group data
were re-examined using measures of social class background and ethnicity, different patterns emerged (Gorard 2000). Middle class boys continued to perform well year on year.
The visibility of the gap in achievement between boys and girls was a consequence
of the use of testing and assessment data that formed an integral part of the
Post-Educational Reform Act (1988) landscape (Goldstein 2001). There have been some
shifts in emphasis behind the political motivations to make achievement data publicly
available, which I now briefly touch on.

Under the UK Conservative government of Margaret Thatcher, initiatives to raise
the educational standards of the population were fuelled, in part, by international

comparisons. The Assessment and Performance Unit (APU) was set up in the 1980s initially to measure accountability through pupil assessments and then later it narrowed its focus to assessing 'key skills' (Gipps and Goldstein 1983). Fears about the futures of boys who had become dispossessed within the labour market, partly due to the decline in manufacturing jobs and the lack of apprenticeships, grew during the 1990s. The debate in the UK media polarised around social class. Some sections of the print media, with primarily working class readerships, blamed middle class, 'child centred' or 'progressive' schooling for boys' lack of motivation in school. Newspapers with a more middle class readership pondered the relationship between gender and learning and remembered a little about the debate over initiatives aimed to encourage girls to study and achieve well in science and technology in the mid-1980s, such as *Girls Into Science and Technology* (GIST) and *Women in Science and Engineering* (WISE) (cf. TES 1998). A popular media story was that the middle class 'trendies' had ruined the educational chances of working class boys through 'progressive' pedagogies. When John Major became the Conservative Prime Minister in 1990, he identified the solution as a need to get 'back to basics', which placed a renewed emphasis on reading, writing and arithmetic, along with computer studies and traditional pedagogic approaches (Ivinson and Murphy 2007). The emphasis on literacy was two-fold: first, it was seen to be essential if the UK was to compete in the so-called knowledge economy in which symbolic labour was epitomised by literacy. Symbolic manipulation had become the desired capital and second, literacy was the subject in which boys were failing most obviously in comparison to girls (ibid.).

The New Labour government under Tony Blair (UK Prime Minister from 1997 to 2007) took up the education standard debate with renewed vigour. The New Labour educational reform agenda was based on arguments about globalisation, changes in labour markets and post-Fordian working patterns that were perceived to require generic skills, flexible workers, casual contracts, technological literacy as well as entrepreneurial skills to compete with Pacific rim countries. The government-led exhortation to raise standards and the high stakes measurement of attainment continued and intensified.

The debate shifted to more technical issues about the instruments required to 'change' pedagogic practice. Arguments for the possibility of raising standards through top-down, centrally imposed, pedagogic and curricular interventions flourished. The pedagogic solutions at the time imposed what have been characterised as centralised, prescriptive and formulaic teaching methods on teachers in primary schools, for example, through the 'literacy' and 'numeracy' hour (Moss 2001). The debate also started to focus increasingly on boys' needs. In particular, social and media concerns over the rise of 'laddishness', a term used to denote a specific kind of male youth culture, was seen to be interfering with boys' academic ambitions (Jackson 2006).

Therefore, a national preoccupation with and conceptualisation of the statistical gap between boys' and girls' achievement levels in education has to been seen as part of a wider social problem which included fears that a faction of the working class was destined to become a permanently unemployed and, therefore, a disenfranchised group, due to shifts in the economic base. These have been termed the 'at-risk' boys, which Skeggs (2004) has argued became identified as the 'bad' working class with 'bad' lifestyles, 'bad' taste, 'bad' manners and 'bad' educational performance. Along with this sense of demonisation, increasingly, working class boys, and boys in general, were also presented as the victims (Burman 2005) of a changing economic structure, in which it was perceived that school cultures had become feminised and that girls were taking boys' jobs. A popular catch phrase frequently used in TV and newspaper media, 'the future is female', reflected a ubiquitous fear that women and girls were taking over and actively contributing to the perceived demise of masculinity.

A general fear circulated that schools, curricula and forms of assessment were disadvantaging boys. One initiative advocated singe-sex classes as a 'solution' to the 'gender gap'. Single sex classes were imagined as spaces that would restore a normative and dominant social representation of masculinity that was perceived to have been weakened through contact with what many imagined were overly feminised school environments (Ivinson and Murphy 2007). Fears and phantasies about the social and school environment as dangerous, stultifying or negative have always been apparent, as the brief overview of some landmark educational reports presented below will suggest. With the decline of the industrial base and the subsequent lack of manual jobs and industrial apprenticeships, the school leaving age in the UK has gradually risen and schools are expected to act as 'holding places' for students from working class communities. Before placing the policy changes described in this section within a temporal context, I describe what is meant in this paper by pedagogy.

Theorising pedagogy: nurture improving on nature

Pedagogy since the seventeenth century has been imagined as nurture improving on nature (Fox-Keller 1985). A dialectical relationship between nature and nurture can be detected even in the writings of John Locke (ibid.). However, up until the educational Acts of the 1870s in the UK, church groups governed schools and knowledge was imagined to belong to God or the gods (Adam and Groves 2007). Accordingly, knowledge was believed to belong to the past; who we were and who we became was fixed by destiny and even the future was thought to be predestined. Therefore, pedagogy in this era was very much a matter of teaching people to know their place in the universe and, in the UK, schooling and pedagogic instruction maintained the historically rooted, social class and gender divides within society. Pedagogy was, in Basil Bernstein's (1996) terms, 'retrospective' and the act of giving the next generation access to the knowledge that had worked in the previous generation was considered to be empowering. However, only groups of higher socio-economic status were considered worthy of inheriting this knowledge. The Hadow Reports (www.educationengland.org.uk/documents/hadow1931/hadow1931.html), discussed later, that appeared in the 1930s were radical and progressive because they advocated pedagogies that would improve on and change the social position of the poorest children in society. In effect, these Reports marked a moment when pedagogies were explicitly presented as nurture: improving on, rather than reproducing, nature.

From the Hadow Reports of the 1930s (Board of Education 1931) to the Plowden Report (Central Advisory Council for Education 1967), also discussed below, pedagogy was increasingly presented as a craft in which teachers were encouraged to create classroom environments to nurture and build on the natural characteristics that children brought with them to school. In a guidance document called 'Confident, Capable and Creative' (Department for Children, Schools and Families 2007), teachers were warned not to misrecognise boys' boisterous behaviour for bad behaviour and, for the first time, pedagogic guidance was explicitly directed at boys.

In the historical section below, I trace the way nature was imagined and represented across this period. My analysis focuses on the early years of education only. The aim will be to demonstrate how the technologies that were available in each period for measuring progress contributed to a changing representation of early years' learners. Before setting off on this brief historical overview, I unpack a little how the controversial 'nurture and nature' dichotomy relates to gender and sex-group.

Gender and sex-group

The arguments about pedagogy presented in this paper are based on the premise that sex-group is different from gender. Sex-group is a form of labelling and categorising persons as either male or female with reference to a biological classification that focuses on genitalia and reproductive organs (Fausto-Sterling 1992).

As far back as 1968, Robert J. Stoller in the USA made the distinction between sex and gender, which, although controversial (Fausto-Sterling 1992), is worth recalling. In his book, *Sex and Gender* (1968), Stoller suggested that a child's gender identity emerges around the age of two years by way of three influences, which are: (1) biological and hormonal; (2) sex assignment at birth and (3) environmental and psychological influences such as imprinting. These influences were conceptualised at the time as either biologically or culturally rooted. Sandra Lipitz Bem also made a strong distinction between sex-group and gender when she devised the controversial Bem Sex Role Inventory (BSRI) in 1971. The inventory requires a respondent to answer a series of questions about their preferences and habits, which are scored and used to measure a person's maleness and femaleness. Thus, a man may be scored as having many female traits and so on. The BSRI was designed to capture gender stereotypes and so probably says more about how a person conforms to those cultural stereotypes than it does about the person. Furthermore, as Bem has pointed out, there is a grave danger that self-reporting questionnaires will serve simply to reinforce stereotypes such as boys being active, inquisitive and risk-takers while girls, on the other hand, being passive, compliant and boringly good. Clearly, if a questionnaire asks a boy or a girl if they prefer to move or sit, study mathematics or English, it is fairly predictable that the results will reflect the cultural gender norms in society at that time. Furthermore, there is a need to be constantly vigilant and not slip from statistical inferences based on self-reporting questionnaires to 'causes'. We cannot reduce gender to a factor or assume that sex-group categories (boy, girl) correspond to, or cause, sociocultural gender norms of masculinity and femininity (Eagley 1987; Stoller 1968).

The need to distinguish gender from sex-group has a strong legacy within feminist scholarship, which has been highly critical of self-reporting questionnaires to measure gender (Crang 2002; Harding 1986; Lott 1981; Stacey, Phoenix, and Hinds 2004; Stanley and Wise 1983; Stanley 1990). Within the UK and in other western European countries, the field of gender and education research emerged within political movements campaigning for women's emancipation. The field reached a critical mass in the 1980s when a number of feminist sociologists, including Madeleine Arnot, Gaby Weiner, Miriam David and Sara Delamont, and psychologists such as Valerie Walkerdine in the UK established theories about how gender dynamics were recreated through institutional practices in schools and universities. Ethnographic studies of schooling burgeoned in the 1980s and were published in academic journals such as *Gender and Education*. Later, studies of masculinity and schooling grew rapidly, following Connell's book *Masculinities* in 1995 and Mac an Ghaill's study, *The Making of Men*, in 1994. The aims of qualitative studies of gender were to understand how gender emerges in the everyday flows of classroom and school practices and, further, how gender can act as sociocultural resources (e.g. Murphy and Gipps 1996) that can be taken up and used by students and teachers in interactions and practices. Ethnographic research demonstrated how such practices often contribute to the reproduction of gender roles and inequalities in education and in life more generally. However, underlying the methods adopted by feminist educational researchers was a strong commitment to understanding epistemology, and how research instruments and technologies construct realities. I return to the epistemological issues around research methods in the discussion. The next section traces the way the child learner was imagined as the technologies used to investigate children's educational achievement developed. I pause at a moment in 2009 when I show how educational policy in England adopted a distinct focus on sex-group and pedagogic guidance became explicitly oriented towards boys.

Representations of pedagogy and the learner: a temporal perspective

This section refers to three educational reports and documents to trace shifts in the way pedagogy was represented from the 1930s to 2009. A brief analysis of these documents maps slippages in the way society, pedagogy and gender were imagined in each period.

The 1930s

Up until the 1870s, the school curriculum was dominated by Latin and Greek texts, grammar, rhetoric and logic. In England, the Hadow Report (Board of Education 1931) shifted the pedagogic gaze from texts to children and marked the beginning of progressive pedagogy in the UK. The drudgery of factory work loomed as an ever-present background image in the document, while malnutrition and disease were cited as the main barriers to development. Children from industrial city centres and rural villages were presented as if they were deprived of adequate stimulation, without which the senses were said to atrophy. Up to the age of five years, development was said to be dominated by senses, motility, movement and energy, and there were many references to children's skeletal and muscular systems within the documents that invoked bodies that could kick, see and touch. Teachers were advised to enable children to move. The Report suggested that learning could not take place when bodies were constrained behind desks bolted to the floor, as they were in Victorian schools built in the late 1800s.

Young children in the early years of development were presented in the Report as a homogenous group and descriptions are dominated by reference to corporeality: the development of bones, muscles and sinews. Apart from its focus on the dirt, malnutrition and unhygienic conditions in working class houses, the Report had little to say about early years pedagogy, because of a general belief that children at that stage were not sufficiently developed to allow meaningful differentiation between them in terms of cognition. A common curriculum and pedagogy were deemed appropriate. The only departure was with respect to physical education, which the Report recommended should take place in single-sex classes, due to a dominant belief that boys were stronger and required move physical movement than girls.

In the report, children were presented through descriptions of bodies with a particular focus on materiality in terms of physiology and the senses. Yet underlying this one can detect a form of vitalism that can be traced back to Locke, who placed the source of knowledge in the senses. According to Locke, one of the qualities inherent in matter is motion and this included mathematical motion; that is, motion as impulse, vital spirit and tension. According to Hadow, the early years' curriculum would, ideally, have been craft based, with an emphasis on the senses and movement because the motivation to learn was imagined to stem from corporeal vitalism rather than the mind.

The 1960s

In the Plowden Report (Central Advisory Council for Education 1967), a shift in lower school pedagogy from an undifferentiated approach to an individualistic approach can be detected. The Report starts with the message that at the heart of the educational process is the child. It suggested that the curriculum should be build on where the child *was* developmentally:

> No advances in policy, no acquisitions of new equipment have their desired effect unless they are in harmony with the nature of the child. (Central Advisory Council for Education 1967, 7)

The hundreds of table and graphs in Volume Two present measurements of various kinds starting with average weights and height for children at specific ages. The Report also draws heavily on the 11 plus tests. The 11 plus test was taken by all children in the UK aged 11 between 1944 and 1976 and determined which kind of secondary (high) school they attended after primary education; either the elite grammar or the non-academic secondary modern school. The 11 plus test was redesigned in the 1960s to reflect Charles Spearman's test for general intelligence 'g' (Sumner 2011). Spearman identified 'g' through factor analysis and correlations from a range of tests that measured, for example, visual perception, abstract reasoning, reading ability and memory. A chapter in the Plowden Report (Central Advisory Council for Education 1967) entitled 'The interaction of heredity and environment' can be read as a detailed lesson in genetics. Normal distribution curves demonstrated that across a range of measures determined by paper and pencil tests, the population of children was highly diverse. Therefore, the Report argued that teachers had to aim their pedagogy at individuals rather than homogeneous groups as in the Hadow Reports, because IQ testing had revealed that within one classroom children had a wide range of abilities. Thus the seeds of the individualistic, child-centred philosophy were well and truly sown.

The Report assumed that teachers could identify intelligence from children's performances in tests. Thus we can trace a shift away from a focus on children's visible corporeality in the Hadow Report towards a focus on the hidden biological matter of genetics. The Plowden Report (Central Advisory Council for Education 1967) presented IQ testing as the new scientific approach to education. The new philosophy that 'everyone is different' invalidated pedagogic practices aimed at groups and the Report advised teachers that every child should be taught according to their ability, where crucially ability was conceptualised as an unquestioned fact discoverable by tests. It was only much later that critiques of the claims that IQ tests detected something genetic such as essential intelligence surfaced (e.g. Gould 1996, Vygotsky 1988). Teachers were extolled to pay attention to the individual variation among children and focus on making pedagogy flexible:

> ... an apple sorting model does not square with the nature of the biological material', (creating a need for) 'a cat's cradle of opportunity, providing multitude of differently developing talents with their own appropriate times and degrees of achievement. (Central Advisory Council for Education 1967, 10)

Pedagogic practice became an ever more sophisticated art of creating the optimum classroom environment to facilitate the natural unfolding of each individual child's potential. The motivation force behind leaning shifted from corporeal vitalism to intelligence.

The late 2000s

In the late 2000s, a new discourse about pedagogic practice emerged. In 2007–2009, in an unusual step, the government's Department for Children, Schools and Families (DCSF) explored the 'gender gap' by consulting academics who understood the sociocultural dynamics of gender. For a brief period, the feminist research community had some influence and managed to broaden the gender gap debate beyond a narrow focus on statistics. For example, Christine Skelton, Becky Francis and Gemma Moss contributed to the DCFS Final Report on 'The Gender Agenda' and the subsequent guidance to educators called *Gender and Education – Mythbusters* (DCSF 2009).

However, their advice seemed to have fallen on deaf ears, for about this time a document called 'Confident, Capable and Creative: supporting boys' achievements' (Primary National Strategy, Department for Children, Schools and Families 2007) appeared on the government's official education website. It provided pedagogic guidance to teachers of children aged three to five years. The documents was not as substantial as the reports mentioned earlier, yet can be seen as a landmark document because it provided teachers with explicit guidance on how to teach boys. It is important to note that no equivalent document to support girls' achievement was published. Teachers were advised to use 'boys' fascinations and learning preferences as starting points' (DCSF 2007, 3) for their pedagogic practice. Creating the right conditions, it suggested, allows children to 'develop self-confidence in themselves as learners, explorers, discovers and as critical thinkers in a rapidly changing world' (ibid.). It stated:

> This is particularly important for boys as their natural exuberance, energy and keen exploratory drive may often be misinterpreted. Unwittingly boys can be labelled and their behaviour be perceived as inappropriate or even challenging. (DCSF 2007, 3)

The Confident, Capable and Creative document explicitly drew on new discourses that suggested boys were losing confidence within an overly feminised school environment. Teachers were told to change the environment by challenging their own common sense notions about boys' attention seeking and disruptive behaviour. It suggested that teachers' ideas and pedagogic approaches 'may be leading boys to 'pick up ideas that their natural curiosity is wrong,' so stifling their exploratory drives (ibid.).

> If they perceive that their strengths, interests and learning preferences are not respected they will lose interest in the leaning process. (Ibid.)

In effect, teachers' (feminine) pedagogy was presented as harmful to masculinity. It needs to be remembered that the majority of primary school teachers in the UK are women. In the booklet, the uniqueness attributed to masculinity was underscored by references to neuroscience.

Connected to this notion of normative masculinity was an argument that boys have different 'learning styles' from girls (for a critique of this, see Younger, Warrington, and Williams 1999; Younger and Warrington, with McLellan 2005). The argument was supported partly by common sense ideas about biological difference in attention spans, boys' supposed over-active hormones and the need for structure, which often drew on non-academic writers making over exaggerated claims about neuroscience (e.g. Gurian 2001; Hoff Sommers 2000). Neuroscience is a nascent scientific field and the exaggerated claims that many educational consultants attribute to neuroscience have been challenged by authors such as Cordelia Fine (2010) who recently identified such claims as neurosexism. Also included in these debates was the idea that boys' and girls' socialisation provided them with different habits and interests, yet no evidence for this was provided. The Confident, Capable and Creative document gave the impression that the motivational force behind leaning is a kind of innate masculinity presented as 'exploratory drive' or 'natural curiosity' that specifically belonged to boys. Masculinity became the vital force that teachers had to learn to recognise and promote.

From bones, to minds, to sex-group

Across this period from the 1930s to the 2000s, teachers have been told to shift their gaze. In the Hadow Report, the pedagogic gaze came to rest on children collectively rather than texts. A science of human development that focused on corporeal change (muscles, bones and tissues) started to inform pedagogy. The Plowden Report (Central Advisory Council for Education 1967) instructed teachers to differentiate their gaze between children. The hegemonic group of early years learners presented in the Hadow Report (Board of Education 1931) became a diverse range of individual children with varying IQs and 'g's. From 2009 onwards, teachers have been instructed to shift their gaze to sex-group differences and specifically to masculinity. Amidst an elongated moral panic about girls winning the achievement race, the Confident, Capable and Creative guidance document (Department for Children, Schools and Families 2007), instead of setting up optimum environments for individuals, instructed teachers to set up optimum environments for boys. This guidance re-established a status quo within education that, except for a short period between the mid-1980s and 1990s, has implicitly assumed that boys' interests are at the centre of education, curricula and pedagogic practices (Arnot, David, and Weiner 1999; Ivinson and Murphy 2007). In 2009, teachers were instructed to develop pedagogic approaches that would allow masculinity to flourish, with an implicit assumption that masculinity is the vital force that could reignite economy recovery. These slippages are summarised below in Table 1.

We can trace slippages in representations of social life, from collective to individual; in pedagogy, from nurture to nature and in gender, from implicit to explicit masculinity.

If the construction of the learner foregrounds sex-group difference, as it has in the UK since 2009, the pedagogic gaze shifts away from nurture and rests on nature. That is, when the focus on gender as a sociocultural phenomenon shifts to a focus on the sex-group, it embeds the notion that children have fixed or innate characteristics. It also elides distinctions between sex-group and gender, implying that gender is a genetic and/or neurological matter. Furthermore, I argue that this shift represents an epistemological crisis that can be placed within the global frame outlined at the beginning of the paper.

Statistical technologies used for reporting achievement data by sex-group have reinstated very conservative gender binaries. By presenting girls in a race always ahead of boys, notions of femininity as *opposite* and so detrimental to masculinity become reified and fixed ideas. [Female] teachers are accused of stifling boys' 'natural exuberant energy' (Confident, Capable and Creative). There is no *a priori* foundation to this binary; it is a political construct instantiated in the Social Contract of the seventeenth century onwards (Pateman 1988) that makes it in the interest of one group to dominate another. I argue that statistical technologies have been used to create an 'iron cage' to protect masculinity. The following section suggests how feminists in the UK are trying to break into the 'iron cage'.

Table 1. Moving from an exterior to an interior gaze in representations of the child in educational reports in the UK.

Child-leaner/ technology	Social gaze	Pedagogy
1930s: Bones – corporeality	Shoulder blades, height: personality types (quick – slow)	Nurture – exercise movement: aimed at social class divides
1970s: Mind – 'g' intelligence	IQ test scores: variation across sample/class (intelligent– unintelligent)	Nurture/nature balance, to differentiate cognitive tasks: aimed at the individual
2000s: Sex-group – genetics/ neuroscience	Boys/girls: (active, nosey, risk-takers – passive, boring, compliant)	Nature – teachers not to interfere with it: aimed at the boy

The epistemological crisis

Since the UK Coalition government came to power in May 2010, there has been a move to make data on school achievement even more widely available and highly accessible. Sophisticated new web tools allow parents to access public examination data for each phase of schooling (known as Key Stage) by geographical region and for specific schools, making it very easy for people to compare examination results (e.g. http://dashboard.ofsted.gov.uk). At the point of writing, such web-based tools present achievement by sex-group and by groups designated as receiving free school meals (FSM), which is used as an indicator of poverty and is often disaggregated by race and ethnic group. The public via interactive web-based tools can access these data. From 2010, data demonstrating year on year progression has been made available by the Department for Education and is easily accessible (http://www.education.gov.uk/researc-handstatistics).

At the point of writing, the general public could find out rates of progression for 2008–10, by geographical region, by school and by subjects (English, mathematics and science). Although national curriculum tests are no longer administered for science at Key Stages 1 and 2, the Department for Education administers tests to a sample of children across England in order to gain their own measures.

The continuous drive to create educational markets has led to increasingly sophisticated presentations of statistics to the extent, I would argue, that the technologies of data presentations have now become one of the most influential cultural artefacts that *produce* gender in education, especially in England (rather than in Scotland, Northern Ireland or Wales). These technologies have unintentionally entrenched a notion of sex-group difference as fact. Public understandings of gender issues have regressed back to a position before second wave feminism which is generally associated with the period when people became aware of gender inequalities in society between the 1960s and mid-1980s. If teachers are constantly presented with the message that boys and girls learn differently due to innate genetic make-up, they are likely to be disempowered and believe that their pedagogic strategies cannot work against boys' and girls' innate genetic features. In effect, they are being told that biology controls learning and that culture or social contexts and, thus, their own classroom environments cannot counter the forces of nature.

Pedagogy: unintended effects

Children in England are the most tested in Europe (Lingard and Ozga 2007). Schools are data rich yet analysis poor. One unintended effect of the intense focus on quantification is that sex-group data about educational achievement presents differences as incontrovertible facts. In a further slippage, policy documents that now almost universally refer to gender as sex-group, conflate a useful distinction between a biologically rooted classification with cultural norms and expectations about what a typical boy or girl should be and do. Achievement data is unremittingly presented according to sex-group, making it almost impossible for teachers or parents to imagine that good common pedagogy could nurture human persons rather than males or females. Increasingly, we hear teachers talking about boys' and girls' preferred learning styles, as if learning style is a direct manifestation of sex-group genetic make-up: yet these relationships are complex and not well understood (Younger and Warrington, with McLellan 2005).

The focus on quantitative studies of achievement using sex-group as a variable creates analysis that deflects attention away from gender as historical, cultural, political and social phenomena. This leaves gender untethered and unrecognised. Specifically, teachers are given few resources to understand how gender operates. We have observed that gender often emerges in classroom practice below the radar of conscious awareness (Ivinson and Murphy 2007). As the teacher's gaze is averted away from gender and fixated on sex-group, gender becomes boundlessly unfretted and unlikely to be addressed explicitly or analysed. This perpetuates its influence often by reproducing deep historical legacies of gender inequality.

An even more extreme version of this argument would suggest that the neo-liberal regimes of accountability, that harness PISA and TIMSS data to investigate gaps in boys' and girls' educational achievement, actively enlist dominant, common sense representations of gender, to create a specific, abstracted construction of 'boy' (as lad in the UK) and 'girl' (as compliant and passive) that serve to reproduce rather than break cycles of underachievement. This is further compounded when guidance documents construct a framework that can be interpreted as privileging boys.

Achievement, even when measured by test scores, is patterned differently depending on which discipline/subject is placed in the spotlight (Murphy and Elwood 1998). How teachers open up a space for talk, activity and negotiation within the constraints of the subject specific classrooms influences *who* can and cannot participate meaningfully. This requires a explicit focus on, and understanding of, classroom context, the imaginaries it invokes, the policing that goes on inside it and how teachers perceive *who* can do *what* within the context (Ivinson and Murphy 2007).

Researchers (Berge with Ve 2000) have suggested that teachers who have personally grappled with questions about gender in their relationships and lives were able to bring considerable awareness to their pedagogic practices. We (Ivinson and Murphy 2007) found, for example, that male teachers who had worked in industry and had had women managers were able to think about gender in their personal lives and were able to bring some of this insight into their pedagogic practices. We cited a male Design and Technology (D&T) teacher who was enthusiastic about encouraging girls to learn to use electric sanding and sawing machines. We have observed some male Physical Education teachers encouraging boys not to develop macho, competitive approaches to sport but to compete with skill and style. Classrooms are contexts where 'play', contestation and resistance as well as compliance are visibly at work (Luke 1995; Singh 2002, both cited in Ivinson 2007). Therefore, the potential for subverting dominant discourses of gender is ever present in classrooms.

Conclusions

In the end, testing and test score analysis involve highly abstracted technologies, which are far removed from the everyday lives of teachers and children. While such abstraction is necessary to hold the world still and allow comparisons to be made (Flyvberg 2001) it also misses processes, flow and the way life is enmeshed in gender cultures. Empirical investigations and 'gap talk' (Gillborn 2010; Martino and Rezai-Rashli 2013) in educational achievement need to be underpinned by strong theoretical contributions if ameliorative strategies and pedagogic approaches are to shift deep-seated and recurring patterns of gender and social inequalities.

Along with others, I argue that politics and educational policies must engage with multiple scales of analysis that capture patterns of inequality and, yet, also recognise the messy, hybrid, complexity of everyday life (Lingard and Rawolle 2011; Rose 1996). Indeed, there is a need to grapple with education systems as complex that belong to multiple universes of various scales and modalities (Taylor and Ivinson 2013). Furthermore, educational researchers, along with teachers, should be encouraged to challenge narrow constructions of subjectivity, such as 'lad' and 'passive girl' as well as 'black', 'working class', and 'poor' rather than accept these as stable and enduring categories.

The challenge is how to make visible and salient the deep historical legacies of gender that work on and in us all. This work needs to be done to break a cycle in which analysis of sex-group gaps in educational achievement actually contributes to what is 'discounted' by the inscription devices and coding technologies of accountability that are deemed, in this particular neoliberal construct, to be 'objective' and so give the allusion of 'truth'.

If we wish to understand the causes of gender variation within education, we need nuanced approaches that use a range of methods and instruments that can genuinely engage with the flows, contingencies and historical legacies of everyday classroom and school life. Of course, we also need to recognise that to study phenomena, researchers are obliged, occasionally, to reify and stabilise the flow of everyday life. Only by stabilising phenomena using categories can we gather a snapshot of life that can then be subjected to complex, quantitative analysis. Yet, we need to be fully aware that the categories, including 'boy' and 'girl' that we create within a quantitative database are abstractions that although they have scientific use, are blunt instruments for understanding gender dynamics in human life. Furthermore, test data is not unbiased data (Elwood 2001; Gipps and Murphy 1994; Gorard, Rees, and Salisbury 1999). We need to remember that whatever factors we choose to focus on, there will be a greater variation within sex-group than between sex-group (cf. Connell 1987; Lloyd and Duveen 1992). The choice of categories requires considerable care. Indeed, we could say that the way we choose to 'cut' phenomena (Barad 2007) is an ethical issue.

In one sense, this challenge goes to the heart of the central problem within this field of research, namely that power relations and gender are always deeply entangled. For example, does multi-level modelling 'feel' like proper science because it aligns with 'hard', 'objective' masculinity while 'soft' qualitative methods align with femininity? This leads to the undesirable possibility that new theoretical work on masculinities, which use qualitative methods (e.g. Connell 1995; Epstein et al. 1998; Frosh, Phoenix, and Pattman 2002) on the one hand, and the new wave of quantitative work on statistical modelling around boys' education in Europe on the other, could develop as independent silos. This would be a great shame because it would mean that important work on the politics of sexuality and queer theory (e.g. Butler 1993: Sedgwick 1990) would be ignored. Such work has pointed out that personal identities can be violated by the compulsory division into either or male or female categories and that the use of labels ignores the lived realities of those who are gay, bisexual and transgender. Bem insisted, in the 1960s, that psychological experimental studies should not start by assigning participants into male and female sex-group categories, but should seek to discover what masculinity and femininity is.

This brings us to the micro-politics of educational research itself. If we are seduced into accepting that 'numbers'-driven, accountability is the only one way of approaching educational policy, then we will not be open to new ways of thinking. All too often, 'big data' analysis is crudely appropriated for political ends. If we cannot tackle, or have no motivation to tackle, the gender dynamics within the field of educational research, including the status afforded to qualitative and quantitative methods (cf. Flyvberg 2001) what chance have we of influencing gender dynamics in school and in everyday life? It was encouraging to participate in a conference hosted by Luxembourg University, which brought together participants from different countries using a range of methodologies to understand gender variations in educational success and which gave rise to this Special Issue.

References

Adam, B., and C. Grove. 2007. *Future Matters*. Leiden: Brill.
Arnot, M., M. David, and G. Weiner. 1999. *Closing the Gender Gap: Postwar Education and Social Change*. London: Polity Press.
Ball, S. 2012. *Global Education inc.: New Policy Networks and the Neo-liberal Imaginary*. London: Routledge.
Barad, K. 2007. *Meeting the Universe Halfway: Quantum Physics and the Entanglement of Matter and Meaning*. Durham and London: Duke University Press.
Berge, B.-M. with H. Ve. 2000. *Action Research for Gender Equity*. Buckingham: Open University Press.
Bernstein, B. 1996. *Pedagogy, Symbolic Control and Identity: Theory, Research, Critique*. London: Taylor and Francis.
Board of Education. 1931. The Hadow Report. Report of the Consultative Committee on the Primary School. London: His Majesty's Stationary Office. www.educationengland.org.uk/documents/hadow1931/hadow1931.html. (accessed 19 January 2014).
Burman, E. 2005. "Childhood, Neo-liberalism and the Feminization of Education." *Gender and Education* 17: 351–367.
Butler, J. 1993. *Bodies that Matter: On the Discursive Limits of Sex*. London and New York: Routledge.
Central Advisory Council for Education (England). 1967. Plowden Report. Children and Their Primary Schools. London: His Majesty's Stationary Office. http://www.educationengland.org.uk/documents/plowden/. (accessed 3 February 2014).
Connell, R. W. 1987. *Gender and Power: Society, the Person and Sexual Politics*. Stanford, CA: Stanford University Press.
Connell, R. W. 1995. *Masculinities*. Cambridge: Polity Press.
Crang, M. 2002. "Qualitative Methods: The New Orthodoxy?" *Progress in Human Geography* 26 (5): 647–655.
Department for Children, Schools and Families. 2007. Confident, Capable and Creative (CCC): Supporting Boys' Achievements. http://www.foundationyears.org.uk/wp-content/uploads/2011/10/Confident_Capable_Boys.pdf. (accessed 19 January 2014).
Department for Children, Schools and Families. 2009. *Gender and Education – Mythbusters: Addressing Gender and Achievement Myths and Realities*. Nottingham: DCSF Publications.

Department for Education. 2013. *National Curriculum Assessments at Key Stage 2 in England, 2013*. London: Department for Education. https://www.gov.uk/government/publications/national-curriculum-assessments-at-key-stage-2-2012-to-2013. (accessed 19 January 2014).

Eagley, A. H. 1987. *Sex Differences in Social Behaviour: A Social-role Interpretation*. Hillsdale, NJ: Lawrence Erlbaum Associates.

Elwood, J., and C. Gipps. 1999. *Review of Recent Research on the Achievement of Girls in Single-sex Schools*. London: Institute of Education University of London.

Elwood, J. 2001. "Examination Techniques: Issues of Validity and Effects on Pupils' Performance." In *Curriculum and assessment*, edited by D. Scott, 83–104. Westport, CT: Ablex Publishing.

Epstein, D., J. Elwood, V. Hey, and J. Maw, eds. 1998. *Failing Boys? Issues in Gender and Achievement*. Buckingham: Open University Press.

Fine, C. 2010. *Delusions of Gender*. New York: Norton.

Fausto-Sterling, A. 1992. *Myths of Gender: Biological Theories about Women and Men*. New York: Basic Books.

Flyvberg, B. 2001. *Making Social Science Matter: Why Social Inquiry Fails and how it can Succeed again*. Cambridge: Cambridge University Press.

Fox Keller, E. 1985. "How Gender Matters or, Why it's so Hard to Count Past Two." In *Perspectives on Gender and Science*, edited by J. Harding, 168–183. Brighton: The Falmer Press.

Foucault, M. 1972. *The Archaeology of Knowledge*. New York: Pantheon Books.

Frosh, S., A. Phoenix, and R. Pattman. 2002. *Young Masculinities: Understanding Boys in Contemporary Society*. Basingstoke: Palgrave.

Gillborn, D. 2010. "The Colour of Numbers: Surveys, Statistics and Deficit Thinking About Race and Class." *Journal of Education Policy* 25 (2): 253–276.

Gipps, C. V., and H. Goldstein. 1983. *Monitoring Children: An Evaluation of the Assessment and Performance Unit*. London: Heinemann Education Books.

Gipps, C. V., and P. Murphy. 1994. *A Fair Test? Assessment, Achievement and Equity: Assessing Assessment*. Maidenhead: Open University Press.

Gorard, S., G. Rees, and J. Salisbury. 1999. "Reappraising the Apparent Underachievement of Boys at School." *Gender and Education* 11 (4): 441–454.

Gorard, S. 2000. *Education and Social Justice: The Changing Composition of Schools and its Implications*. Cardiff: University of Wales Press.

Goldstein, H. 2001. Using Pupil Performance Data for Judging Schools and Teachers: Scope and Limitations. http://www.bristol.ac.uk/cmm/team/hg/using-pupil-performance-data-for-judging-schools-and-teachers.pdf. (accessed 31 January 2014).

Gould, S. J. 1996. *The Mismeasure of Man: Revised and Expanded Education*. New York: Penguin.

Gurian, M. 2001. *Boys and Girls Learn Differently!*. San Francisco, CA: Jossey-Bass.

Harding, S. ed. 1986. *The Science Question in Feminism*. Milton Keynes: Open University Press.

Hoff Sommers, C. 2000. *The War Against Boys: How Misguided Feminism is Harming Our Young Men*. New York: Simon and Schuster.

Ivinson, G. 2007. "Pedagogic Discourse and Sex Education: Insights from Bernstein and Moscovici's Work." *Sex Education* 7 (2): 201–216.

Ivinson, G., and P. Murphy. 2007. *Rethinking Single-sex Teaching: Gender, School Subjects and Learning*. Maidenhead: Open University Press/McGraw Hill.

Jackson, C. 2006. *Lads and Laddettes in Education*. Maidenhead: McGraw Hill.

Lingard, B., and S. Rawolle. 2011. "New Scalar Politics: Implications for Education Policy." *Comparative Education* 47 (4): 489–502.

Lingard, B., and J. Ozga, eds. 2007. *The RoutledgeFalmer Reader in Education and Policy Practice*. Oxford: RoutledgeFarmer.

Lloyd, B., and G. Duveen. 1992. *Gender Identities and Education*. Hemel Hempstead: Harvester Wheatsheaf.

Lott, B. 1981. "A Feminist Critique of Androgyny: Towards the Elimination of Gender Attribution of Learned Behavior." In *Gender and Nonverbal Behavior*, edited by C. Mayo and N. Henley, 171–180. New York: Springer-Verlag.

Mac an Ghaill, M. 1994. *The Making of Men: Masculinities, Sexualities and Schooling*. Buckingham: Open University Press.

Martino, W., and G. Rezai-Rashti. 2013. "Gap Talk' and the Global Rescaling of Educational Accountability in Canada." *Journal of Education Policy* 28 (5): 589–611.

Miller, P., and N. Rose. 2008. *Governing the Present*. Cambridge: Polity.

Moss, G. 2001. *Language and Education*. London: Taylor and Francis.

Murphy, P., and C. Gipps, eds. 1996. *Equity in the Classroom: Towards Effective Pedagogy for Girls and Boys*. London: Falmer/UNESCO.

Murphy, P., and J. Elwood. 1998. "Gendered Experiences, Choices and Achievement: Exploring the Links." *International Journal of Inclusive Education* 2 (2): 95–118.

Murphy, P., and E. Whitelegg. 2006. *Girls in the Physics Classroom: A Review of the Research into the Participation of Girls in Physics*. London: Institute of Physics Publishing.

Pateman, C. 1988. *The Sexual Contract*. Cambridge: Polity Press.

Rogoff, B. 1995. "Observing Sociocultural Activity on Three Planes: Participatory Appropriation, Guided Participation, and Apprenticeship." In *Sociocultural Studies of Mind*, edited by J. Wertsch, P. Del Rio, and A. Alvarez, 139–165. Cambridge: Cambridge University Press.

Rogoff, B. 2003. *The Cultural Nature of Human Development*. Oxford: Oxford University Press.

Rose, N. 1996. *Inventing Our Selves: Psychology, Power and Personhood*. Cambridge: Cambridge University Press.

Rose, N. 1999. *Governing the Soul: The Shaping of the Private Self*. London: Free Association Books.

Sedgwick, E. K. 1990. *Epistemologies of the Closet*. Berkeley, CA: University of California Press.

Skeggs, B. 2004. *Class, Self, Culture*. London: Routledge.

Skelton, C. 2001. *Schooling the Boys: Masculinities and Primary School Education*. Buckingham: Open University Press.

Stacey, J., A. Phoenix, and H. Hinds. 2004. *Working Out: New Directions for Women's Studies*. London: Falmer Press/Women's Studies Network.

Stanley, L. ed. 1990. *Feminist Praxis: Research, Theory and Epistemology in Feminist Sociology*. London: Routledge.

Stanley, L., and S. Wise. 1983. *Breaking Out: Feminist Consciousness and Feminist Research*. London: Palgrave and Kegan Paul.

Stoller, R. J. 1968. *Sex and Gender: On the Development of Masculinity and Femininity*. New York: Science House.

Sumner, C. 2011. 1945–1965: "The Long Road to Circular 10/65." *Reflecting Education* 6 (1): 90–102.

Taylor, C., and G. Ivinson. 2013. "Material Feminisms: New Directions for Education." *Gender and Education* 25 (6): 665–670.

Thomas, S., and P. Mortimore. 1996. "Comparing Value-added Models for Secondary-school Effectiveness." *Research Papers in Education* 11 (1): 5–33.

Tikly, L. 2001. "Globalisation and Education in the Postcolonial World: Towards a Conceptual Framework." *Comparative Education* 37 (2): 151–171.

Vygotsky, L. 1988. *Thought and Language*, edited by A. Kozulin. Cambridge, MA: MIT Press.

Whitty, G. 2002. *Making Sense of Education Policy: Studies in the Sociology and Politics of Education*. London: Sage.

Younger, M., M. Warrington, and J. Williams. 1999. "The Gender Gap and Classroom Interactions: Reality and Rhetoric." *British Journal of Sociology of Education* 20 (3): 325–341.

Younger, M., M. Warrington, and with R. McLellan. 2005. *Raising Boys' Achievement in Secondary Schools: Issues, Dilemmas and Opportunities*. Buckingham: Open University Press.

Troubling discourses on gender and education

Elina Lahelma

Research Community Cultural and Feminist Studies in Education, University of Helsinki, Helsinki, Finland

Background: In educational policies, two discourses on gender have existed since the 1980s. I call them the 'gender equality discourse' and the 'boy discourse'. The gender equality discourse in education is based on international and national declarations and plans, and is focused predominantly on the position of girls and women. The boy discourse, which has gained popularity through the media, draws on the gender gap in school achievement, attainment and behaviour.

Purpose: The purpose of the article is to describe and analyse the history of these discourses in Finland since the 1970s, with contextualisations to the international and European equality politics.

Sources of evidence: The analysis is based on international and Finnish policy documents, earlier ethnographic research and the author's own experiences as an activist in the field of research, administration and teaching in gender and education. Methodologically, the article uses the ideas of multi-sited ethnography and auto-ethnography.

Main argument: I will suggest that, despite constant efforts, sustainable change has not been achieved by the gender equality discourse. It has encountered problems because equality work in education has been conducted in short-term projects. Another reason is that issues of gender and gender equality are difficult to grasp and politically sensitive. I will also argue that the measures suggested by the boy discourse have been ineffective. Theoretical problems with the boy discourse lie in the categorisation of genders as if girls and boys were two different species. Moreover, in Finland currently, boys' achievements in school, even if (on average) weaker than girls' achievements, seem not to lead to weaker positions in further education and in the labour market. I suggest further that, despite the widespread media publicity about underachieving boys, efforts by teachers and administrators to give boys extra support have resulted in little impact. Some projects that started from the boy discourse continued by developing measures that drew on the gender equality discourse, with no special emphasis on boys. This would be a positive step if the gender equality discourse actually led to changes in educational practices. Unfortunately, this does not seem to happen.

Conclusions: I will conclude by suggesting that gender awareness is needed at all levels of education. This involves consciousness of social and cultural differences, inequalities and otherness, all of which should be built into educational practices, as well as a belief that these practices can be changed. It also includes understanding gender as being intertwined with other categories of difference.

Introduction

In 1979, the United Nations General Assembly adopted a global women's rights treaty (CEDAW 1979). This treaty is often referred to as the international bill of rights for women. The goal of eliminating all forms of discrimination against women included a special focus on education. At that time most European countries had already instituted gender equality policies. Since the 1970s, numerous international and national declarations, action plans and projects have been tried as means of creating gender equality in education, with emphasis on the position of girls and women.

At the same time, another discourse in education has travelled around the so-called Western countries. This travelling discourse (Arnesen, Lahelma, and Öhrn 2008), sometimes called 'Moral Panic' (Epstein et al. 1998) or 'Boy Crises' (Kimmel 2010), is a discourse on gender gaps in attendance, achievement and behaviour in school. This discourse on the problems of boys has lately been strengthened by the increased emphasis on achievement as measured by achievement tests. Whilst this discourse points to an important issue, it has also regularly been a populist theme in the anti-feminist men's movement and has been publicised by the media. This makes it difficult to address the real problems in a serious and unbiased way.

Using examples mainly from Finland, I will try to suggest some of the reasons why neither the official policy discourse on gender equality nor the media discourse on boys' underachievement in school seems to lead to sustainable changes in educational policies or practices. I also suggest that educational authorities and politicians often seem inclined to listen to the media discourses rather than listening to researchers or heeding official policies and resolutions on gender equality. Yet measures adopted from the media-initiated discourse on boys seem to be sporadic and ineffective.

Finland offers an interesting case study because the achievements on the PISA study, in all subjects, are consistently amongst the best, while at the same time the gender gap in reading is one of the largest amongst participating countries (http://www.oecd.org/pisa/).[1] Finland is also interesting because of the relatively good position of women in society, as suggested by several indicators of gender equality.

This paper draws on analyses of international and national policy documents. However, I also use reflections from my earlier ethnographic studies in schools (e.g. Gordon, Holland, and Lahelma 2000) and life historical studies on young people's transitions to adulthood (e.g. Gordon and Lahelma 2003; Lahelma 2011), as well as my own experiences. For three decades, I have been a feminist activist in the field of research, administration and teaching in gender and education. By reflecting the policy documents with my earlier ethnographic data, I use the idea of multi-sited ethnography (Marcus 1995); by presenting my own memories in their social, historical and cultural contexts, I also use some auto-ethnographical methodologies (e.g. Allen and Piercy 2005).

Policy discourses and the work towards gender equality

During the last 30 years, work towards gender equality in education has been repeatedly conducted in various networks and projects. This has been a worldwide mission: repeatedly, the important role of educators in promoting gender equality has been underlined in statements of such bodies as the United Nations, the OECD and the Council of Europe, as well as in national legislation and decisions. In several countries around the world, gender research and feminist studies in education have achieved a respectable status in universities. An example of policy documents at the European level is a study by the European Commission on gender differences in educational outcomes, known as EURYDICE 2010. The overview presented in the EURYDICE report suggests that, with a few exceptions, all European countries have, or plan to have, gender equality policies in education. The primary aim, according to this overview, is to challenge traditional gender roles and stereotypes. Other objectives include enhancing the representation of women in decision-making bodies, countering gender-based attainment patterns and combating gender-based harassment in schools (EURYDICE 2010, 13).

In Finland, gender equality had already been addressed in educational legislation in the late 1970s. In the 1980s a Commission on Gender Equality in Education was charged, by the Ministry of Education, with exploring the changes needed in education as required by the new legislation (Ministry of Education 1988).[2] The thorough report, which was based on three years of research and development work in experimental schools, included dozens of recommendations pertaining to educational structures and curricula, school textbooks, counselling and teacher education. The Act on Equality between Women and Men (1986/2005), which also delineated concrete responsibilities for educational authorities to promote gender equality, came into effect 1987. Soon after that, the general comments concerning gender equality were abolished from the school legislation – as if the question of gender equality in education no longer needed a special initiative in educational legislation.

From the 1990s onwards, education in Finland has sometimes been addressed in Government programmes and action plans for gender equality, but education has not been given a central position. Even if several indicators suggest the strong position of Finnish women in terms of gender equality, there is much to be done, including within the field of education. In the UN Convention on the Elimination of All Forms of Discrimination against Women, which evaluated Finland (CEDAW 2008), a request was made for the introduction of gender-sensitive curricula[3] and for teaching methods that address the structural and cultural causes of discrimination against women. Teacher training was also addressed (CEDAW 2008, 6).

In 2010, the first Government Report on Gender Equality was given by the Ministry of Social Affairs and Health. In this report, the Government outlined its views on future gender equality policy up to the year 2020. The report was based on six studies conducted by experts from different sectors and used as background information for evaluating the impact of gender equality policy. One of these studies was on education (Kuusi, Jakku-Sihvonen, and Koroma 2009). The main recommendations for education included the task of incorporating goals and actions to promote gender equality in educational policy planning and development. The report noted that legislation concerning the education sector and development plans concerning education, training and research had included very few gender equality goals in the past ten years. Suggestions were aimed at curriculum planning and teaching methods, student counselling, early childhood education, equality planning in educational institutions and teaching materials. The main problems in education, as defined in the report, were that gender segregation[4] remains, both in the labour market and in education, and that gender awareness is lacking (Ministry of Social Affairs and Health 2010). Unlike the EURYDICE report, issues such as sexual harassment or women in leadership positions were not specifically mentioned in the suggestions for the educational sector. However, these recommendations existed in the other sections; accordingly, they should carry the same obligations for the educational authorities to comply with national policies.

The Government report noted the slowness of change in the field of gender equality. Today, looking at the report from 1988 (Ministry of Education 1988), it is also easy to see that the changes have indeed been minimal, that many of the problems noted still exist and that the recommendations given in 1988 are still needed (Lahelma 2011). This is true, even if a great deal of equality work has been carried out over the last several decades, involving co-operation with schools, universities, vocational training, teachers, students, researchers, ministries of education, officials, as well as with employers and employees in the private and public sectors (Brunila, Heikkinen, and Hynninen 2005; Brunila 2009; Lahelma 2011).

Why is it that the move towards the stated aims for gender equality seems an almost impossible mission (Lahelma 2011)? Drawing on my experience and several studies, I will reflect on some reasons for this. An analysis by Kristiina Brunila (2009) suggests that equality work has been conducted in short-term projects, and the good practices that repeatedly have been found in these projects have not been sustained, but, instead, have withered without the extra resources that the projects provided. Another reason is that the concepts around gender and gender equality are complex. Gender is so deeply entrenched in the structures and cultures of a society, as well as in our embodied subjec- tivities that it is difficult to grasp. I will return to this issue below. The third reason lies in the power relations that are embedded in issues of gender equality, in general, and in education more specifically. Gender projects are often regarded as feminist issues that challenge a society's current structures and cultures. Anyone who has had the experi- ence of lecturing on gender and education is familiar with hostile student comments – along with most enthusiastic responses (Lahelma 2011). One male teacher educator, interviewed in a study by Vidén and Naskali (2010), put it like this:

> It is difficult to find an objective point of view in teaching gender awareness. The issue is easily politicised, and it turns into a sermon preached from one perspective. (Vidén and Naskali 2010, 45, translation[5] Lahelma)

This difficulty is especially problematic because the 'boy discourse' focusing on boys' underachievement, which has received a great deal of media attention and is explored below, suggests that boys are the actual losers in education, while the 'gender equality discourse' speaks more about girls and women.

The 'boy discourse'

At the same time as the official gender equality discourse has been promoted, especially since the late 1980s, there has been another discourse on gender and education. This discourse, which I call the 'boy discourse', is fed by concerns about boys' school achievement, attainment and behaviour, all of which contribute to a 'moral panic' (e.g. Epstein et al. 1998; Francis and Skelton 2005; Kimmel 2010) that travels from one country to another. The discourse has its background in current statistics and achieve- ment tests instituted by restructuring policies, with a neo-liberal focus on standards and competition and a neo-conservative focus on basic skills. Measurable results are easily regarded as school outcomes, and categories on which comparisons are made are regarded as the essential ones (Arnesen, Lahelma, and Öhrn 2008). For example, the PISA results (e.g. http://www.oecd.org/pisa) suggest that gender differences in reading achievements seem to be rather universal in European countries. Girls' higher performance is consistent across countries, age groups, survey periods and study groups. In mathematics and the sciences, the situation is more varied, with girls performing at lower levels in approximately one-third of the European educational systems (EURYDICE 2010).

The fact that girls' educational achievement is, on average, better than boys has been known for a long time. However, it has not always and in all contexts been regarded as a problem, but rather as a self-evident gender pattern that does not destabilise the power position of men in a society (e.g. Epstein et al. 1998). Behind this new concern have been structural changes in many Western countries in which direct routes from school to manual work have been limited, and the futures of working-class boys have been challenged. Boys from higher socio-economic backgrounds have also experienced difficulties because more and more girls are applying for the same fields of education.

In Finland, the first round of discussion on boys' underachievement started relatively early, in 1982, and I happened to be involved. As a planner on Finland's National Board of Education, I conducted a study of student routes to upper secondary education. I made use of a new national register that included students' final grades in all subjects. What surprised me was that, despite their better grades on average, girls were accepted into their fields of choice in upper secondary education less often than boys. This result was not picked up by the Finnish media; what did emerge was a huge debate on what was, in fact, old news: namely that girls achieved more highly than boys. 'School oppresses boys!' This title in a comment on the results in a professional journal became a slogan repeated in public, but it was also challenged by researchers (Lahelma 1992, 2005).

Since then, the public discourse on boys' underachievement has been periodically highlighted. It received considerable attention after the first PISA results in 2002. Finnish boys scored better in reading literacy than students in all countries on average, better than boys in any other OECD country and better than girls in many of the participating countries (e.g. Välijärvi et al. 2002). However, concerns were expressed by the media and educational authorities. The problem was that the gender gap was at its widest in Finland: although Finnish boys scored very well, they scored worse than Finnish girls. The main daily newspaper, *Helsingin Sanomat*, published a huge report titled 'Rescue the boys!' An interview about the PISA results included the following assumptions: boys lag behind girls; working methods are such that boys lack the eagerness to learn: boys at a 'difficult age' learn better by doing (for the direct quotation in Finnish, see Lahelma 2009, 140).

One aspect of the boy discourse that receives regular media attention is what is commonly referred to as the feminisation of certain professions. For example, in 2010, a discussion in *Helsingin Sanomat* started with an anxious comment about the vocational education of painters, a field which now draws more and more girls with excellent grades, whilst before, in comparison, it had been an education for boys with poor grades. This discourse was rather startling, because – according to official policies intended to eliminate gender segregation in education – changes in this direction should have been very welcome.

The media discourse on boys is often supported by recognised psychiatrists and based on developmental theories that suggest the slower development of boys compared with girls. It is a powerful discourse and well received by teachers who have experience with boys having difficulty in achievement, attainment and behaviour in school more often than girls. There are numerous examples of teacher statements suggesting that school practices and working methods are not suitable for boys, carrying with them the tacit belief being that these practices and methods are suitable for girls. These kinds of assumptions were repeated in teacher interviews and informal discussions in the context of our ethnographic study in Finnish lower secondary schools, conducted in the 1990s (e.g. Gordon, Holland, and Lahelma 2000). Many of the teachers were concerned about boys' problems and actively encouraged the boy pupils whenever the boys showed any small sign of effort. One example from our fieldwork is a teacher who allowed two boys to present a horrifying sexist and violent video during the lesson; she explained that 'the boys get practice in performing, and they will remember that they have been allowed to choose for themselves'. These boys were low achieving, but they were central in the class's informal hierarchy. This kind of 'pedagogy for boys' surely emphasises the very masculinity that contributes to these boys' underachievement. Moreover, it does not improve the learning environment for girls or for other boys. This was not, however, the whole picture of the teachers that we worked with. Many of them had also considered gendered practices from other perspective. Some were aware of the tendency of paying more attention to boys at the expense of girls and felt bad about it.

Similar patterns are also found in new studies. National statistics on school achievement suggest that boys, on average, are given better grades in the Finnish language than their test scores merit (Kuusi, Jakku-Sihvonen, and Koroma 2009).[6] A female teacher who was interviewed in the study by Vidén and Naskali (2010, 46) said: 'I am not able to pay attention to the needs of the boys. They probably would need more active working methods'.

Concerns about the problems of boys are culturally shared with parents, due to the widespread media publicity. According to the ethnographic study in the 1990s (e.g. Gordon, Holland, and Lahelma 2000), for example, the following comment by a head teacher during a parents' evening was received with understanding laughter: 'Girls, they would come to school even if they were not compelled to. Boys, those starry-eyed young rascals, would not come voluntarily.' It is possible to interpret this statement as a shared positive evaluation of the boys who did not like school. This attitude is not new; in her historical analysis of boys' underachievement, Cohen (1998) refers to the concept of the 'healthy idleness' of young boys, referring to documents of English school authorities in the early 1900s.

The discourse on boys' achievement also seems to have had its impact on administrative decisions, and some policy initiatives are based on the achievement gap. The discourse tends to provoke 'intuitive' strategies, which may actually be counterproductive for boys. Pedagogy that draws on assumptions about negative 'boyish' attitudes to school can easily turn to solutions that allot more time for competitive sports or media products, which some of the underachieving boys are expected to enjoy (Francis 2000).

There are examples in Finland for single-sex groups in which boys are 'allowed to be boys', preferably with a male teacher. In one of our research schools in the 1990s, one group was a boys-only classroom. The official reasons were of practical nature, but the male class tutor, according to field notes, made a joke with the boys about the privilege of being 'without women'. The results, however, turned out to be negative, and the school moved back to co-educational groups. Single-sex groupings have generally been regarded as problematic, as the idea is based on generalised expectations that all boys enjoy the same kinds of activities.

In the following section, I suggest that the 'boy discourse', as it manifests itself in the Finnish context, falls into several practical, theoretical and political problems and is not helpful for those boys who have difficulties in school. I have already commented on some practical problems above, but below I will go further into discussions that are more theoretical and political. First, I address categorisation, and second, I address the problem of narrowing the scope of analysis to school only.

The problems of categorising girls and boys into separate groups

Assumptions that girls and boys are two different species are often implicitly behind the boy discourse. Many of the potential strategies to help boys, such as the efforts to add course content that is supposed to interest boys, actually are based on the classification of boys' needs and development as 'natural' and fundamentally different from those of girls. It is possible to read the statement on gender in the amendments to the Finnish Act on Basic Education as suggesting that girls and boys belong in different categories:

> In teaching, special attention should be given to the different needs and the differences in growth and development of girls and boys. (Act on Basic Education, Amendments 1998/ 2001)

Teachers are, of course, aware of differences within the genders. They might at the same time, however, think of categories. The teacher quoted below starts with a general statement about boys, but then adds a comment on the talent of some of the boys. It has often been suggested in school studies that high-achieving boys are easily regarded as talented, which is not a term that is regularly used for girls (Walkerdine 1989; Lahelma and Öhrn 2003).

> Boys do not have the patience for systematic work. But then [...] especially amongst boys there are many who are so talented that whatever goes down well with them. (Extract from a teacher interview, author's ethnographic data in the 1990s)

A more recent example is from a small-scale ethnographic study conducted by three students during their own teacher education. During the practice period, a teacher educator urged the student teachers to tolerate the boys' breaches of discipline and order, saying: 'Creating a disturbance is a phase in boys' development' (Norema, Pietilä, and Purtonen 2010).

Following the theoretical reflections of Floya Anthias (2002), I suggest some consequences that stemmed from categorising girls and boys. The first consequence is returning to biological differences that are regarded as essential. Several examples of this were given above; for example, in the Act on Basic Education the different needs of boys and girls are suggested. The second consequence is generalisation, in which the characteristics of some boys – for example, those without the patience for systematic work – are regarded applying to all boys. The third consequence is seeing categories as related dichotomies. For instance, girls' outperformance on the PISA tests is regarded as a problem for boys.

One aspect of categorisation is evaluating girls' success as something problematic and boys' lack of success as something heroic, as was suggested earlier through the extract from the parents' evening. Also given above are examples in which reasons for the taken-for-granted attribution of boys' lack of success are sought in the working methods and feminisation of the schools (Lahelma 2005, 2009).

Categorisation means that differences are not analysed in relation to other dimensions, i.e. intersectionally (e.g. Yuval-Davies 2006). Minor differences in achievement between boys and girls are talked about as a major 'problem' requiring immediate intervention, whereas more important differences, based on social backgrounds of class and ethnicity, are toned down or focused on separately from gender. Ignoring social background in making comparisons between girls and boys makes the problems of working-class girls and the privilege of middle-class students of both genders invisible. Also, the strong focus on achievement in certain subjects (instead of other subjects or other aspects of schooling) means that complexities in terms of gender are reduced. Furthermore, working-class and/or minority ethnic boys' low achievement in school (on average) is often framed as a question of gender, instead of a matter of class or ethnicity, or something arising from changes in the opportunities caused by the ongoing restructuring of the economy in post-industrial societies (Arnesen, Lahelma, and Öhrn 2008).

The fact that there is a male majority among students who receive poor grades and who have problems in school should not be neglected. But research that draws on an understanding of masculinities suggests different explanations from those given in the 'boy discourse'. Some researchers have asked what kinds of masculinities are being emphasised in contemporary schools' official and informal pedagogies (Phoenix 2004; Francis and Skelton 2005; Epstein et al. 1998; Martino and Pallotta-Chiarollli 2003). If 'healthy idleness' (Cohen 1998) is valued by school authorities and 'laddiness' (e.g. Willis 1977) is respected in informal boys' cultures at school, then it is not difficult to understand why some boys are underachievers. Several studies suggest that boys who do well in school are often the targets of teasing, and this might happen more often in schools with students from working-class backgrounds. In our ethnographic study, in which one of the schools was more working class, the other more middle class, this pattern was clear. In my student interviews in the first of the schools, one of the reasons given why a certain boy was the target of teasing was that he was 'professor-like'. Being good at sports is appreciated in boys' cultures, not necessarily 'being good in school'.

From school onwards: gender equality through education

It is important to remember that the aim of gender equality policies is not only to promote gender equality *in* education, but also *through* education. According to the Finnish Act on Equality between Women and Men (1986/2005),[7] education should improve the status of women, particularly in working life. Even if, according to the Government Report on Gender Equality (Ministry of Social Affairs and Health 2010, 10), modern gender equality policy is intended for all, the law is not gender-neutral. The report addresses the main problem in education as follows:

> Even if both genders have equal access to education, the fields of education are, however, strongly gender divided. In this dichotomy, essential changes have not taken place during the last ten years. Gender-specific traditional educational and occupational choices have an impact on inequalities between women and men in working life and wages. Even if Finnish women have, because of their educational status and success, good prerequisites for achievement in working life, the contribution that they have made to education is not sufficiently visible in career and wages; neither is their education made maximal use of in working life. The lower educational status of men on average in relation to women does not cause lower salaries. Low educational status can, however, cause problems in employment opportunities. (Ministry of Social Affairs and Health 2010, 110)

I have presented above some memories from my early studies in the 1980s. It was then that I found, for the first time, that girls on average, even if they achieved better than boys in school, had more difficulty in obtaining a study place in upper secondary education. The main reason for this was the strong gender segregation in post-compulsory education. In the Finnish educational structure, entrance tests and criteria were, in general, more selective in the fields for which women applied than in the male-dominated fields. In education and the labour market, women with a good education and excellent marks typically competed with other women with a good education and excellent marks. This pattern has not changed in recent decades (Brunila et al. 2011).

In Finland women pursue higher education more than men, as also is the case in many other countries, but this gender difference is minor in relation to the very pointed gender segregation in the fields of further education and the labour market. Formal schooling is organised so that education leading to traditional male occupations is often found at the upper-secondary school level rather than in higher (university) education, unlike the traditional female occupations; this means, for example, that electricians need upper-secondary education, whereas pre-school teaching requires a university education.

A master's degree is more often expected in status jobs in predominantly female fields than in male-dominated fields, and competition for education is harder in the female fields (Lahelma 2009). Moreover, grades or achievement on the matriculation examination (which in Finland is the nation-wide test after the general secondary high school) do not have much importance in the competition for entry into the most popular fields of higher education, particularly in the fields to which women usually apply.

In effect, gender segregation in further education and the labour market has benefited boys, whose opportunities to compete in education and the labour market are often better than would be expected, based on their school achievement. Thus, educational achievement is a different resource for men in comparison with women. In these respects it might be said that girls, as a group, earn higher marks, but as a group they are also more dependent on marks to gain entry into higher education and the labour market (Arnesen, Lahelma, and Öhrn 2008). This situation may change, however, and higher levels of education are needed in the professions of the future. In many countries, the male-dominated technical sectors are diminishing more quickly than the female-dominated service sectors. As was mentioned in the Government report (Ministry of Social Affairs and Health 2010) above, low educational status can cause problems in employment opportunities.

From 'boy discourse' to gender awareness in the official policies

Even if many teachers are making the effort to help boys and though concerns about boys in public discourse are constant, often expressed by educational authorities, official measures addressing this discourse are not often realised. At the European level, the EURYDICE (2010) study in 29 countries suggests that only a few countries address boys' underachievement in official policy. In Finland, analysis of gender equality projects from the 1970s onwards suggests the same (Brunila 2009).

The need to address school achievement in relation to other dimensions of difference, intersectionally (e.g. Yuval-Davies 2006), is often explicitly argued in official reports, as if to challenge the boy discourse. The EURYDICE study does not suggest any specific measures for improving boys' achievement, but drawing on Tinklin et al. (2003), recommends interplay between different sources of inequality:

> The interplay between gender, social class and ethnic background affects behaviour and consequently pupil performance. A policy focus on only one source of social inequality might hide the complexity of experiences within a specific group and lead to over-simplistic solutions. (EURYDICE 2010, 112)

The importance of dismantling the stereotypical models of manhood and taking into account differences between men and boys was suggested in the Government Report on Gender Equality in Finland (Ministry of Social Affairs and Health 2010, 22). The report also included a section on Men and Gender Equality, with the main conclusion for education being that a gender perspective should be strengthened in all educational policies, instead of implementing extensive special measures addressed to boys only (Ministry of Social Affairs and Health 2010, 160).

There are interesting examples that suggest the authorities' difficulties in resolving these issues. Sometimes, policy initiatives start with concerns about boys' underachievement, but end with more general recommendations about gender equality or gender awareness. For example, in 2009 I participated as one of the invited speakers in a European Union Conference with the title Gender Differences in Educational Achievement (European Union 2009), held in Sweden. The conference opened with questions such as 'Why are boys falling behind in education? What is the relationship between gender and literacy?' Most of the speakers and participants, many of whom were well-known gender researchers, challenged the dichotomising boy discourse, and numerous suggestions were made related to the general policy aims of gender equality, rather than to supporting boys as a group.

In Finland, the gender gap in achievement has recently been on the political agenda again, when the Government expressed its concerns about the exclusion of young people. In the Finnish Government's Development Plan for Education and Research for the years 2011–16, an action programme for promoting equal opportunities in education is defined and charged with the following task:

> The Government will undertake comprehensive action to even out gender differences in learning outcomes, participation in education and completion of studies and to minimise the effect of the socio-economic background on participation in education. (Ministry of Education and Culture 2010, 10)

All educational levels were mentioned in more detail, and the objective was to halve the impact of gender, social and ethnic background on educational participation and attainment by the year 2020. Interlinking dimensions of difference was not mentioned, which suggests that certain measures should be used to address issues related to ethnic and social backgrounds with other measures used to close the gender gap. A working group in the Ministry of Education and Culture was given the responsibility of devising the measures to achieve these aims. Dozens of researchers were consulted in drawing up the report, and the 35 recommendations were informed by their studies. Gender was not given a central position in the report (Ministry of Education and Culture 2012), and the recommendations did not include any measures that explicitly addressed minimising gender differences. Students' family background was mentioned as the most important factor in learning outcomes at the comprehensive school level, as well as in continued education thereafter. The report did not refer to the recent Government Report on Gender Equality (Ministry of Social Affairs and Health 2010). Recommendations concerning gender, however, were in line with those in this report and included aims for gender awareness at all levels of education.

It appears that, despite the widespread media publicity about underachieving boys, efforts by teachers and administrators to give boys extra support have turned out to have little impact. Some projects that started from the boy discourse turned out to develop measures that drew on the gender equality discourse, with no special emphasis on boys. This would be a positive step if the gender equality discourse actually led to changes in educational practices and raised gender awareness. As I have suggested earlier, this does not seem to have happened; at least, not very quickly.

Conclusions

In this article, I have dealt with two educational discourses in relation to gender: the 'gender equality discourse' and the 'boy discourse', with special focus in the case of Finland. I have suggested that both have strong supporters, but that relatively little sustainable change has been achieved by either discourse. I have suggested that the gender equality discourse has encountered problems because equality work has been conducted in short-term projects instead of through sustainable policy directives (Brunila 2009; Lahelma 2011). I have suggested, in addition, that for teachers and teacher educators, issues of gender and gender equality are difficult to grasp (Lahelma 2011). There are also political problems involved: boys' lower school achievement on average is presented as an argument to counter feminism, and the interests of girls are regarded as if they are in opposition to the interests of boys.

I have also argued that, even if problems in school achievement and behaviour are more usual amongst boys than girls, the measures suggested by the boy discourse are sporadic and ineffective. Theoretical problems with the boy discourse lie in the categorisation of genders as if girls and boys were two different species. Moreover, the assumptions behind the boy discourse that boys' poor achievement (on average) has an impact on boys' weak position in further education (on average) and in the labour market are empirically false in Finland's current society.

One significant conclusion from the study is that, despite the strength of the boy discourse in Finland and in Europe as a whole, very few of the measures that have been implemented have drawn on this discourse. Instead, as shown by recent Finnish policies, political projects that began as boy discourses ended up making suggestions about gender awareness.

I will conclude with a short discussion of the concept gender awareness. It was further elaborated upon in a national project (2008–11) on gender awareness in teacher education under my leadership (Lahelma 2011; Lahelma and Hynninen 2012). Gender awareness, as defined in the project, means consciousness of social and cultural differences, inequalities and otherness, all of which are built into educational practices, as well as a belief that these practices can be changed. It also includes understanding gender as being intertwined with other categories: ethnicity, age, sexuality and health, as well as with local and cultural opportunities and differences (Lahelma and Hynninen 2012). I will close by suggesting that gender awareness is needed in order to combat the dualistic and confrontational positions of the gender equality discourse and the boy discourse.

It should be remembered, moreover, that women's participation in education is still not taken for granted in all countries. In Finland, the achievements of girls and women in education should be celebrated as an important example. There is a danger that the achievements of the women's movement will be reversed and women's interests will again become obscured if there is excessive focus on the boy discourse.

Notes

1. In the most recent PISA study (2012) Finland's overall performance was not as strong as previous performance, but still relatively strong.
2. The author served as a secretary of this commission during the years 1985–88.
3. Gender-sensitivity and gender awareness are often used in gender equality documents almost as synonyms. In Finland gender awareness has recently been used more regularly in relation to teachers' responsibilities and education. I will return to the question in the discussion section.
4. Gender segregation is the term used for gender separation in the English translation of the report. Therefore I use the term segregation in this article.
5. Further on, all the citations that are drawn from publications written in Finnish or from research data are translated by the author.
6. On the other hand, there is a small tendency for girls to receive better grades than their tests merit in mathematics, but here the difference is very small.
7. '§1. The objectives of this Act are to prevent discrimination based on gender, to promote equality between women and men, and thus to improve the status of women, particularly in working life. [...] §5 Authorities, educational institutions and other bodies providing education and training shall ensure that women and men have equal opportunities for education, training and professional development, and that teaching, research and instructional material support attainment of the objectives of this Act' (The Act on Equality between Women and Men 1986, with amendments until 2005).

References

Act on Equality between Women and Men (609/1986, amendments 232/2005). Statutes of Finland.

Act on Basic Education (608/1998, amendments in government decision 1435/2001). Statutes of Finland.

Allen, Katherine R., and Fred P. Piercy. 2005. "Feminist Autoethnography." In *Research Methods in Family Therapy*. 2nd ed., edited by Douglas Sprenkle and Fred P. Piercy, 155–169. New York: Guilford.

Anthias, Floya. 2002. "Diasporic Hybridity and Transcending Racisms: Problems and Potential." In *Rethinking Anti-racisms from Theory to Practice*, edited by Floya Anthias and Cathie Lloyd. London: Routledge.

Arnesen, Anne-Lise, Elina Lahelma, and Elisabet Öhrn. 2008. "Travelling Discourses of Gender and Education: The Case of Boys' Underachievement." *Nordisk Pedagogik* 28 (1): 1–14.

Brunila, Kristiina, Mervi Heikkinen, and Pirkku Hynninen. 2005. *Difficult but Doable. Good Practices for Equality Work*. Kajaani: Oulu University, Kajaani University Consortium.

Brunila, Kristiina. 2009. *Parasta Ennen. Tasa-arvotyön Projektitapaistuminen* [Best Before. Projectisation of Equality Work]. Helsinki: Helsingin yliopisto. Kasvatustieteen laitoksen tutkimuksia 222.

Brunila, K., T. Kurki, E. Lahelma, J. Lehtonen, R. Mietola, and T. Palmu. 2011. "Multiple Transitions: Educational Policies and Young People's Post-compulsory Choices." *Scandinavian Journal of Educational Research* 55 (3): 1–18.

CEDAW. 1979. *The Convention on the Elimination of All Forms of Discrimination Against Women*. New York: United Nations.

CEDAW. 2008. *Concluding Observations of the Committee on the Elimination of Discrimination Against Women: Finland*. New York: United Nations.

Cohen, Michèle. 1998. "'A Habit of Healthy Idleness': Boys' Underachievement in Historical Perspective." In *Failing Boys? Issues in Gender and Achievement*, edited by Debbie Epstein, Jannette Elwood, Valerie Hey, and Janet Maw, 19–34. Buckingham: Open University Press.

Epstein, Debbie, Jannette Elwood, Valerie Hey, and Janet Maw. 1998. *Failing Boys? Issues in Gender and Education*. Buckingham: Open University Press.

European Union. 2009. *Gender Differences in Educational Achievement*. Documentation (2009). se2009.eu.

EURYDICE. 2010. *Gender Differences in Educational Outcomes: Study on the Measures Taken and the Current Situation in Europe*. Brussels: European Commission.

Francis, Becky. 2000. *Boys, Girls and Achievement: Addressing the Classroom Issues*. London: Routledge/Falmer.

Francis, Becky, and Christine Skelton. 2005. *Reassessing Gender and Achievement*. London: Routledge.

Gordon, Tuula, Janet Holland, and Elina Lahelma. 2000. *Making Spaces: Citizenship and Difference in Schools*. London: Macmillan, and New York: St. Martin's Press.

Gordon, Tuula, and Elina Lahelma. 2003. "From Ethnography to Life History: Tracing Transitions of School Students." *International Journal of Social Research Methods: Theory and Practice* 6 (3): 245–254.

Kimmel, Michael. 2010. *Boys and School: A Background Paper on the 'Boy Crises'*. Swedish Government Inquiries. Swedish Government Official Reports. SOU 2010:53.

Kuusi, H., R. Jakku-Sihvonen, and M. Koramo. 2009. *Koulutus ja Sukupuolten Tasa-arvo* [Education and Gender Equity]. Ministry of Education, Reports 2009: 52.

Lahelma, Elina. 1992. *Sukupuolten Eriytyminen Peruskoulun Opetussuunnitelmassa* [Gender Differentiation in the Curriculum of the Comprehensive School]. Helsinki: Yliopistopaino.

Lahelma, Elina. 2005. "School Grades and Other Resources: The 'Failing Boys' Discourse Revisited." *NORA, Nordic Journal of Women's Studies* 13 (2): 78–89.

Lahelma, Elina. 2009. "Tytöt, Pojat ja Keskustelu Koulumenestyksestä [Girls, Boys and Discussion on School Achievement]." In *Sukupuoli ja Toimijuus Koulutuksessa* [Gender and Agency in Education], edited by Hanna Ojala, Tarja Palmu, and Jaana Saarinen, 136–156. Tampere: Vastapaino.

Lahelma, Elina. 2011. "Gender Awareness into Teacher Education: An Impossible Mission?" *Education Inquiry* 2 (2): 263–276.

Lahelma, Elina, and Pirkko Hynninen. 2012. "Gender Equality in Finnish Teacher Education – With Reflections from Nordic and European Collaboration." In *Education for Social Justice, Equity and Diversity. A Honorary Volume for Professor Anne-lise Arnesen. Studies on Education*. Vol. 1, edited by Torill Strand, and Merethe Roos, 109–130. Berlin: Lit Verlag.

Lahelma, Elina, and Elisabet Öhrn. 2003. "'Strong Nordic Women' in the Making? Educational Politics and Classroom Practices." In *Democratic Education: Ethnographic Challenges*, edited by Dennis Beach, Tuula Gordon, and Elina Lahelma, 39–51. London: Tufnell Press.

Marcus, George E. 1995. "Ethnography in/of the World System: The Emergence of Multi-sited Ethnography." *Annual Review of Anthropology* 24: 95–117.

Martino, Wayne, and Maria Pallotta-Chiarolli. 2003. *So What's a Boy? Addressing Issues of Masculinity and Schooling*. Maidenhead: Open University Press.

Ministry of Education. 1988. *Tasa-arvokokeilutoimikunnan Mietintö* [Report of the Commission of Equal Opportunities in Education]. Komiteanmietintö 1988:17. Helsinki: Valtion Painatuskeskus.

Ministry of Education and Culture. 2012. *Ehdotus Valtioneuvoston Strategiaksi Koulutuksellisen tasa-arvon Edistämiseksi* [Proposal for the Government's Strategy for Educational Equality]. Opetus- ja Kulttuuriministeriön Työryhmämuistioita ja Selvityksiä 2012:28. Helsinki: Opetusministeriö.

Ministry of Social Affairs and Health. 2010. *Valtioneuvoston Selonteko Naisten ja Miesten Välisestä tasa-arvosta* [Government Report on Gender Equality]. Sosiaali- ja Terveysministeriö. Julkaisuja 2010:8.

Norema, Anne, Penni Pietilä, and Tanja Purtonen. 2010. *Pipot Tiedon Tiellä. Sukupuolihuomioita Opettajankoulutuksessa* [Caps on the Way to Knowledge. Gendered Observations in Teacher Education]. Helsinki: Yliopistopaino.

Phoenix, Ann. 2004. "Using Informal Pedagogy to Oppress Themselves and Others." *Nordisk Pedagogik* 24 (1): 19–38.

Tinklin, Teresa, Linda Croxford, Alan Ducklin, and Barbara Frame. 2003. "Inclusion. A Gender Perspective." *Policy Futures in Education* 1 (4): 640–652.

Vidén, Sari, and Päivi Naskali. 2010. *Sukupuolitietoisuus Lapin Yliopiston Opettajankoulutuksessa* [Gender Awareness in Teacher Education at the University of Lapland]. Lapin Yliopiston Kasvatustieteellisiä Julkaisuja 22. Rovaniemi.

Välijärvi, Jouni, Pirjo Linnakylä, Pekka Kupari, Pasi Reinikainen, and Inga Arffman. 2002. *The Finnish Success in PISA – and Some Reasons Behind it*. Helsinki: National Board of Education.

Walkerdine, V. and the Girls and Mathematics Unit. 1989. *Counting Girls Out*. London: Virago.

Willis, P. 1977. *Learning to Labour: How Working Class Kids get Working Class Jobs*. Farnborough: Saxon House.

Yuval-Davies, Nira. 2006. "Intersectionality and Feminist Politics." *European Journal of Women's Studies* 13 (3): 193–209.

Reversal of gender differences in educational attainment: an historical analysis of the West German case

Rolf Becker

Department of Sociology of Education, University of Bern, Bern, Switzerland

Background information: During the late 1970s and the early 1980s, West Germany witnessed a reversal of gender differences in educational attainment, as females began to outperform males.

Purpose: The main objective was to analyse which processes were behind the reversal of gender differences in educational attainment after 1945. The theoretical reflections and empirical evidence presented for the US context by DiPrete and Buchmann (Gender-specific trends in the value of education and the emerging gender gap in college completion, *Demography* 43: 1–24, 2006) and Buchmann, DiPrete, and McDaniel (Gender inequalities in education, *Annual Review of Sociology* 34: 319–37, 2008) are considered and applied to the West German context. It is suggested that the reversal of gender differences is a consequence of the change in female educational decisions, which are mainly related to labour market opportunities and not, as sometimes assumed, a consequence of a 'boy's crisis'.

Sample: Several databases, such as the German General Social Survey, the German Socio-economic Panel and the German Life History Study, are employed for the longitudinal analysis of the educational and occupational careers of birth cohorts born in the twentieth century.

Design and methods: Changing patterns of eligibility for university studies are analysed for successive birth cohorts and gender. Binary logistic regressions are employed for the statistical modelling of the individuals' achievement, educational decision and likelihood for social mobility – reporting average marginal effects (AME).

Results: The empirical results suggest that women's better school achievement being constant across cohorts does not contribute to the explanation of the reversal of gender differences in higher education attainment, but the increase of benefits for higher education explains the changing educational decisions of women regarding their transition to higher education.

Conclusions: The outperformance of females compared with males in higher education might have been initialised by several social changes, including the expansion of public employment, the growing demand for highly qualified female workers in welfare and service areas, the increasing returns of women's increased education and training, and the improved opportunities for combining family and work outside the home. The historical data show that, in terms of (married) women's increased labour market opportunities and female life-cycle labour force participation, the raising rates of women's enrolment in higher education were – among other reasons – partly explained by their rising access to service class positions across birth cohorts, and the rise of their educational returns in terms of wages and long-term employment.

Introduction

All modern Western societies have experienced educational expansion since the beginning of the twentieth century, particularly after 1945 (Müller and Kogan 2010). Moreover, recent empirical studies provide evidence for declining social and gender inequalities in terms of educational opportunities in most of these countries (Breen et al. 2010). In the case of West Germany, Breen et al. (2012) show that the offspring of working and lower-middle-class people also benefited from educational expansion in regard to both participation in higher education and the attainment of educational quali-fications. Other distinct developments are the gender reversal in educational attainment (DiPrete and Buchmann 2013) and the reduction in women's disadvantage in the educa-tional system (Buchmann and DiPrete 2006). This change of gender-specific disparities in educational attainment has occurred in nearly all OECD member countries since the late 1970s and early 1980s (Buchmann, DiPrete, and McDaniel 2008, 328). In Germany, this is particularly true for the attainment of the higher education entrance qualification (*Abitur*) at academic high schools (*Gymnasium*), as well as the enrolment in university training in West Germany and then in East Germany after the German reunification in 1990 (Becker and Müller 2011; Helbig 2013).

Against the background of the formation of the Federal Republic of Germany (other-wise known as West Germany) in 1949, the question arises as to why there was a gen-der reversal in educational attainment during the late 1970s and the early 1980s. Why have women caught up to and then outpaced men in both academic high school comple-tion and enrolment in university studies? How can the reversal of gender differences in enrolment in the academic high school and in the attainment of higher education entrance qualifications be explained? There are several empirical studies seeking expla-nations for this long-term process, considering for the most part the situation in the USA. The empirical evidence for the West German case is, however, somewhat poor (Becker and Müller 2011; Hadjar and Berger 2010). Today, German research focuses on the structures and mechanisms of the current gender-specific inequality of educational opportunities and behaviour in school using a static cross-sectional design (e.g. Hadjar 2011). Therefore, it is of interest to analyse the *dynamics of the changing gender inequalities* in the West German context over a long historical period and consecutive birth cohorts in order to contribute to a sociological explanation of this phenomenon (e.g. Blossfeld and Rohwer 1997).

The remainder of this empirical study is structured in the following way. In the next section, a structural–individualistic explanation will be suggested, which could contribute to an explanation of the reversal of gender differences in educational attainment in West Germany. With regard to DiPrete and Buchmann's (2013) empirical study, the impact of both the increasing labour market demand for qualified and highly qualified women and their increasing returns to education will be focused upon. The third section involves discussion on the databases and variables used for empirical analysis. The findings are presented in the fourth section. Finally, the fifth section provides the conclusion.

Theoretical background

In order to contribute to an explanation of the gender reversal from a male advantage to a female one in *Gymnasium* enrolment and completion, one has to consider that women have 'caught up' with men and outpaced them in academic high school completion. The pattern of this social change in the West German context since 1949 indicates that this change did not arise from a so-called 'boy crisis' (DiPrete and Buchmann 2013). Although the female rate of attaining the *Abitur* (the higher education entrance qualification) accelerated after the 1950s, men's likelihood has not declined since that time. According to empirical findings for West Germany, it seems to be obvious that these gender disparities are not due to different changes in men and women in terms of the effects of social origin on educational opportunity (Breen et al. 2012). Recently, Becker and Müller (2011) found indications that this cannot be explained by a change of gender-specific school achievements in favour of West German women. It is assumed by the authors that the reversal of gender differences in attainment is rather a consequence of the changes in female educational decisions. Thus, in order to reveal the mechanisms of this process, it is useful to distinguish between the so-called primary and secondary effect of gender (Boudon 1974). It has to be noted that the outcomes of these mechanisms are linked to the historical change of other structural parameters, such as those related to the economic cycle, labour market, family demography (timing of marriage and motherhood) and the educational system (e.g. Blossfeld and Rohwer 1997; Müller, Willms, and Handl 1983).

The *primary effect of gender* – the correlation between gender and achievement in school after controlling for social origin – is empirically evident (Buchmann, DiPrete, and McDaniel 2008). As a consequence of their socialisation and education in the parental home, it has been suggested that girls are better prepared for schooling than boys (Hadjar 2011). As such, girls receive better grades if their competences and intelligence are controlled for. Furthermore, they have advantages in social skills and classroom behaviour (Jacob 2002):

> During adolescence, high school teachers consistently rate girls as putting forth more effort and as being less disruptive than boys. [...] Adolescent girls also possess higher levels of other non-cognitive skills such as attentiveness and organizational skills, [...] self-discipline [...], leadership qualities, and interest in school, all of which facilitate academic success. (Buchmann, DiPrete, and McDaniel 2008, 322)

In West Germany, girls received better marks and grade point averages (GPA) than boys – even when their social origin has been controlled for. They were also more likely to become recommended for upper secondary education at the end of elementary school (Neugebauer 2011). These gender disparities have remained stable since the 1980s (Becker and Müller 2011). The observations by Jacob (2002) and Buchmann, DiPrete, and McDaniel (2008) cited above appear to hold true for West Germany: girls have greater non-cognitive skills (Hadjar and Lupatsch 2010; Kunter and Stanat 2002), whereas boys provide low willingness for achievement and effort in school (Helbig 2012; Neugebauer 2011). Recently, Legewie and DiPrete (2012) explained boys' underperformance in Berlin schools by the effects of school environment, particularly their conception of masculinity in peer culture and their anti-school attitudes and behaviour.

While this primary effect of gender sufficiently explains the female advantage in school for each of the historical periods, the question of whether it contributes to the explanation of the *reversal* of gender differences in attaining the *Abitur* is still unsolved. However, in spite of some empirical evidence that girls have always had better marks and GPAs than boys and also provided better school achievements (DiPrete and Buchmann 2013), clarification is still needed as to whether this primary effect of gender to the advantage of girls and young women already existed in the past (Becker and Müller 2011). If there is no change in the primary effect of gender over the course of historical time, the gender disparities in achievement (and their causes and consequences) do not actually contribute to the explanation of the *reversal* of gender differences in educational attainment (*hypothesis 1*).

Although girls have long gained better grades in school, they did not translate their better performance into higher levels of educational attainment relative to men (Buchmann, DiPrete, and McDaniel 2008, 320, 322; Mickelson 1989). Therefore, it is crucial to analyse the *secondary effect of gender*: the gendered educational decision for enrolling in the *Gymnasium* and becoming eligible for university training when achievement has been controlled for (Jacobs 1996, 177). That means that there are different educational decisions among groups (although while there, achievement is similar). Given different alternatives at a transition point in the educational system, individuals' decisions depend on the benefits and costs of each of the alternatives. Individuals are more likely to choose educational alternatives if the benefits exceed the costs. Since the costs of these alternatives are the same for each gender, the different choices of men and women depend mainly on the different benefits. While in the past boys or young men were more likely to have decided in favour of continuing education compared with girls or women demonstrating the same achievement, it is assumed that this correlation has reversed in the period after 1945.

For West Germany, in particular, analysis has to reveal which incentives and constraints have shaped young women's expectations and decisions regarding the attainment of higher education. While individual and institutional restrictions have been emphasised for describing the gender disparities in educational opportunities, the impact of gender-specific incentives in the labour market – in terms of the changing value of education on individuals' investment in their education (in terms of achievement and skills, attainment of higher education certificates and duration of enrolment in educational system) – and its variation across historical periods has so far been neglected for West Germany. In addition, the resources needed for families' investment in their children's education (in terms of economic, cultural and social capital) and their plans for their children's life course have to be taken into account (Buchmann and DiPrete 2006, 519). For example, it is assumed that 'status maintenance' was once a key reason for parents to invest in their sons' education. For the same reason, it is assumed that they were more likely to invest in their daughters' education in order to prepare them for the 'marriage market' rather than for the labour market (Blossfeld and Timm 2003; Breen and Goldthorpe 1997; Wirth and Schmidt 2003).

However, after the formation of the Federal Republic of Germany in 1949, parents' investment in their daughters' higher education may have become more rational due to growing demand for qualified and highly qualified female labour in the course of the economic development and the expansion of the welfare state during the 1960s and 1970s (Becker 2007; Hecken 2006). Educational expansion was the by-product of both the German economic boom and the expansion of public employment. This might have significantly contributed to increasing educational opportunities for both women and men. These developments in the economic cycle and the expansion of administrative and service jobs were interrelated with an increase in employers' demand for female labour (Blossfeld and Rohwer 1997). In particular, women were recruited for jobs in the state administration (law, business and social insurance), as well as for the semi-professional and professional tasks in the rapidly expanding welfare areas such as education, public health, and social work (Becker and Blossfeld 1991). Therefore, it becomes subjectively rational for women to invest in academic high school education, and subsequently in earning the *Abitur* or a university degree, in order to become employed in the state labour market. For women, these jobs were highly attractive due to privileged working conditions, absence of wage discrimination, the opportunity of long-term part-time and full-time employment across the life course (for integration of married women and mothers into the labour market), and the likelihood of upward mobility into the lower and upper service classes (Becker 1991). These investments in education and training seemed to be less risky, as well as less costly, because jobs and returns to education are rather more certain in the state sector than they are in the private sector. Therefore, across several birth cohorts born after the world economic crisis at the end of the 1920s, more women entered prestigious and often better-paid positions in the West German state sector.[1] Since the 1980s, private employers began to recruit well-trained female graduates for better-paid administrative and service jobs requiring training in higher education (Schubert and Engelage 2006), while the expansion of public employment started to slow after the mid-1970s (Becker and Blossfeld 1991). Due to these developments in the post-1945 period, the reversal of gender differences in educational attainment might have been pushed and accelerated across generations.

Therefore, it is posited that the rising labour wages and class positions of West German women may have provided incentives for their attainment of degrees in higher education (Mayer 1991; Schömann 1994). In particular, the educational returns of clerical and service occupations – the latter requiring high skill levels, as well as providing high living standards and insurance against poverty (Buchmann and DiPrete 2006) – were significant 'pull factors' inciting females to invest in higher education and professional employment (*hypothesis 2*). Overall, as in the USA, a chief reason behind the rising rates of women's enrolment in upper secondary school (*Gymnasium*) was that the educational returns of an upper secondary school degree (*Abitur*) on the labour market had been increasing more for women than for men (Buchmann, DiPrete, and McDaniel 2008, 328).

However, other social changes in the 1960s and 1970s supported this process. On the one hand, women's changing expectations of future labour force participation – as well as age at first marriage and first motherhood in the late 1960s – might be crucial explanatory factors for their *Gymnasium* enrolment and completion of the *Abitur* (Blossfeld and Huninik 1991; Blossfeld and Jaenichen 1992). On the other hand, access to reliable contraception (birth control pill) in the second half of the 1960s positively impacted women's academic high school attendance, since it lowered the costs of engaging in long-term investments in education and career, as well as in delaying the first marriage and birth (Buchmann, DiPrete, and McDaniel 2008, 329; Charles and Luoh 2003, 573–74; Goldin and Katz 2002; Goldin, Katz, and Kuziemko 2006).[2]

Data, variables, and statistical procedures

Databases

Several databases have been employed for the empirical analysis. Firstly, the German General Social Survey (ALLBUS) was used as main database, providing detailed information on the educational attainment of women and men in West Germany. ALLBUS is a biennial cross-sectional survey that has been conducted since 1980 in the western part of Germany, and since 1990 in East Germany (Koch and Wasmer 2004). Combining these surveys, it is possible to reconstruct the reversal of gender differences in attainment across several birth cohorts (consisting of respondents resident in Germany), as well as for a long historical period. From 1980 to 1990, each of the samples consists of about 3000 respondents living in West Germany and West Berlin. Since 1992, the sample of 3500 respondents consists of two-thirds of persons in West Germany and one-third of people living in the eastern states of Germany. For statistical estimations, only West German persons older than 18 years and born between 1919 and 1988 are considered.

Secondly, the longitudinal data of the German Life History Study (GLHS) has been utilised, particularly in terms of providing extremely detailed retrospective data on the intergenerational transmission of education and educational careers, and the occupational careers and dynamics of labour earnings over the life course of West Germans born between 1919 and 1971 (Mayer 2008; Schömann 1994). With the longitudinal data, it is possible to investigate life courses and educational careers in Germany across the entire twentieth century. For our purposes, the GLHS compromises information on the West German respondents' educational achievement, as well as on the self-report of educational success.

Thirdly, the German Socio-economic Panel (GSOEP) is a longitudinal study of private households in Germany (Wagner, Frick, and Schupp 2007). Every year, nearly 11,000 households and more than 20,000 people were sampled. While the GSOEP started in 1984, the biographical retrospective data provides information on the educational and working career for a long historical period until the present age, with detailed time references to the start and end of each of the training and employment spells. In the empirical part, only West German women will be considered.

Fourthly, in order to analyse the impact of gender on both the GPAs of the 9th graders (born around 1985, being around 15 years of age at the time of survey) at the end of the compulsory secondary and the transition to the *Gymnasium* in order to attain the *Abitur*, the cross-sectional data of the enlarged German sample of PISA (Programme for International Student Assessment) 2000 (PISA-E) has been employed (Baumert, Stanat, and Demmrich 2001).

Variables

In order to describe the historical patterns of educational returns, *wages* will be considered. These labour earnings are operationalised as net hourly wages and have been deflated for prices in 1980 (Schömann 1994).

The respondents' *social origin* and their *class destination* are measured by the class scheme suggested by Erikson and Goldthorpe (1992). This class scheme has been tested in several empirical studies on social inequality and mobility. In terms of returns to education, the class destination is an appropriate indicator for returns to education, including dimensions such as income, social status, standard of living and other socio-economic privileges (e.g. Müller and Shavit 1998). For the sake of simplicity, the original class scheme has been reduced to three class categories: working class, middle classes, and service classes. The upper service class consists of higher-grade professionals (e.g. physicians, lawyers and professors), administrators and officials, as well as managers in large industrial establishments and large proprietors. In the lower service class, there are lower-grade professionals (e.g. nurses, teachers in primary school or in lower secondary school), administrators and officials, higher-grade technicians, as well as managers in small industrial establishments and supervisors of non-manual employees. The middle class is rather heterogeneous: routine non-higher-grade manual employees (both administration and commerce), lower-grade routine non-manual employees (sales and services), small proprietors and artisans (with or without employees) and farmers, as well as smallholders and other self-employed workers in primary production.

Finally, the working class comprises lower-grade technicians, supervisors of manual workers, skilled manual workers, semi-skilled and unskilled manual workers (i.e. not in agriculture, etc.) as well as agricultural and other workers in primary production.

In terms of the school education attained by the respondents, three categories are distinguished. The *Hauptschulabschluss* (lower secondary school) is the lowest degree that could be earned in West German schools. The next higher certificate (*Mittlere Reife*) is the graduation obtained after successfully completing an intermediate secondary school (*Realschule*), while the higher education entrance certificate (*Abitur*) could be earned in the academic high school (*Gymnasium*).

Statistical procedure

Binary logistic regressions are employed for the statistical modelling of the individuals' achievement, educational decision and likelihood for social mobility (Long 1997). For statistical reasons, the average marginal effects (AME) will be estimated, allowing comparisons across groups such as birth cohorts, social classes and genders (Hinz and Auspurg 2011). AMEs indicate the change (in terms of percentage points) in the expected likelihood of the interesting event (dependent variable), as one independent variable increases by unity while all other variables are kept constant in terms of their group-specific average.

Empirical results

The change of primary effects of gender

In the first step, the historical process of the reversal of gender differences for enrolment in the *Gymnasium* and attainment of the *Abitur* is reconstructed for several birth cohorts by controlling for their social origin (Table 1). Among the older cohorts born before the 1960s, men were more likely to be eligible for university training than women. However, young women born in the 1960s have caught up with the men of the same age, and the men have been outpaced by women in becoming eligible for university studies in the cohorts born between 1969 and 1978. In the younger cohorts born between 1979 and 1988, the likelihood of attaining an *Abitur* exceeds those for men.

The comparison of the cohort-specific patterns of educational attainment of the *Abitur* with the likelihood of being excellent at school provide an indication that the reversal of gender differences in attainment could not be explained by female improvement in school achievement or by the men's decreases in educational performances (Table 2). For the older birth cohorts born around 1940, women are more likely to be the successful pupils in school. This gender disparity remained rather constant across the younger birth cohorts. Even for the youngest cohort born 1959–61, it is found that women have exceeded men in terms of school achievement (last column in Table 2), but women in the same cohort have had significantly better opportunities in attaining the *Abitur* than men (Table 1). This could be explained by the secondary effects of the female disadvantage only. If the reversal in gender differences had arisen due to changes in the primary effect of gender, then one would expect that women born after the 1960s would show lower achievements. However, this is obviously not the case.

If the primary and secondary effects are considered at the end of compulsory secondary school for young women and men born around 1985, our interpretation stands for the cohort born after the gender reversal at the end of the 1970s (Table 3). Notice

Table 1. Development of inequality of educational opportunity across birth cohorts in West Germany – the likelihood of higher education entrance qualification attainment.

Cohorts	1919–28	1929–38	1939–48	1949–58	1959–68	1969–78	1979–88
Gender							
Male							
Female	−0.060*	−0.084*	−0.102*	−0.074*	−0.055*	0.021*	0.037*
Social origin							
Working class							
Middle classes	0.099*	0.095*	0.110*	0.139*	0.170*	0.162*	0.191*
Service classes	0.301*	0.282*	0.312*	0.359*	0.402*	0.409*	0.382*
Pseudo R^2	0.213	0.217	0.161	0.117	0.123	0.125	0.093
N	3301	3672	4588	5440	5751	2452	995

Note: *$p \leq 0.05$ at least; AME, average marginal effects – estimated by logistic regression.
Source: ALLBUS 1980–2010; own calculations.

Table 2. Primary effects of gender in West Germany – self-reported excellent school achievements.

Birth cohorts	1939–41	1949–51	1954–56	1959–61
Gender				
Male	Reference	Reference	Reference	Reference
Female	0.102*	0.060†	0.055†	0.086*
School certificate				
Lower secondary school	−0.119†	−0.146*	−0.091*	−0.072†
Intermediate secondary school	−0.127†	−0.156*	−0.138*	−0.065
Upper secondary school	Reference	Reference	Reference	Reference
Social origin				
Working class	−0.099*	−0.030	−0.029	0.011
Middle classes	−0.098*	−0.059	0.049	0.066†
Service classes	Reference	Reference	Reference	Reference
Pseudo-R^2	0.031	0.023	0.018	0.014
N	652	686	801	782

Note: $^†p\le0.1$; *$p\le0.05$ at least; AME, average marginal effects, estimated by logistic regression (Reference: average or poor achievement).
Source: German Life History Study I and III (West); own calculations.

Table 3. Primary and secondary effect of gender (9th graders in 2000 – birth cohort 1985).

	Boys		
	(Very) good	Average	Poor
Provide grade points average:	25.9%	50.3%	23.8%
– and would become eligible for university studies:	54.5%	41.9%	32.7%

	Girls		
	(Very) good	Average	Poor
Provide grade points average:	28.9%	50.4%	20.7%
– and would become eligible for university studies:	59.9%	47.3%	33.6%

Source: PISA-E 2000; own calculations.

that 43% of the male 9th graders (mostly at age 15 in 2000), but 48% of the girls of the same age want to continue on to higher education, namely in the academic high school (*Gymnasiale Oberstufe*), in order to become eligible for university studies. If one looks on the average rates of the juveniles with (very) good or average GPA, the girls are more likely to decide in favour of the *Abitur*.

If one takes into account the recently published results on gender disparities in GPAs (e.g. Becker and Müller 2011; Helbig 2012; Neugebauer 2011), it has to be concluded that these findings provide evidence for the first hypothesis, since it seems that the primary effect of gender did *not* contribute to the reversal of gender differences in higher education attainment. This result reinforces the point that we have to reveal the mechanisms of the secondary effect of gender in order to explain the *reversal* of gender differences in attainment during the 1970s and 1980s in West Germany.

The impact of secondary effects of gender on the reversal of gender differences in educational attainment

It was stressed in the theoretical section that the increasing returns to higher-educated women in the labour market may have provided a significant incentive for women to translate their better school performance into higher levels of educational attainment. This should result in increasing female life-cycle employment as a precondition for receiving these (subjectively optimal) benefits in terms of wages or class positions. This process is empirically evident for West Germany (Figure 1).

If the same birth cohorts are considered for reconstructing this long-term process of rising rates in women's overall economic activity, it is found that their employment rates actually increased *before* the reversal in gender differences in attainment took place (Figure 1). Across cohorts and generations, education became increasingly important for their employment prospects. In correspondence with the findings by Blossfeld and Rohwer (1997, 187), it is evident on the left part of Figure 1 that women born after 1948 – who benefited from educational expansion – are more likely to be employed continuously. In particular, the birth cohorts that were affected by the *gender reversal* firstly provide the highest employment rate across their life course. While the increasing employment rates of the older cohorts of (married) women – particularly the birth cohort 1939–48 – could be interpreted as a supply response to increased job opportunities, empirical evidence by Blossfeld and Rohwer (1997, 168–70) suggests that the younger cohorts are more likely than women in the older cohorts to combine family and occupation in all phases of the family cycle, and to also turn their education into better job opportunities. The increasing opportunity for part-time employment might have supported the compatibility of work and family, as well as the relatively stable and highly elastic female labour supply function since the late 1960s and early 1970s, when women born after 1948 entered the labour market (see the right part of Figure 1).[3] It seems to be clear that the educational expansion in West Germany fostered the (part-time and full-time) employment of women in the post-1945 period. As a result, part-time work seemed to act as a bridge between 'housewife status' and full-time employment, particularly for highly qualified mothers (Blossfeld and Rohwer 1997, 182). Women in the younger birth cohorts participated in education in order to become employed, as well as to be employed in all phases of their motherhood. These processes could have contributed to the reversal of gender differences in attainment in West Germany.

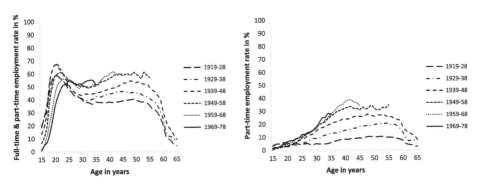

Figure 1. Changing patterns of female employment in the life course across birth cohorts in West Germany.
Source: GSOEP 1984–2009; own calculations.

Now the question arises whether women who have profited from educational expansion have received increased benefits in terms of wages. The development of labour earnings – indicated by average net hourly wages (in German marks) – in the occupational career of several birth cohorts in the West German post-1945 period provide evidence that the improvement of economic welfare and educational expansion *did* result in higher wages across the younger cohorts (Figure 2). However, this cohort-specific development is valid for both men and women, and differences in wages at the entrance to the labour market remained constant across the work history. Compared with the starting wages of women and men born around 1930 and 1940, the increases across the younger birth cohorts are rather similar. The average wages are lower for women in each of the cohorts, but the rates of growth are identical for each of the genders. However, previous studies provide empirical evidence that West German women across birth cohorts have particularly benefited from higher education in terms of earnings (Schömann 1994), allocation to better-paid jobs in the state sector (Hannan, Schömann, and Blossfeld 1990) and continuous further training in terms of wages (Schömann and Becker 2002). Overall, the returns to education in terms of labour earnings become similar between the genders in terms of advantages to well-educated women in the younger birth cohorts. Thus, this finding indirectly provides empirical support for the second hypothesis: that the returns to education were one of the incentives for female human capital investments.

In the theoretical section, it has been argued that women in West Germany entered prestigious and often better-paid positions as a result of employers – and particularly the state sector – demanding a well-trained labour force in administrative and welfare areas after 1949. Now it has to be analysed whether the educational returns for these clerical and service occupations were significant 'pull factors' stimulating female investment in higher education and professional employment. The test of this second hypothesis is an indirect one again, and focuses on social mobility into the lower and upper service classes.

The educational returns estimated for the likelihood of access to the lower and upper service classes support this interpretation (Table 4). The results also provide evidence for the second hypothesis. In other words, the higher the educational degree, the higher the propensity for entering a position in the service classes – even if social origin has been controlled for. For both women and men, educational expansion has improved access to lower and upper service classes, since returns to education have increased

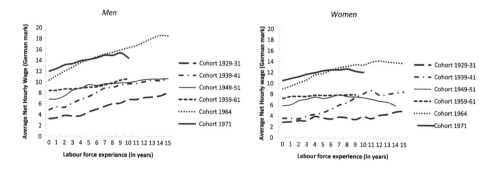

Figure 2. Dynamics of male and female average labour earnings over the life course across birth cohorts in West Germany.
Source: German Life History Study I, III and IV (West); own calculations.

Table 4. Female returns to education – social mobility in service classes.

Cohorts	1919–28	1929–38	1939–48	1949–58	1959–68	1969–78
Lower service class						
School certificate – women						
Hauptschulabschluss	Reference	Reference	Reference	Reference	Reference	Reference
Mittlere Reife	0.209*	0.250*	0.243*	0.271*	0.391*	0.378*
Abitur	0.213*	0.286*	0.254*	0.336*	0.444*	0.463*
School certificate – men						
Hauptschulabschluss	Reference	Reference	Reference	Reference	Reference	Reference
Mittlere Reife	0.240*	0.207*	0.252*	0.252*	0.205*	0.107*
Abitur	0.169*	0.133*	0.163*	0.285*	0.279*	0.242*
Upper service class						
School certificate – women						
Hauptschulabschluss	Reference	Reference	Reference	Reference	Reference	Reference
Mittlere Reife	0.063*	0.038*	0.028*	0.084*	0.077*	0.037*
Abitur	0.138*	0.097*	0.139*	0.196*	0.188*	0.140*
School certificate – men						
Hauptschulabschluss	Reference	Reference	Reference	Reference	Reference	Reference
Mittlere Reife	0.127*	0.188*	0.184*	0.149*	0.068*	0.041*
Abitur	0.251*	0.316*	0.348*	0.303*	0.222*	0.188*
Upper or lower service class						
School certificate – women						
Hauptschulabschluss	Reference	Reference	Reference	Reference	Reference	Reference
Mittlere Reife	0.206*	0.237*	0.221*	0.248*	0.366*	0.345*
Abitur	0.361*	0.410*	0.441*	0.494*	0.543*	0.531*
School certificate – men						
Hauptschulabschluss	Reference	Reference	Reference	Reference	Reference	Reference
Mittlere Reife	0.277*	0.274*	0.285*	0.268*	0.212*	0.104*
Abitur	0.443*	0.455*	0.467*	0.476*	0.433*	0.350*

Note: *$p \leq 0.05$ at least; average marginal effects (controlled for social origin) – estimated by logistic regression. Hauptschulabschluss, lower secondary school certificate; Mittlere Reife, intermediate secondary school certificate; Abitur, higher education entrance certificate.
Source: ALLBUS 1980–2010; own calculations.

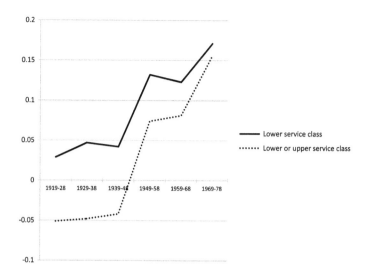

Figure 3. Gender differences in returns to education: the trend of female mobility into service classes.
Source: ALLBUS 1980–2010 (average marginal effects, controlled for social origin and education); own calculations.

across cohorts. For women born after 1958, in particular, the attainment of the *Abitur* significantly provides privileged opportunities for allocation into the higher social classes. This result indicates an interaction of the demand for well-trained female workers, educational expansion, the increase of female labour market participation, and finally, the rising returns to higher education to the advantage of women.

Finally, it needs to be assessed whether gender differences in the changing returns to education in terms of social mobility to the service classes are significant but random. In Figure 3, women's likelihood of access to the service classes (controlled for education and social origin) compared with the men's mobility rates are documented. For the cohorts born between 1919 and 1948, gender differences for the allocation to service classes were rather lower, but men have had significantly better chances for entry to the upper service class. For the younger cohorts born after 1948, gender differences increased to the advantage of women. Women born after 1948 are more likely to have access to service classes than men. Thus, the investment in higher education and continuous employment became more effective for women. The increasing gender disparity of social mobility into service classes in favour of women might correlate with the reversal of gender differences in educational attainment in the late 1970s and the early 1980s in West Germany. This interpretation might be valid, since the birth cohorts who profited the most from this return to education – maybe in regard to economic independence and social approval by education, employment and occupational success – are the same cohorts who have carried out the so-called gender reversal in higher education. Thus, our results provide empirical evidence for the second hypothesis again.

Conclusions

The aim of our empirical analysis was to contribute to the empirical description and explanation of the reversal of gender differences in educational attainment – particularly focusing on eligibility for university studies – which took place in the late 1970s and the early 1980s in West Germany. While men have had better opportunities for enrolment in higher education for a long time, in recent decades women have benefited from educational expansion and outpaced men in attaining higher credentials. Due to the limitations of the data, it has to be stressed that the results remain rather descriptive, but they might serve to illustrate one explanation as to how women's increasing returns to higher education acted as a crucial factor in the reversal of gender differences in educational attainment.

In order to explain the process in which women have caught up to and outpaced men in this period, the theoretical reflections and empirical evidence presented in the US context by DiPrete and Buchmann (2006) and Buchmann, DiPrete, and McDaniel (2008) have been considered. In order to understand the nature, causes and consequences of the changing gender gap in higher education, the theoretical model suggested by Boudon (1974) for the genesis and reproduction of inequality of educational opportunity has been adapted for the scope of our study (see also Becker 2003). In the theoretical section, it has been stressed that the primary effect of gender – the correlation of educational achievement and gender (in favour of women) – does not contribute significantly to the long-term reversal of gender differences to the advantage of women. Therefore, the processes and mechanisms resulting in the secondary effect of gender – the gender-specific educational decision to continue into higher education – have to be revealed. Taking several opportunities and constraints for educational decision into account, it has been claimed that the expansion of welfare areas in public employment, as well as an increasing number of administrative and service positions in the private labour market requiring high occupational skills, was an important incentive for West German women to invest in education and training in order to become employed in service class positions. It becomes evident that there are several important 'pull factors' impacting on female educational careers across birth cohorts, such as the supply of prestigious and better-paid positions in the labour market. In particular, women's increased access to the service classes since the 1980s has provided a higher standard of living, as well as improved insurance against poverty.

The empirical analysis provides evidence that the *investment risk* (the relation between the cost of higher education and successful completion of higher education) was always lower for women relative to men. It became obvious that achievement differences across gender and time did not contribute to the explanation of the reversal of gender differences in attainment during the late 1970s and early 1980s. Due to increasing returns on their education in terms of wages and occupational positions, women translated their better educational achievements into increased *educational motivation*. The results indicate that the increase in economic benefits corresponds with the reversal of gender differences in women's higher education attainment, possibly driven by increased educational motivation. This is due to the structural and institutional change of the labour markets in the course of the tertiarisation of economic sectors and occupations. Overall rates of women's enrolment in the *Gymnasium* and university studies might have increased due to the increased returns that the *Abitur* and university degrees provides in terms of social mobility to the service classes, which is much higher than it is for men in the same birth cohorts.

After the union of the Federal Republic of Germany and the GDR, the former substantive vertical gender segregation in enrolment in university training to the disadvantage of women in Germany has been reversed to the men's disadvantage when continuing in university training. However, the horizontal gender segregation in choice of vocational training and university studies has persisted over time (Becker, Haunberger, and Schubert 2010; see also Jonsson 1999, 392). If we take the causes of the gender reversal in the 1970s and 1980s into account, it becomes obvious that the horizontal segregation corresponds with men's and women's *'feasible set'* of choice alternatives. As in previous periods after 1945, women mainly prefer the types of education and training resulting in occupations that provide them with subjectively optimal benefits.

Since the incentives for the different alternatives are not constant in time, it is not impossible that the horizontal segregation will change in the next centuries. Just as in other countries, the German history of female employment and gender segregation of occupations and industries has taught us that horizontal and vertical gender segregation in education and occupation are not constant (Müller, Willms, and Handl 1983). However, there are no indications that the gender pay gap will diminish over the course of these most recent structural trends, since the relationships between gender, occupation and income have remained constant over the course of educational expansion. Amongst other things, women are paid less than men because women tend to select professions and jobs that are 'valued' at financially lower rates by employers (Schömann 1994).

Acknowledgements

The article is dedicated to my teacher and friend, Hans-Peter Blossfeld, on his 60th anniversary. For helpful comments on earlier drafts, I wish to thank the editors, the anonymous reviewers, and Walter Müller and Andreas Hadjar.

Notes

1. The significant increase in female labour force participation after 1945 might have resulted in the suspension of the 'housewife wedlock' in 1977 – supporting women's economic independence from their husbands (as wives did not have to ask their husbands for permission to gain professional employment outside the private household any more) and also resulting in greater acceptance of married women in the labour force. However, it seems to be clear that the suspension was a reaction of law-makers to the increase of long-term female employment.
2. In several studies, processes such as female emancipation or changing gender stereotypes have been mentioned as crucial causes for the increasing enrolment of women in higher education. There are good reasons to assume that these processes have been the consequence of increasing female education, rather than causes for female enrolment (DiPrete and Buchmann 2013).
3. It could also be argued that, for women, the increasing supply of marketable goods and services has facilitated these processes by reducing the time and effort involved in private household duties. It might be also true that mothers' feasibility of continuous employment in the course of life has positively influenced the educational and occupational aspirations of their daughters, and pushed women's increasing economic activities across generations, in addition to the integration of women into the labour market across the birth cohorts.

References

Baumert, Jürgen, Petra Stanat, and Anke Demmrich. 2001. "PISA 2000: Untersuchungsgegenstand, theoretische Grundlagen und Durchführung der Studie." In *PISA 2000: Basiskompetenzen von Schülerinnen und Schülern im internationalen Vergleich*, edited by Deutsches PISA-Konsortium, 15–68. Opladen: Leske + Budrich.

Becker, Rolf. 1991. "Karrieremuster von Frauen in der Privatwirtschaft und im öffentlichen Dienst." In *Vom Regen in die Traufe. Frauen zwischen Beruf und Familie*, edited by Karl Ulrich Mayer, Jutta Allmendinger, and Johannes Huinink, 119–141. Frankfurt am Main: Campus.

Becker, Rolf. 2003. "Educational Expansion and Persistent Inequalities of Education: Utilizing the Subjective Expected Utility Theory to Explain the Increasing Participation Rates in Upper Secondary School in the Federal Republic of Germany." *European Sociological Review* 19: 1–24.

Becker, Rolf. 2007. "State and Private Sector Employees." In *Blackwell Encyclopedia of Sociology*, edited by George Ritzer, 4734–4737. Oxford: Blackwell.

Becker, Rolf, and Hans-Peter Blossfeld. 1991. "Cohort-specific Effects of the Expansion of the Welfare State on Job Opportunities: A Longitudinal Analysis of Three Birth Cohorts in the Federal Republic of Germany." *Sociologische Gids* 38: 261–284.

Becker, Rolf, Sigrid Haunberger, and Frank Schubert. 2010. "Studienfachwahl als Spezialfall der Ausbildungsentscheidung und Berufswahl." *Zeitschrift für Arbeitsmarktforschung* 42: 292–310.

Becker, Rolf, and Walter Müller. 2011. "Bildungsungleichheiten nach Geschlecht und Herkunft im Wandel." In *Geschlechtsspezifische Bildungsungleichheiten*, edited by Andreas Hadjar, 55–75. Wiesbaden: VS Verlag für Sozialwissenschaften.

Blossfeld, Hans-Peter, and Johannes Huinink. 1991. "Human Capital Investments or Norms of Role Transition? How Women's Schooling and Career Affect the Process of Family-formation." *American Journal of Sociology* 97: 143–168.

Blossfeld, Hans-Peter, and Ursula Jaenichen. 1992. "Educational Expansion and Changes in Women's Entry into Marriage and Motherhood in the Federal Republic of Germany." *Journal of Marriage and the Family* 54: 302–315.

Blossfeld, Hans-Peter, and Götz Rohwer. 1997. "Part-time Work in West Germany." In *Between Equalization and Marginalization: Part-time Working Women in Europe and the United States*, edited by Hans-Peter Blossfeld and Catherine Hakim, 164–190. Oxford: Oxford University Press.

Blossfeld, Hans-Peter, and Andreas Timm. 2003. "Who Marries Whom in West Germany?" In *Who Marries Whom – Educational Systems as Marriage Markets in Modern Societies*, edited by Hans-Peter Blossfeld and Andreas Timm, 19–35. Dordrecht: Kluwer Academic Publishers.

Boudon, Raymond. 1974. *Education, Opportunity, and Social Inequality*. New York: Wiley.

Breen, Richard, and John H. Goldthorpe. 1997. "Explaining Educational Differentials. Towards a Formal Rational Action Theory." *Rationality and Society* 9: 275–305.

Breen, Richard, Ruud Luijkx, Walter Müller, and Reinhard Pollak. 2010. "Long-term Trends in Educational Inequality in Europe: Class Inequalities and Gender Differences." *European Sociological Review* 26: 31–48.

Breen, Richard, Ruud Luijkx, Walter Müller, and Reinhard Pollak. 2012. "Bildungsdisparitäten nach Sozialer Herkunft und Geschlecht im Wandel – Deutschland im internationalen Vergleich." In *Soziologische Bildungsforschung. Sonderheft 52 der Kölner Zeitschrift für Soziologie und Sozialpsychologie*, edited by Rolf Becker and Heike Solga, 346–373. Wiesbaden: Springer+VS Verlag für Sozialwissenschaften.

Buchmann, Claudia, and Thomas A. DiPrete. 2006. "The Growing Female Advantage in College Completion: The Role of Family Background and Academic Achievement." *American Sociological Review* 71: 515–541.

Buchmann, Claudia, Thomas A. DiPrete, and Anne McDaniel. 2008. "Gender Inequalities in Education." *Annual Review of Sociology* 34: 319–337.

Charles, Kerwin Kofi, and Ming-Ching Luoh. 2003. "Gender Differences in Completed Schooling." *The Review of Economics and Statistics* 85: 559–577.

DiPrete, Thomas A., and Claudia Buchmann. 2006. "Gender-specific Trends in the Value of Education and the Emerging Gender Gap in College Completion." *Demography* 43: 1–24.

DiPrete, Thomas A., and Claudia Buchmann. 2013. *The Rise of Women: The Growing Gender Gap in Education and What it Means for American Schools*. New York: Russell Sage Foundation.

Erikson, Robert, and John H. Goldthorpe. 1992. *The Constant Flux: A Study of Class Mobility in Industrial Societies*. Oxford: Clarendon Press.

Goldin, Claudia, and Lawrence F. Katz. 2002. "The Power of the Pill: Oral Contraceptives and Women's Career and Marriage Decision." *Journal of Political Economy* 110: 730–770.

Goldin, Claudia, Lawrence F. Katz, and Ilyana Kuziemko. 2006. "The Homecoming of American College Women: The Reversal of the College Gender Gap." *Journal of Economic Perspectives* 20: 133–156.

Hadjar, Andreas. 2011. "Einleitung." In *Geschlechtsspezifische Bildungsungleichheiten*, edited by Andreas Hadjar, 7–19. Wiesbaden: VS Verlag für Sozialwissenschaften.

Hadjar, Andreas, and Joel Berger. 2010. "Dauerhafte Bildungsungleichheiten in Westdeutschland, Ostdeutschland und der Schweiz: Eine Kohortenbetrachtung der Ungleichheitsdimensionen soziale Herkunft und Geschlecht." *Zeitschrift für Soziologie* 39: 182–201.

Hadjar, Andreas, and Judith Lupatsch. 2010. "Der Schul(miss)erfolg der Jungen. Die Bedeutung von sozialen Ressourcen, Schulentfremdung und Geschlechterrollen." *Kölner Zeitschrift für Soziologie und Sozialpsychologie* 62: 599–622.

Hannan, Michael T., Klaus Schömann, and Hans-Peter Blossfeld. 1990. "Sex and Sector Differences in the Dynamics of Wage Growth in the F.R.G." *American Sociological Review* 55: 694–713.

Hecken, Anna Etta. 2006. "Bildungsexpansion und Frauenerwerbstätigkeit." In *Die Bildungsexpansion. Erwartete und Unerwartete Folgen*, edited by Andreas Hadjar and Rolf Becker, 124–155. Wiesbaden: VS Verlag für Sozialwissenschaften.

Helbig, Marcel. 2012. "Warum Bekommen Jungen Schlechtere Schulnoten als Mädchen? Ein Sozial Psychologischer Erklärungsansatz." *Zeitschrift für Bildungsforschung* 2: 41–54.

Helbig, Marcel. 2013. "Geschlechtsspezifischer Bildungserfolg im Wandel. Eine Studie zum Schulverlauf von Mädchen und Jungen an allgemeinbildenden Schulen für die Geburtsjahrgänge 1944–1986 in Deutschland." *Journal for Educational Research Online (JERO)* 5: 141–183.

Hinz, Thomas, and Karin Auspurg. 2011. "Gruppenvergleiche bei Regressionen mit Binären Abhängigen Variablen – Probleme und Fehleinschätzungen am Beispiel von Bildungschancen im Kohortenverlauf." *Zeitschrift für Soziologie* 40: 62–73.

Jacob, Brian A. 2002. "Where the Boys aren't: Non-cognitive Skills, Returns to School and the Gender Gap in Higher Education." *Economics of Education Review* 21: 589–598.

Jacobs, Jerry A. 1996. "Gender Inequality and Higher Education." *Annual Review of Sociology* 22: 153–185.

Jonsson, Jan O. 1999. "Explaining Sex Differences in Educational Choice: An Empirical Assessment of a Rational Choice Model." *European Sociological Review* 15: 391–404.

Koch, Achim, and Martina Wasmer. 2004. "Die Allgemeine Bevölkerungsumfrage der Sozialwissenschaften (ALLBUS). Rückblick und Ausblick in die neunziger Jahre." *ZUMA-Nachrichten* 29: 7–28.

Kunter, Mareike, and Petra Stanat. 2002. "Soziale Kompetenz von Schülerinnen und Schülern. Die Rolle von Schulmerkmalen für die Vorhersage Ausgewählter Aspekte." *Zeitschrift für Erziehungswissenschaft* 5: 49–71.

Legewie, Joscha, and Thomas A. DiPrete. 2012. "School Context and the Gender Gap in Educational Achievement." *American Sociological Review* 77: 463–485.

Long, J. Scott. 1997. *Regression Models for Categorical and Limited Dependent Variables*. Thousand Oaks, CA: Sage.

Mayer, Karl Ulrich. 1991. "Berufliche Mobilität von Frauen in der Bundesrepublik Deutschland." In *Vom Regen in die Traufe: Frauen zwischen Beruf und Familie*, edited by Karl Ulrich Mayer, Jutta Allmendinger, and Johannes Huinink, 57–90. Frankfurt am Main: Campus Verlag.

Mayer, Karl Ulrich. 2008. "Retrospective Longitudinal Research: The German Life History Study." In *Handbook of Longitudinal Research: Design, Measurement and Analysis*, edited by Scott Menard, 85–106. San Diego, CA: Elsevier.

Mickelson, Roslyn Arlin. 1989. "Why does Jane Read and Write Well? The Anomaly of Women's Achievement." *Sociology of Education* 62: 47–63.

Müller, Walter, and Irena Kogan. 2010. "Education." In *Handbook of European Societies. Social Transformations in the 21st Century*, edited by Stefan Immerfall and Göran Therborn, 217–289. New York: Springer.

Müller, Walter, and Yossi Shavit. 1998. "The Institutional Embeddedness of the Stratification Process: A Comparative Study of Qualifications and Occupations in Thirteen Countries." In *From School to Work: A Comparative Study of Educational Qualifications and Occupational Destinations*, edited by Walter Müller and Yossi Shavit, 1–48. Oxford: Oxford University Press.

Müller, Walter, Angelika Willms, and Johann Handl. 1983. *Strukturwandel der Frauenarbeit 1880–1980*. Frankfurt am Main: Campus.

Neugebauer, Martin. 2011. "Werden Jungen von Lehrerinnen bei den Übergangsempfehlungen für das Gymnasium benachteiligt? Eine Analyse auf Basis der IGLU-Daten." In *Geschlechtsspezifische Bildungsungleichheiten*, edited by Andreas Hadjar, 235–260. Wiesbaden: VS Verlag für Sozialwissenschaften.

Schömann, Klaus, and Rolf Becker. 2002. "A Long-term Perspective on the Effects of Training in Germany." In *Education, Training and Employment Dynamics: Transitional Labour Markets in the European Union*, edited by Klaus Schömann and Philip J. O'Connell, 153–185. Cheltenham: Edward Elgar.

Schömann, Klaus. 1994. *The Dynamics of Labor Earnings Over the Life Course: A Comparative and Longitudinal Analysis of Germany and Poland*. Berlin: Max-Planck-Institut für Bildungsforschung/edition sigma.

Schubert, Frank, and Sonja Engelage. 2006. "Bildungsexpansion und berufsstruktureller Wandel." In *Die Bildungsexpansion. Erwartete und unerwartete Folgen*, edited by Andreas Hadjar, and Rolf Becker, 93–122. Wiesbaden: VS Verlag für Sozialwissenschaften.

Wagner, Gert G., Joachim R. Frick, and Jürgen Schupp. 2007. "The German Socio-Economic Panel Study (SOEP) – Scope, Evolution and Enhancements." *Schmollers Jahrbuch* 127: 139–169.

Wirth, Heike, and Simone Schmidt. 2003. "Bildungspartizipation und Heiratsneigung: Die Entwicklung des Bildungsselektiven Heiratsverhaltens in Westdeutschland zwischen 1970 und 1997." *ZUMA-Nachrichten* 52: 89–124.

The gendered interplay between success and well-being during transitions

Robin Samuel

Center on Poverty and Inequality, Stanford University, Stanford, USA; Department of Sociology, University of Cambridge, Cambridge, UK; Department of Social Sciences, University of Basel, Basel, Switzerland

Background: Young females have been found to out-perform males in terms of grades and university degrees in many studies. At the same time, young women seem to exhibit lower levels of well-being compared with men. Interestingly, little work has evaluated the interplay between educational success and well-being. However, antecedents and consequences of educational success will likely affect life chances and further educational and occupational trajectories.

Purpose: This paper contributes to this important, but as of yet, underdeveloped topic. The interplay between educational success – conceptualised as successful intergenerational educational mobility – and well-being is analysed as a dynamic, reciprocal and gendered process.

Sample: Panel data from the Transition from Education to Employment Project (TREE) is used to study the gendered interplay between educational success and well-being. TREE focuses on post-compulsory educational and labour market pathways of the PISA 2000 cohort in Switzerland. It is based on a sample of 6343 young people who left compulsory schooling in 2000. Data were collected annually from 2001 to 2007. At the time of the first interview, the age range of the middle 50% of the youths was between 16.5 and 17.3 years.

Design and methods: As previous research shows, episodes of educational mobility will not be evenly distributed over the observed period. Thus, an autoregressive cross-lagged mixture model framework is employed to account for the expected unequal distribution of the variables over time and the multilevel structure of the data. Within this framework, two modelling approaches are combined to test the implied reciprocal relationship between educational success and well-being. In the Latent Transition Analysis part of the model, success is measured as latent classes with fixed outcome categories. In the Autoregressive Structural Equation part of the model, well-being is specified to correlate over time. Models were estimated separately for males and females to allow for different error variances.

Results: The models reveal that mechanisms of social comparison are gendered and operate differently at various stages of the observed period. Young females seem to be more likely to succeed and to experience positive effects in terms of well-being during successful episodes when compared to males. On the downside, females' well-being seems to be more strongly affected by failure.

Conclusions: This paper shows that well-being is a gendered personal resource during the transition to adulthood. These findings contribute to the literature on gender differences in educational success as they show how gender, as a social process, operates to create different success and well-being outcomes.

Introduction

It is one of the major social changes of our time that women now outperform men in the field of education in many countries (Buchmann, DiPrete, and McDaniel 2008; Hadjar 2011; Logan and Medford 2011). The implications of this shift are profound. Those who are successful in education will likely benefit from a wider range of life choices and may go on to have better jobs, health and well-being. As with educational achievement, well-being appears to have a gendered dimension. It is a consistent finding that young males report higher levels of well-being and related mental health factors, such as self-esteem (Bayard et al. 2014). Instances of lower well-being among young females have been attributed towards a tendency to have more critical stances with respect to their own physical appearance and the quality of their friendships (Feingold and Mazzella 1998; McHale et al. 2001; Salmela-Aro and Tuominen-Soini 2010). However, a few studies provide evidence that young men's well-being might become increasingly sensitive to life events and social comparison across cohorts. Young men are increasingly likely to compare themselves to the muscular male ideal as portrayed in the mass media (Barlett, Vowels, and Saucier 2008; Ogbeide et al. 2010). Yet, levels of interpersonal orientation – 'the tendency to be concerned with the status of one's relationships and the opinions others hold of oneself' – are still lower among young men (Nolen-Hoeksema 2001, 175). Even though well-being has been described as an end in and of itself since Aristotle (2012 [approx. 330 BC]), research has shown that it might act as a personal resource (Jencks 1979; Lyubomirsky, King, and Diener 2005). In fact, several studies link educational achievement to well-being (e.g. Kriesi, Buchmann, and Jaberg 2012; Michalos 2008). In the context of educational success, Hascher and Hagenauer (2011) emphasise the centrality of well-being. Still, it is unclear how well-being may foster educational success.

From a gender equality perspective, it is crucial, for three reasons, to study how success and well-being are related over time for females and males. First, in labour markets with high levels of occupational sex segregation, as is the case with Switzerland and Germany, there is typically little horizontal occupational mobility (Kriesi, Buchmann, and Sacchi 2010). Thus, educational pathways are especially interesting, as post-compulsory schooling performance and experience shape the course of life to a greater extent than in other countries (Blossfeld and Maurice 2011; Krüger and Levy 2000). Second, well-being is an indication of how well people feel about themselves and their achievements (Diener 1984; Veenhoven 1984). If men and women's well-being is variously affected by success and failure, this may indicate different cultural beliefs about gender roles (Connell and Messerschmidt 2005; Correll 2001, 2004; West and Zimmerman 1987). Third, if well-being is used as a gendered resource to encourage success in education, this will contribute to the explanation of why females more often succeed in education.

This paper will explore the patterns underlying the interplay between educational success and well-being. Educational success may entail different concepts (Kriesi et al. 2012). In this research, I use the example of successful and unsuccessful intergenerational educational mobility. This is a relative notion of success as it relates to a person's educational attainment in respect to parental educational attainment. Two questions will be addressed. First, how are effects of success or failure on well-being gendered? Second, how are effects of well-being on successful outcomes gendered?

The interplay between successful inter-generational educational mobility, well-being and gender

The study of various types of success and well-being as reciprocally linked is a relatively new development in economic, educational, psychological and sociological literature. For example, Samuel, Bergman, and Hupka-Brunner (2013) provide evidence that the interplay between educational and early occupational success and well-being is reciprocal and gendered. However, most of the research focuses on either the effects of educational and occupational success on well-being, or, to a lesser extent, the effects of well-being on success.

Recent examples of the former perspective are Hadjar, Haunberger, and Schubert (2008), who identify effects of educational attainment on life satisfaction. Samuel et al. (2011) show that successful or unsuccessful intergenerational transfer of educational attainment affects the stability of well-being. Kriesi et al. (2012) set out to analyse the relative significance of various types of educational success by testing a comprehensive model, which assesses academic achievement in compulsory schooling and post-compulsory education, the expected transition to the type of post-compulsory education, successful intergenerational transmission of educational status and educational goal achievement. They find that well-being at the age of 18 is best predicted by lower-secondary status attainment and the transition success to post-compulsory education. Although these studies use different data and concepts of educational success, they all make the case that social comparison seems to be one of the main drivers behind well-being, apart from traits such as extraversion and neuroticism.

This observation has been made in numerous other studies (Festinger 1954; Michalos 1985; Oesch and Lipps 2013; Wolbring, Keuschnigg, and Negele 2013). Basically, well-being is thought of as a function of a person's self-evaluation with respect to a reference point, such as another person's educational achievements. Accordingly, if another person has superior educational credentials than oneself, one's well-being might be negatively affected and vice versa. From a gender perspective, Bayard et al. (2014) examine trajectories in upper secondary education and the development of well-being using self-esteem as an indicator, taking a social comparison perspective. They find young women's well-being to be more influenced by educational attainment and men's well-being to be inert to the characteristics of their educational trajectories. Hankin and Abramson (2001) show that females are more likely to be negatively affected by life events in terms of depression, which governs later behaviour negatively (Bergman and Scott 2001). Similarly, De Coster (2005) finds that females are more likely to have their well-being influenced by family stress. But why are young women more sensitive to life events and social comparison effects?

One strand of explanation might be found in socialisation theory and theories of social interaction (Bourdieu 1998; Gilligan 1990). Women are socialised to take a more comparative perspective, while men are more likely to 'deemphasize their connection to others' (Kort-Butler 2008, 123). Males and females differ in how they evaluate the opinions others hold of themselves. The levels of interpersonal orientation are consistently higher among girls (Nolen-Hoeksema 2001). Consequently, failing to attain the parents' educational attainment might negatively affect well-being as females are socialised to be more socially orientated and to base their self-concept on interpersonal relations. Another strand within gender socialisation theory emphasises different coping styles (Compas, Orosan, and Grant 1993). For example, Nolen-Hoeksema (2001) points out that life events might affect females more as they tend towards (emotional) rumination.

Young men act more according to expected norms of masculinity (Kort-Butler 2008). This includes controlling emotions as well as emphasising positive aspects in the face of failure. Because females have been found to be more susceptible to social comparison effects, I expect them to be more affected by failure than males. Furthermore, gender-specific coping styles predict a negative effect on well-being.

As for the effect of well-being on success, the research is comparably sparse (Diener 2009, 268). Lyubomirsky and colleagues (2005) reviewed studies that implied causal relationships between happiness – specifically, the long-term propensity to frequently experience positive emotions – and successful outcomes. They report weighted mean effect sizes in the longitudinal studies ranging from 0.05 to 0.29 (n=62). Hascher and Hagenauer describe well-being as a central aspect of educational success (2011). A few other studies show that well-being fosters successful academic outcomes (Gilman and Huebner 2006; Suldo, Thalji, and Ferron 2011). In line with Heineck and Anger (2010), I propose that the effects of well-being on successful intergenerational educational mobility might be understood analogously to the effects of non-cognitive characteristics on labour market outcomes. More likely, well-being is associated with success because it is rewarded as a desirable characteristic (Bowles, Gintis, and Osborne 2001). The display of a positive attitude toward life might be considered as an indication of commitment, correct conduct and even academic performance.

In addition, much like reading skills, well-being might be conceived of as a part of an individual's set of productive traits (Borghans et al. 2008; Heckman, Stixrud, and Urzua 2006). That is, well-being is associated with higher productivity in educational contexts, which will lead to the potential for better marks and signal suitability for promotion to more selective educational pathways. Both views, supply and demand, are complimentary and in this paper I assume that both are at play. In sum, well-being might be associated with desirable educational outcomes and thus successful intergenerational educational mobility because its display is rewarded, and well-being might act as a resource because a generally more positive attitude toward life will likely support goal attainment. I hypothesise that well-being is positively associated with successful intergenerational educational mobility. There is, however, no theoretical basis on which to expect gender differences in how well-being is used as a personal resource.

Data

The reciprocal relationship between successful intergenerational educational mobility, well-being and gender is analysed using the Swiss youth panel TREE. It is a nationally representative PISA 2000 follow-up (Adams and Wu 2002; OECD/PISA 2001; TREE 2011). The sample was drawn from a school leaver cohort in 2000, which participated in PISA at the end of compulsory schooling (9th grade). It was surveyed annually from 2001 to 2007. An additional wave was collected in 2010. I use the data obtained between 2001 and 2006. For computational reasons, data from 2007 and 2010 cannot be included. However, this will not affect the analyses as gendered pathways have been shown to converge six years after compulsory schooling in Switzerland (Hupka-Brunner et al. 2011). The final sample used for the analyses comprised 2345 men and 2982 women. As the models for men and women are estimated separately, the uneven distribution of gender does not affect the results.

Measures

Successful intergenerational educational mobility is measured as the difference between parents' level of International Standard Classification of Education (ISCED) 97 and their offspring's educational or occupational position during each wave (Samuel, Bergman, and Hupka-Brunner 2013). This variable takes on three values: success, stable and failure. For example, a daughter attending university and her parents having an ISCED 97 level of I (i.e. without compulsory education) will create a positive success differential, which is treated as success. If the parent and offspring's educational or occupational levels are the same, this is treated as stable. If the offspring does not attain the parents' level of education, this is conceived of as a failure. Importantly, this variable is treated as nominal. I do not assume that the success categories will exhibit any intrinsic or extrinsic order.

Well-being is quantified as a positive attitude toward life (Grob et al. 1991, 1996). This five-item construct was measured at each wave. Exemplary items are: 'My future looks bright', 'I am happy with the way my life plan unfolds' and 'My life seems to be meaningful'. The Tucker–Lewis Index of 0.953 for an autoregressive model over six waves with autocorrelation indicates excellent measurement quality of this construct even over time.

There are a series of variables to be accounted for, because well-being and success – and their interplay – depend on several factors (Bourdieu and Passeron 1970; Breen and Jonsson 2000; Desjardins 2008; DiPrete and Eirich 2006; Krais 1983; Michalos 2008; Samuel, Bergman, and Hupka-Brunner 2013). The variables and scales relating to social background, individual factors and institutional context were all measured in the PISA 2000 survey and are internationally tested (Adams and Wu 2002).

Economic capital

Economic capital or wealth is a multi-item variable measuring different aspects of familial wealth, for example, the number of cars, bathrooms, computers and cell phones, and whether the adolescents have a room of their own (standard deviation, SD=0.81).

Highest International Socio-Economic Index of Occupational Status (HISEI)

HISEI is measured by the International Socioeconomic Index of Occupational Status. It provides information on the socio-economic status of the parents' main job. The highest value of the parents was chosen (HISEI; SD=16.28).

Cultural possession

This variable is operationalised using a multi-item composite variable. Information on the quantity of books, paintings, etc. was combined with more qualitative information on the kind of the cultural goods, e.g. whether the household owns classical literature (SD=6.31).

Reading skills

This is a PISA measure of reading literacy and combines three aspects of reading: 'Retrieving, interpreting and reflecting upon and evaluating information' (Adams and Wu 2002, 200; SD=89.00).

Structure of educational and occupational systems

In Switzerland, the French-speaking and German-speaking regions differ from each other with regard to educational and occupational mobility (OPET 2008). Also, there is evidence that young people in the French-speaking region of Switzerland exhibit lower levels of well-being than those in the German-speaking region (Semmer et al. 2005). I thus include a dummy for the French and Italian-speaking regions of Switzerland (i.e. Latin; 53.2%).

State and path dependency

A young person's educational situation at a given time will determine, to some extent, later educational and occupational outcomes as well as the pathways in their entirety (DiPrete and Eirich 2006). Similarly, well-being at a given time will predict future well-being. I include autoregressive elements in the models to account for this. Future values are modelled as a function of all past values.

Analytical plan

This paper will analyse the effects of successful and unsuccessful intergenerational educational mobility on well-being as well as the effects of well-being on successful and unsuccessful intergenerational educational mobility. As previous research shows, episodes of educational mobility will not be evenly distributed over the observed period (e.g. Mare 1980). I use an autoregressive cross-lagged mixture model framework to account for the expected unequal distribution of the variables over time and the multilevel structure of the data. Within this framework, two modelling approaches are combined to test the implied reciprocal relationship between success and well-being. More precisely, the model is a combination of Latent Transition Analysis (Humphreys and

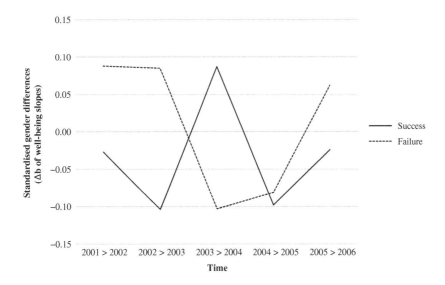

Figure 1. Effects of success and failure on well-being slope differences between males and females over time.

Janson 2000; Nylund 2007) and Autoregressive Structural Equation Modelling (Curran and Bollen 2001), conditional on a series of time-invariant control variables. In the Latent Transition Analysis part of the model, successful and unsuccessful intergenerational educational mobility is measured as latent classes with fixed outcome categories. In the Autoregressive Structural Equation part of the model, well-being is specified to correlate over time. Intercepts and slopes of autoregressive parts (well-being) are allowed to vary across classes and time. Slopes for time-invariant control variables are allowed to vary across classes and time. Two models, one for females and one for males were estimated using random starts and starting values (Samuel, Bergman, and Hupka-Brunner 2013). This allows for different error variances for males and females (Correll 2001).

Results

Gendered effects of intergenerational educational mobility on well-being

Figure 1 displays standardised gender differences (Δb) between slopes of the autoregressive parts of well-being for the categories success and failure. A negative Δb indicates that the slope is steeper for females, and a positive Δb steeper for males. The steepness of these slopes indicates the effect of success or failure on every single transition between all waves controlling for a series of other of other variables (Appendices 1, 2 and 5). Note that the slopes for well-being between every time point will always be positive, as well-being at one time point predicts well-being at the subsequent time point. However, the difference Δb between two slopes can be negative. The general picture does not hint at a systematic gendered pattern (Appendices 1 and 2). Based on this model, females seem to make better use of successful episodes in terms of well-being. Their slopes for well-being are steeper than the males' 80% of the time. Males exhibit steeper slopes in the context of failure more often, i.e. 60% of the time. That is, their well-being is less affected by failure.

These findings are in line with other research that shows that young women cope less well with adverse external effects, and thus report lower well-being (Salmela-Aro and Tynkkynen 2010). Again, this may be caused by unsuccessful intergenerational educational mobility. As for males, one could hypothesise that failure may affect well-being negatively as anticipated traditional roles as male 'breadwinner' are at risk (see operationalisation of positive attitude toward life; Connell and Messerschmidt 2005). Critical phases are, typically, labour market entry after completing an apprenticeship. In many cases, this occurs between three and five years upon completion of compulsory schooling (transitions 2003–2004 and 2004–2005 in Figure 1).

Gendered effects of well-being on intergenerational educational mobility

The estimates for well-being on success are all positive (in logit scale; Figure 2). Well-being increases the likelihood to experience success. By and large, females seem to make better use of well-being as a personal resource to foster successful outcomes controlling for various social and personal resources (Appendices 3 and 4). However, this ability seems to decrease over time. The pattern for males is less clear. Their ability to use well-being as a personal resource to be successful seems to increase three years after completion of compulsory schooling.

These findings are consistent with the idea that well-being can be thought of as a personal resource, as some of the literature finds (Bandura 1989; Salmela-Aro and Tuominen-Soini 2010). It allows a person to master challenging situations in an education context.

Discussion and conclusion

In this paper, I set out to analyse one of the major social changes of our time: that women now outperform men in education. The analyses support this idea, in line with previous literature. I would like to emphasise three key findings, which extend previous studies both theoretically and empirically in that they relate to gender as a social process.

First, the models show that it is a reasonable assumption to conceive of the interplay between well-being and successful and unsuccessful intergenerational educational mobility as a gendered reciprocal relationship. Well-being and successes affect each other, not only on the level of states but also in the form of trajectories. This goes beyond previous research in that the interplay is explicitly modelled as a reciprocal relationship. Second, in the context of success, females seem to benefit more in terms of well-being. Males seem to be less affected by failure. These findings go some way to corroborate the hypothesis that females are more susceptible to social comparison effects and that gendered coping styles are at play mostly due to socialisation processes (De Coster 2005; Hankin and Abramson 2001; Kort-Butler 2008). Research focusing on how status group membership is associated with well-being might, additionally, help to understand these findings (Branscombe 1998; O'Brien and Major 2005). If females are considered to have, on average, lower societal status than males, they are more likely to be adversely affected by unsuccessful episodes but also to experience a greater positive effect on their well-being when successful. Conversely, males as members of a higher status group in the gender dimension, will likely display a more inert well-being pattern (Bayard et al. 2014). Their evaluation of life will, on average, not be as susceptible to events and social comparison. Importantly, the relative inertia of male well-being patterns might also conceal more complex masculinities. For example, low-status men might report constant levels of well-being as a form of compensatory masculinity (Pyke 1996).

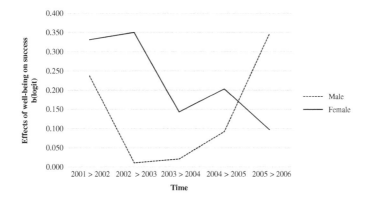

Figure 2.   Effects of well-being on success over time (reference category: failure).

The third key finding considers well-being as a personal resource. Young women seem to make better use of this asset to foster successful intergenerational educational mobility. This extends the literature on well-being as a resource by bringing in a gender perspective. Different societal expectations for men and women might explain this finding (West and Zimmerman 1987). In Switzerland, the norm for males is still to be successful and to become a 'breadwinner'. This is regardless of radical economic shifts and dynamics such as the decline of the male breadwinner model due to increased female labour market participation (Crompton 1999). Controlling for common determinants of educational success, this will likely leave less headroom for any other resources to affect educational outcomes. Conversely, it can be argued that women are less expected to succeed by society norms and might, therefore, need every available resource. It is then possible to hypothesise that well-being is a precondition for females to attain success. The decreasing utility of well-being as personal resource for females could be an age effect (Fonseca and Matos 2011). As the data being used are drawn from a school leaver cohort, there is not much variation in age and this assumption will have to be tested in another study.

Further research should address more precisely the mechanisms moderating the gendered interplay between intergenerational educational mobility and well-being. Specifically, the variation across intersections of social class will be sizeable (Browne and Misra 2003; Pyke 1996). Furthermore, self-esteem could moderate the effects of social comparison on well-being. Moreover, it would be crucial to apply other concepts of well-being and success likewise to test whether the findings in this study hold for affective well-being and subjective success (Keller et al. 2014). This could take the form of goal attainment against the backdrop of gendered self-assessments (Correll 2001, 2004). From a social comparison perspective, it would be interesting to examine how the increasing proportion of academically successful young women affects the personal perception of their achievements. This development might fuel new gendered expectations. Likewise, the meaning of failure could change with the declining hegemony of the male breadwinner model. Especially with regard to gender differences, the relationship between success and well-being is likely to continue to be dynamic beyond the examined period. The nature and implications of this interplay could shed light on the challenges females face transforming their credentials and capacities to match occupational positions. This is particularly true in the case of motherhood (Avellar and Smock 2003; Correll, Benard, and Paik 2007).

Acknowledgements

I am grateful to Manfred Max Bergman, Shelley J. Correll, Andreas Hadjar, Anna Heilbronner Samuel, Sandra Hupka-Brunner, Shireen Kanji, Chris Mitchell, Olga Samuel, the editors of Educational Research, and the participants of the International Conference: 'Gender Variations in Educational Success' in Luxembourg, 3–5 October 2011, for comments on earlier versions of this paper.

Funding

This research was supported by the Swiss National Science Foundation (grant PBBSP1_141399).

References

Adams, Ray, and Magaret Wu, eds. 2002. *PISA 2000 Technical Report*. Paris: OECD/PISA.

Aristotle. 2012. *Nicomachean Ethics*. Chicago, IL: University of Chicago Press.

Avellar, Sarah, and Pamela J. Smock. 2003. "Has the Price of Motherhood Declined Over Time? A Cross-cohort Comparison of the Motherhood Wage Penalty." *Journal of Marriage and Family* 65 (3): 597–607.

Bandura, A. 1989. "Regulation of Cognitive Processes Through Perceived Self-efficacy." *Developmental Psychology* 25 (5): 729–735.

Barlett, Christopher P., Christopher L. Vowels, and Donald A. Saucier. 2008. "Meta-analyses of the Effects of Media Images on Men's Body-image Concerns." *Journal of Social and Clinical Psychology* 27 (3): 279–310.

Bayard, Sybille, Monika Staffelbach, Philipp Fischer, and Marlis Buchmann. 2014. "Upper-secondary Educational Trajectories and Young Men's and Women's Self-esteem Development in Switzerland." In *Psychological, Educational and Sociological Perspectives on Success and Well-being in Career Development*, edited by Anita C. Keller, Robin Samuel, Manfred Max Bergman, and Norbert K. Semmer. New York: Springer.

Bergman, Manfred Max, and Jacqueline Scott. 2001. "Young Adolescents' Wellbeing and Health-risk Behaviours: Gender and Socio-economic Differences. *Journal of Adolescence* 24 (2): 183–197.

Blossfeld, Hans-Peter, and Jutta von Maurice. 2011. "Education as a Lifelong Process." *Zeitschrift für Erziehungswissenschaft* 14 (2): 19–34.

Borghans, Lex, Angela Lee Duckworth, James J. Heckman, and Bas ter Weel. 2008. "The Economics and Psychology of Personality Traits." *Journal of Human Resources* 43 (4): 972–1059.

Bourdieu, Pierre. 1998. *La domination masculine*. Paris: Ed. du Seuil.

Bourdieu, Pierre, and Jean-Claude Passeron. 1970. *La Reproduction. Élements Pour une théorie du système d'Enseignement*. Paris: Ed. de Minuit.

Bowles, Samuel, Herbert Gintis, and Melissa Osborne. 2001. "The Determinants of Earnings: A Behavioral Approach." *Journal of Economic Literature* 39 (4): 1137–1176.

Branscombe, N. R. 1998. "Thinking About One's Gender Group's Privileges or Disadvantages: Consequences for Well-being in Women and Men." *British Journal of Social Psychology* 37 (2): 167–184.

Breen, Richard, and Jan O. Jonsson. 2000. "Analyzing Educational Careers: A Multinomial Transition Model." *American Sociological Review* 65 (5): 754–772.

Browne, Irene, and Joya Misra. 2003. "The Intersection of Gender and Race in the Labor Market." *Annual Review of Sociology* 29: 487–513.

Buchmann, Claudia, Thomas A. DiPrete, and Anne McDaniel. 2008. "Gender Inequalities in Education." *Annual Review of Sociology* 34: 319–337.

Compas, B. E., P. G. Orosan, and K. E. Grant. 1993. "Adolescent Stress and Coping: Implications for Psychopathology During Adolescence." *Journal of Adolescence* 16 (3): 331–349.

Connell, R. W., and James W. Messerschmidt. 2005. "Hegemonic Masculinity Rethinking the Concept." *Gender & Society* 19 (6): 829–859.

Correll, Shelley J. 2001. "Gender and the Career Choice Process: The Role of Biased Self-assessments." *American Journal of Sociology* 106 (6): 1691–1730.

Correll, Shelley J. 2004. "Constraints into Preferences: Gender, Status, and Emerging Career Aspirations." *American Sociological Review* 69 (1): 93–113.

Correll, Shelley J., Stephen Benard, and In Paik. 2007. "Getting a Job: Is There a Motherhood Penalty?" *American Journal of Sociology* 112 (5): 1297–1339.

Crompton, Rosemary. 1999. *Restructuring Gender Relations and Employment: The Decline of the Male Breadwinner*. Oxford: Oxford University Press.

Curran, Patrick J., and Kenneth A. Bollen. 2001. "The Best of Both Worlds: Combining Autoregressive and Latent Curve Models." In *New Methods for the Analysis of Change*, edited by L. M Collins and A. G. Sayer, 105–136. Washington, DC: American Psychological Association.

De Coster, Stacy. 2005. "Depression and Law Violation: Gendered Responses to Gendered Stresses." *Sociological Perspectives* 48 (2): 155–187.

Desjardins, Richard. 2008. "Researching the Links Between Education and Well-being." *European Journal of Education* 43 (1): 23–35.

Diener, ed. 1984. "Subjective Well-being." *Psychological Bulletin* 95 (3): 542–575.

Diener, ed. 2009. *The Science of Well-being: The Collected Works of Ed Diener*. New York: Springer.

DiPrete, T. A., and G. M. Eirich. 2006. "Cumulative Advantage as a Mechanism for Inequality: A Review of Theoretical and Empirical Developments." *Annual Review of Sociology* 32: 271–297.

Feingold, Alan, and Ronald Mazzella. 1998. "Gender Differences in Body Image are Increasing." *Psychological Science* 9 (3): 190–195.

Festinger, Leon. 1954. "A Theory of Social Comparison Processes." *Human Relations* 7 (2): 117–140.

Fonseca, Helena, and Margarida G. Matos. 2011. "Are Adolescent Weight-related Problems and General Well-being Essentially an Issue of Age, Gender or Rather A Pubertal Timing Issue?" *Journal of Pediatric Endocrinology and Metabolism* 24 (5–6): 251–256.

Gilligan, Carol. 1990. *In A Different Voice: Psychological Theory and Women's Development.* Reissue edition. Cambridge, MA: Harvard University Press.

Gilman, Rich, and Scott E. Huebner. 2006. "Characteristics of Adolescents Who Report Very High Life Satisfaction." *Journal of Youth and Adolescence* 35 (3): 293–301.

Grob, Alexander, Ruth Lüthi, Florian G. Kaiser, August Flammer, and Andrew Mackinnon. 1991. "Berner Fragebogen Zum Wohlbefinden Jugendlicher (BFW)." *Diagnostica* 37 (1): 66–75.

Grob, Alexander, Todd D. Little, Brigitte Wanner, and Alexander J. Wearing. 1996. "Adolescents' Well-being and Perceived Control Across 14 Sociocultural Contexts." *Journal of Personality and Social Psychology* 71 (4): 785–795.

Hadjar, Andreas, ed. 2011. *Geschlechtsspezifische Bildungsungleichheiten.* Wiesbaden: VS Verlag für Sozialwissenschaften.

Hadjar, Andreas, Sigrid Haunberger, and Frank Schubert. 2008. "Bildung Und Subjektives Wohlbefinden Im Zeitverlauf, 1984–2002. Eine Mehrebenenanalyse." *Berliner Journal für Soziologie* 18 (3): 1–31.

Hankin, B. L., and L. Y. Abramson. 2001. "Development of Gender Differences in Depression: An Elaborated Cognitive Vulnerability-transactional Stress Theory." *Psychological Bulletin* 127 (6): 773–796.

Hascher, Tina, and Gerda Hagenauer. 2011. "Wohlbefinden und Emotionen in der Schule als Zentrale Elemente des Schulerfolgs unter der Perspektive Geschlechtsspezifischer Ungleichheiten." In *Geschlechtsspezifische Bildungsungleichheiten*, edited by Andreas Hadjar, 285–308. Wiesbaden: VS Verlag für Sozialwissenschaften.

Heckman, James J., Jora Stixrud, and Sergio Urzua. 2006. "The Effects of Cognitive and Noncognitive Abilities on Labor Market Outcomes and Social Behavior." *Journal of Labor Economics* 24 (3): 411–482.

Heineck, Guido, and Silke Anger. 2010. "The Returns to Cognitive Abilities and Personality Traits in Germany." *Labour Economics* 17 (3): 535–546.

Humphreys, Keith, and Harald Janson. 2000. "Latent Transition Analysis with Covariates, Nonresponse, Summary Statistics and Diagnostics: Modelling Children's Drawing Development." *Multivariate Behavioral Research* 35 (1): 89–118.

Hupka-Brunner, Sandra, Robin Samuel, Evéline Huber, and Manfred Max Bergman. 2011. "Geschlechterungleichheiten im Intergenerationalen Bildungstransfer in der Schweiz." In *Geschlechtsspezifische Bildungsungleichheiten*, edited by Andreas Hadjar, 77–98. Wiesbaden: VS Verlag für Sozialwissenschaften.

Jencks, Christopher. 1979. *"Who Gets Ahead? The Determinants of Economic Success in America."* New York: Basic Books.

Keller, Anita C., Norbert K. Semmer, Robin Samuel, and Manfred Max Bergman. 2014. "The Meaning and Measurement of Well-being as an Indicator of Success." In *Psychological, Educational and Sociological Perspectives on Success and Well-being in Career Development*, edited by Anita C. Keller, Robin Samuel, Manfred Max Bergman, and Norbert K. Semmer. New York: Springer

Kort-Butler, Lisa A. 2008. "Coping Styles and Sex Differences in Depressive Symptoms and Delinquent Behavior." *Journal of Youth and Adolescence* 38 (1): 122–136.

Krais, Beate. 1983. "Bildung als Kapital. Neue Perspektiven für die Analyse der Sozialstruktur?" In *Soziale Ungleichheiten*, edited by Reinhard Kreckel, 201–220. Göttingen: Verlag Otto Schwartz.

Kriesi, Irene, Marlis Buchmann, and Andrea Jaberg. 2012. "Educational Success and Adolescents' Well-being in Switzerland." *Schweizerische Zeitschrift für Soziologie* 38 (2): 245–265.

Kriesi, Irene, Marlis Buchmann, and Stefan Sacchi. 2010. "Variation in Job Opportunities for Men and Women in the Swiss Labor Market 1962–1989." *Research in Social Stratification and Mobility* 28 (3): 309–323.

Krüger, H., and R. Levy. 2000. "Masterstatus, Familie und Geschlecht. Vergessene Verknüpfungslogiken zwischen Institutionen des Lebenslaufs." *Berliner Journal für Soziologie* 10 (3): 379–401.

Logan, Sarah, and Emma Medford. 2011. "Gender Differences in the Strength of Association Between Motivation, Competency Beliefs and Reading Skill." *Educational Research* 53 (1): 85–94.

Lyubomirsky, Sonja, Laura King, and Ed Diener. 2005. "The Benefits of Frequent Positive Affect: Does Happiness Lead to Success?" *Psychological Bulletin* 131 (6): 803–855.

Mare, Robert D. 1980. "Social Background and School Continuation Decisions." *Journal of the American Statistical Association* 75 (370): 295–305.

McHale, Susan M., Devon A. Corneal, Ann C. Crouter, and Leann L. Birch. 2001. "Gender and Weight Concerns in Early and Middle Adolescence: Links with Well-being and Family Characteristics." *Journal of Clinical Child & Adolescent Psychology* 30 (3): 338–348.

Michalos, Alex C. 1985. "Multiple Discrepancies Theory (MDT)." *Social Indicators Research* 16 (4): 347–413.

Michalos, Alex C. 2008. "Education, Happiness and Wellbeing." *Social Indicators Research* 87 (3): 347–366.

Nolen-Hoeksema, Susan. 2001. "Gender Differences in Depression." *Current Directions in Psychological Science* 10 (5): 173–176.

Nylund, Karen Lynn. 2007. *Latent Transition Analysis*. Los Angeles, CA: University of California.

O'Brien, L. T., and B. Major. 2005. "System-justifying Beliefs and Psychological Well-being: The Roles of Group Status and Identity." *Personality and Social Psychology Bulletin* 31 (12): 1718–1729.

OECD/PISA, ed. 2001. *Knowledge and Skills for Life: First Results from PISA 2000*. Paris: OECD/PISA.

Oesch, Daniel, and Oliver Lipps. 2013. "Does Unemployment Hurt Less if there is More of it Around? A Panel Analysis of Life Satisfaction in Germany and Switzerland." *European Sociological Review* 29 (5): 955–967.

Ogbeide, Stacy A., Christopher A. Neumann, Brian E. Sandoval, and C. Diane Rudebock. 2010. "Gender Differences Between Body Weight and Psychological Well-being During Young Adulthood: A Brief Report." *The New School Psychology Bulletin* 8 (1): 41–46.

OPET. 2008. *Vocational Education and Training in Switzerland 2008: Facts and Figures*. Federal Office for Professional Education and Technology (OPET).

Pyke, Karen D. 1996. "Class-based Masculinities, the Interdependence of Gender, Class, and Interpersonal Power." *Gender & Society* 10 (5): 527–549.

Salmela-Aro, K., and H. Tuominen-Soini. 2010. "Adolescents' Life Satisfaction During the Transition to Post-comprehensive Education: Antecedents and Consequences." *Journal of Happiness Studies* 11 (6): 683–701.

Salmela-Aro, K., and L. Tynkkynen. 2010. "Trajectories of Life Satisfaction Across the Transition to Post-compulsory Education: Do Adolescents Follow Different Pathways?" *Journal of Youth and Adolescence* 39 (8): 870–881.

Samuel, Robin, Manfred Max Bergman, and Sandra Hupka-Brunner. 2013. "The Interplay Between Educational Achievement, Occupational Success, and Well-being." *Social Indicators Research* 111 (1): 75–96.

Samuel, Robin, Sandra Hupka-Brunner, Barbara E. Stalder, and Manfred Max Bergman. 2011. "Successful and Unsuccessful Intergenerational Transfer of Educational Attainment on Wellbeing in the Swiss Youth Cohort TREE." *Swiss Journal of Sociology* 37 (1): 57–78.

Semmer, N. K., F. Tschan, A. Elfering, W. Kälin, and S. Grebner. 2005. "Young Adults Entering the Workforce in Switzerland: Working Conditions and Well-being." In *Contemporary Switzerland*, edited by H. Kriesi, P. Farago, M. Kohli, and M. Zarin-Nejadan, 163–189. New York: Palgrave Macmillan.

Suldo, Shannon, Amanda Thalji, and John Ferron. 2011. "Longitudinal Academic Outcomes Predicted by Early Adolescents' Subjective Well-being, Psychopathology, and Mental Health Status Yielded from a Dual Factor Model." *The Journal of Positive Psychology* 6 (1): 17–30.

TREE, ed. 2011. *Project Documentation 2000–2010*. Basel: TREE.

Veenhoven, Ruut. 1984. *Conditions of Happiness*. Dordrecht: D. Reidel.

West, Candace, and Don H. Zimmerman. 1987. "Doing Gender." *Gender & Society* 1 (2): 125–151.

Wolbring, Tobias, Marc Keuschnigg, and Eva Negele. 2013. "Needs, Comparisons, and Adaptation: The Importance of Relative Income for Life Satisfaction." *European Sociological Review* 29 (1): 86–104.

Appendix 1. Robust maximum likelihood estimates for predictors of well-being, males (n=2345).

	b	S.E.(b)	b	S.E.(b)	b	S.E.(b)
t_1_well-being	*Successful*		*Stable*		*Unsuccessful*	
Cultural poss.	0.01	0.00	0.01	0.00	0.01	0.00
HISEI	0.00*	0.00	0.00*	0.00	0.00*	0.00
Economic cap.	0.07*	0.03	0.07*	0.03	0.07*	0.03
Reading skills	0.00	0.00	0.00	0.00	0.00	0.00
Latin	−0.25***	0.04	−0.25***	0.04	−0.25	0.04***
Intercept	0.11***	0.03	0.11***	0.03	0.11***	0.03
t_2_well-being	*Successful*		*Stable*		*Unsuccessful*	
Cultural poss.	0.00	0.01	0.00	0.01	0.00	0.01
HISEI	0.00	0.00	0.00	0.00	0.00	0.00
Economic cap.	−0.07	0.05	−0.02	0.04	0.00	0.05
Reading skills	0.00	0.00	0.00	0.00	0.00*	0.00
Latin	−0.10	0.07	−0.02	0.06	−0.04	0.09
Well-being_t_1	0.55***	0.05	0.65***	0.04	0.65***	0.06
Intercept	0.03	0.05	−0.02	0.04	0.00	0.05
t_3_well-being	*Successful*		*Stable*		*Unsuccessful*	
Cultural poss.	0.00	0.01	0.00	0.01	−0.01	0.01
HISEI	0.00	0.00	0.00	0.00	0.00	0.00
Economic cap.	0.08+	0.04	−0.04	0.04	0.11*	0.06
Reading skills	0.00	0.00	0.00	0.00	0.00	0.00
Latin	−0.14*	0.07	−0.08	0.06	−0.06	0.09
Well-being_t_2	0.57***	0.04	0.64***	0.04	0.72***	0.05
Intercept	0.03	0.05	0.08	0.05	−0.02	0.05
t_4_well-being	*Successful*		*Stable*		*Unsuccessful*	
Cultural poss.	0.00	0.01	0.00	0.01	0.00	0.01
HISEI	0.00	0.00	0.00*	0.00	0.00	0.00
Economic cap.	0.03	0.05	0.04	0.05	0.05	0.06
Reading skills	0.00	0.00	0.00+	0.00	0.00	0.00
Latin	−0.04	0.07	−0.11+	0.06	−0.24**	0.09
Well-being_t_3	0.72***	0.04	0.77***	0.03	0.57***	0.05
Intercept	0.06	0.05	0.02	0.05	0.14**	0.05
t_5_well-being	*Successful*		*Stable*		*Unsuccessful*	
Cultural poss.	−0.01	0.01	0.00	0.01	0.01	0.01
HISEI	0.00	0.00	−0.01*	0.00	0.00	0.00
Economic cap.	0.06	0.06	0.06	0.04	−0.07	0.05
Reading skills	0.00	0.00	0.00	0.00	0.00	0.00
Latin	0.01	0.08	0.06	0.07	−0.19*	0.09
Well-being_t_4	0.57***	0.05	0.72***	0.03	0.63***	0.05
Intercept	−0.07	0.06	−0.01	0.05	0.08	0.06
t_6_well-being	*Successful*		*Stable*		*Unsuccessful*	
Cultural poss.	0.00	0.01	0.00	0.01	0.01	0.01
HISEI	0.00	0.00	0.00	0.00	0.00	0.00
Economic cap.	−0.01	0.05	0.01	0.05	0.02	0.05
Reading skills	0.00	0.00	0.00	0.00	0.00	0.00

(Continued)

Appendix 1. (*Continued*).

	b	S.E.(b)	b	S.E.(b)	b	S.E.(b)
Latin	−0.11	0.07	−0.12+	0.07	−0.09	0.10
Well-being_t_5	0.65***	0.05	0.72***	0.04	0.70***	0.05
Intercept	0.10	0.06	0.06	0.05	0.00	0.06

***$p<0.001$; **$p<0.01$; *$p<0.05$; +$p<0.1$. b, standardised effect of variable; S.E.(b), standard error of standardised effect of variable. Cultural poss., quantity and kind of cultural goods in the household; HISEI, socio-economic status of the parents; Economic cap., familial wealth; Reading skills, PISA measure of reading literacy; Latin, a variable indicating whether the young person lives in the French and Italian-speaking regions of Switzerland (reference category: German-speaking region); Well-being_t_j, well-being measured in previous data collection; Intercept, constant term of the equation.

Appendix 2. Robust maximum likelihood estimates for predictors of well-being, females ($n=2982$).

	b	S.E.(b)	b	S.E.(b)	b	S.E.(b)
t_1_well-being	*Successful*		*Stable*		*Unsuccessful*	
Cultural poss.	0.01	0.00	0.01	0.00	0.01	0.00
HISEI	0.00	0.00	0.00	0.00	0.00	0.00
Economic cap.	0.03	0.03	0.03	0.03	0.03	0.03
Reading skills	0.00	0.00	0.00	0.00	0.00	0.00
Latin	−0.39***	0.04	−0.39***	0.04	−0.39***	0.04
Intercept	0.19***	0.03	0.19***	0.03	0.19***	0.03
t_2_well-being	*Successful*		*Stable*		*Unsuccessful*	
Cultural poss.	0.00	0.01	0.00	0.01	−0.01	0.01
HISEI	0.00	0.00	0.00	0.00	0.00	0.00
Economic cap.	0.03	0.03	0.04	0.04	−0.01	0.05
Reading skills	0.00+	0.00	0.00	0.00	0.00	0.00
Latin	−0.09+	0.05	−0.19***	0.05	−0.19*	0.08
Well-being_t_1	0.58***	0.03	0.62***	0.03	0.56***	0.05
Intercept	0.02	0.04	0.07+	0.04	0.12*	0.05
t_3_well-being	*Successful*		*Stable*		*Unsuccessful*	
Cultural poss.	0.01	0.00	0.01	0.01	0.00	0.01
HISEI	0.00*	0.00	0.00	0.00	0.00	0.00
Economic cap.	0.04	0.03	−0.02	0.04	−0.06	0.06
Reading skills	0.00	0.00	0.00	0.00	0.00	0.00
Latin	−0.08+	0.05	−0.13*	0.06	−0.18+	0.10
Well-being_t_2	0.67***	0.03	0.68***	0.04	0.63***	0.06
Intercept	0.04	0.04	0.02	0.04	0.12+	0.06
t_4_well-being	*Successful*		*Stable*		*Unsuccessful*	
Cultural poss.	0.00	0.00	0.00	0.00	0.01	0.01
HISEI	0.00+	0.00	0.00	0.00	0.00	0.00
Economic cap.	−0.03	0.03	0.05	0.03	−0.10	0.07
Reading skills	0.00+	0.00	0.00	0.00	0.00*	0.00
Latin	−0.17***	0.05	−0.08	0.05	−0.10	0.10
Well-being_t_3	0.63***	0.03	0.64***	0.03	0.68***	0.06
Intercept	0.10**	0.04	0.05	0.04	0.04	0.07
t_5_well-being	*Successful*		*Stable*		*Unsuccessful*	
Cultural poss.	−0.01*	0.01	0.00	0.01	−0.01	0.01

(*Continued*)

Appendix 2. (*Continued*).

	b	S.E.(*b*)	*b*	S.E.(*b*)	*b*	S.E.(*b*)
HISEI	0.00	0.00	0.00	0.00	0.00	0.00
Economic cap.	0.06	0.04	−0.02	0.04	−0.01	0.06
Reading skills	0.00	0.00	0.00	0.00	0.00	0.00
Latin	−0.08	0.05	−0.12*	0.06	−0.22**	0.09
Well-being_t_4	0.67***	0.04	0.65***	0.03	0.71***	0.05
Intercept	0.04	0.04	0.07+	0.04	0.01	0.06
t_6_well-being	*Successful*		*Stable*		*Unsuccessful*	
Cultural poss.	0.01	0.01	0.01	0.01	0.00	0.01
HISEI	0.00	0.00	0.00	0.00	−0.01*	0.00
Economic cap.	0.07+	0.04	0.02	0.05	0.06	0.05
Reading skills	0.00	0.00	0.00	0.00	0.00	0.00
Latin	−0.09	0.06	−0.14*	0.06	−0.19*	0.08
Well-being_t_5	0.68***	0.03	0.69***	0.04	0.63***	0.05
Intercept	0.07+	0.04	0.02	0.04	0.12*	0.05

***$p<0.001$; **$p<0.01$; *$p<0.05$; +$p<0.1$. *b*, standardised effect of variable; S.E.(*b*), standard error of standardised effect of variable. Cultural poss., quantity and kind of cultural goods in the household; HISEI, socio-economic status of the parents; Economic cap., familial wealth; Reading skills, PISA measure of reading literacy; Latin, a variable indicating whether the young person lives in the French and Italian-speaking regions of Switzerland (reference category: German-speaking region); Well-being_t_j, well-being measured in previous data collection; Intercept, constant term of the equation.

Appendix 3. Maximum likelihood robust logit estimates for predictors of success and stable achievement for males (reference category: failure; *n*=2345; autoregressive elements not shown).

	b	S.E.(*b*)	*b*	S.E.(*b*)
	t1_success		t1_stability	
Latin	0.67***	0.12	0.58***	0.11
Reading skills	0.01***	0.00	0.00***	0.00
Economic cap.	−0.40***	0.08	−0.25***	0.07
HISEI	−0.05***	0.00	−0.01***	0.00
Cultural poss.	−0.01	0.01	0.01	0.01
Constant	−0.01	0.08	0.38***	0.08
	t2_success		t2_stability	
Latin	−0.37	0.32	0.50*	0.26
Reading skills	0.00	0.00	0.00*	0.00
Economic cap.	−0.46*	0.19	−0.38*	0.17
HISEI	−0.05***	0.01	−0.02*	0.01
Cultural poss.	0.01	0.03	0.02	0.02
Well-being_t_1	0.24	0.17	0.30*	0.12
Constant	−4.67***	0.53	−2.23***	0.18
	t3_success		t3_stability	
Latin	−0.98*	0.46	−0.42	0.34
Reading skills	0.00	0.00	0.00	0.00
Economic cap.	−0.16	0.27	−0.12	0.19
HISEI	−0.01	0.02	0.00	0.01

(*Continued*)

Appendix 3. (*Continued*).

	b	S.E.(b)	b	S.E.(b)
Cultural poss.	0.02	0.04	0.02	0.03
Well-being_t_2	0.01	0.31	−0.19	0.24
Constant	−5.71***	1.05	−3.19***	0.26
	t4_success		t4_stability	
Latin	1.89***	0.30	1.13***	0.21
Reading skills	−0.01***	0.00	0.00**	0.00
Economic cap.	0.27	0.17	0.18	0.13
HISEI	−0.02*	0.01	−0.01*	0.01
Cultural poss.	0.02	0.02	0.00	0.02
Well-being_t_3	0.02	0.16	0.09	0.10
Constant	−14.16***	0.31	−3.60***	0.30
	t5_success		t5_stability	
Latin	−0.13	0.22	−0.18	0.17
Reading skills	0.00	0.00	0.00	0.00
Economic cap.	−0.11	0.14	−0.08	0.11
HISEI	−0.02*	0.01	0.00	0.01
Cultural poss.	−0.01	0.02	−0.01	0.01
Well-being_t_4	0.09	0.11	0.10	0.09
Constant	−12.99***	0.18	−1.95***	0.16
	t6_success		t6_stability	
Latin	−0.36	0.23	−0.20	0.18
Reading skills	0.00*	0.00	0.00	0.00
Economic cap.	0.24	0.15	0.05	0.11
HISEI	−0.02*	0.01	0.01+	0.01
Cultural poss.	−0.03+	0.02	−0.01	0.01
Well-being_t_5	0.35**	0.13	0.20*	0.10
Constant	−5.88***	0.81	−1.37***	0.15

***$p<0.001$; **$p<0.01$; *$p<0.05$; +$p<0.1$. b, standardised effect of variable; S.E.(b), standard error of standardised effect of variable. Cultural poss., quantity and kind of cultural goods in the household; HISEI, socio-economic status of the parents; Economic cap., familial wealth; Reading skills, PISA measure of reading literacy; Latin, a variable indicating whether the young person lives in the French and Italian-speaking regions of Switzerland (reference category: German-speaking region); Well-being_t_j, well-being measured in previous data collection; Intercept, constant term of the equation.

Appendix 4. Maximum likelihood robust logit estimates for predictors of success and stable achievement for females (reference category: failure; $n=2982$; autoregressive elements not shown).

	b	S.E.(b)	b	S.E.(b)
	t1_success		t1_stability	
Latin	0.94***	0.11	0.44***	0.11
Reading skills	0.01***	0.00	0.00***	0.00
Economic cap.	−0.17*	0.07	−0.13+	0.07
HISEI	−0.02***	0.00	0.00	0.00
Cultural poss.	−0.03**	0.01	−0.01	0.01

(*Continued*)

Appendix 4. (*Continued*).

	b	S.E.(b)	b	S.E.(b)
Constant	0.31***	0.08	0.65***	0.07
	t2_success		t2_stability	
Latin	0.18	0.23	0.65***	0.19
Reading skills	0.00	0.00	0.01***	0.00
Economic cap.	−0.17	0.14	−0.09	0.12
HISEI	−0.04***	0.01	−0.01	0.01
Cultural poss.	−0.03	0.02	−0.02	0.02
Well-being_t_1	0.33**	0.12	0.20+	0.11
Constant	−2.79***	0.23	−1.22***	0.14
	t3_success		t3_stability	
Latin	−1.29***	0.32	−0.25	0.26
Reading skills	0.00	0.00	0.00**	0.00
Economic cap.	−0.34+	0.20	−0.21	0.16
HISEI	−0.02*	0.01	−0.01	0.01
Cultural poss.	−0.03	0.02	−0.02	0.02
Well-being_t_2	0.35*	0.15	0.14	0.14
Constant	−3.13***	0.35	−1.90***	0.19
	t4_success		t4_stability	
Latin	1.07***	0.20	0.45**	0.15
Reading skills	0.00**	0.00	0.00*	0.00
Economic cap.	−0.16	0.12	−0.05	0.09
HISEI	−0.01*	0.01	−0.01	0.01
Cultural poss.	0.00	0.02	0.00	0.01
Well-being_t_3	0.14	0.09	0.01	0.07
Constant	−5.22***	0.60	−2.31***	0.20
	t5_success		t5_stability	
Latin	−0.91***	0.19	−0.60***	0.15
Reading skills	0.00	0.00	0.00+	0.00
Economic cap.	−0.05	0.13	−0.14	0.10
HISEI	−0.02*	0.01	0.00	0.01
Cultural poss.	0.00	0.02	0.02	0.01
Well-being_t_4	0.20*	0.09	0.03	0.07
Constant	−4.43***	0.54	−1.77***	0.17
	t6_success		t6_stability	
Latin	−0.42+	0.22	−0.35*	0.18
Reading skills	0.00*	0.00	0.00	0.00
Economic cap.	−0.33*	0.13	−0.07	0.10
HISEI	0.00	0.01	0.01	0.01
Cultural poss.	−0.02	0.02	0.01	0.01
Well-being_t_5	0.10	0.11	0.01	0.09
Constant	−5.81***	0.94	−1.76***	0.17

***$p<0.001$; **$p<0.01$; *$p<0.05$; +$p<0.1$. b, standardised effect of variable; S.E.(b), standard error of standardised effect of variable. Cultural poss., quantity and kind of cultural goods in the household; HISEI, socio-economic status of the parents; Economic cap., familial wealth; Reading skills, PISA measure of reading literacy; Latin, a variable indicating whether the young person lives in the French and Italian-speaking regions of Switzerland (reference category: German-speaking region); Well-being_t_j, well-being measured in previous data collection; Intercept, constant term of the equation.

Appendix 5. Model fit indices for all models.

Covariates	LogL	AIC	BIC	BIC adj.	n	No. of parameters
none	−33992.481	68218.962	68977.450	68605.667	4831	117
Cultural poss.	−45625.854	91525.709	92437.950	92002.604	5760	137
Cultural poss., HISEI	−41900.174	84110.348	85130.477	84637.937	5332	155
Cultural poss., HISEI, economic cap.	−41847.432	84040.865	85179.428	84629.690	5331	173
Cultural poss., HISEI, economic cap., reading skills	−41706.784	83795.569	85052.453	84445.516	5327	191
Cultural poss., HISEI, economic cap., reading skills, female	−41619.015	83656.030	85031.364	84367.229	5327	209
Cultural poss., HISEI, economic cap., reading skills, female, Latin	−41365.891	83185.783	84679.566	83958.233	5327	227

All covariates (see above), covariates allowed to vary across classes and time:	LogL	AIC	BIC	BIC adj.	n	No. of parameters
Latin	−41360.301	83194.602	84754.191	84001.081	5327	237
Latin, female	−41355.507	83205.014	84830.408	84045.521	5327	247
Latin, female, reading skills	−41346.309	83206.618	84897.818	84081.155	5327	257
Latin, female, reading skills, economic cap.	−41343.490	83218.979	84969.404	84124.141	5327	267
Latin, female, reading skills, economic cap., HISEI	−41335.290	83222.580	85038.810	84161.770	5327	277
Latin, female, reading skills, economic cap., HISEI, cultural poss.	−41331.274	83234.548	85116.584	84207.768	5327	287
Females only	−24489.328	49496.655	51050.746	50227.803	2982	259
Males only	−16638.027	33794.054	35285.905	34463.009	2345	259

Log Likelihood (LogL), Akaike information criterion (AIC), Bayesian information criterion (BIC) and sample size adjusted BIC (BIC adj.) for the different models. HISEI, socio-economic status of the parents. Note that they are not strictly nested due to Full Information Maximum Likelihood estimation.

How gender differences in academic engagement relate to students' gender identity

Ursula Kessels, Anke Heyder, Martin Latsch and Bettina Hannover

Department of Education and Psychology, Freie Universität Berlin, Berlin, Germany

Background: Gender differences in educational outcomes encompass many different areas. For example, in some educational settings, boys lag behind girls on indicators of educational success, such as leaving certificates and type of school attended. In studies testing performance, boys typically show lower competence in reading compared with girls, yet tend to show higher competence in school subjects related to mathematics. While such differences in competence between the genders can be relatively small, they coincide with much greater differences in motivation-related variables emerging during the school years, and thus seem to channel students into lifelong gendered pathways via gendered educational and occupational preferences.

Purpose: From a psychological perspective, we propose the *Interests as Identity Regulation Model* (IIRM) as a useful tool for understanding many of the gender differences in educational outcomes. Specifically, the focus is on two areas of research: girls' and women's under-representation in subjects such as maths and science; and boys' lower engagement at school in general.

Sources of evidence: Findings from recent research, mostly from a psychological perspective using quantitative measures and empirical studies testing the IIRM, are reported to illustrate different aspects of the interplay between students' gender identity and gendered social meanings of academic domains (such as maths), as well as academic engagement in general.

Main argument: IIRM suggests that the perceived fit between students' gender identity and the gendered social meanings associated with different possible behaviours at school (e.g. choosing a subject, investing effort or not) is a relevant heuristic for students' directing of their learning activities. The male stereotyping of maths and science implies a greater misfit between girls' gender identity and engagement in these domains. The perception that displaying effort and engagement at school is feminine leads to a misfit between boys' gender identity and academic engagement in general.

Conclusions: Attempts to alleviate gender differences in educational outcomes that channel students into lifelong gendered pathways with regard to qualifications and occupations will benefit from an understanding of how closely these academic choices are related to students' gender identity. Interventions should aim at enhancing the individually perceived fit between a student's gender identity and engagement in specific subjects or learning activities. The nature of such interventions will be an important topic of future research.

Gender differences in academic outcomes

Gender differences in educational achievement transpire to be different depending on whether we look at boys' and girls' participation in education and acquisition of education-related certificates on the one hand, or at their acquired cognitive competencies on the other. With respect to participation in education, in countries that 'track' students into different school types, girls are overrepresented in higher tracks because of their better grades, and are therefore more likely to obtain the entrance qualification for college or university studies. In contrast, boys are overrepresented in lower school tracks and among students leaving school without a certificate (e.g. for Germany: Statistisches Bundesamt 2011; for England: Department for Education and Skills 2007; for Europe: EACEA 2010; for the USA: Snyder and Dillow 2011; for a review, see Hadjar 2011).

With respect to cognitive competences, studies employing standardised performance tests, such as the cross-national school achievement studies PIRLS and PISA, yield a somewhat different picture. While effect sizes for gender differences in performance vary cross-nationally (e.g. for mathematics Else-Quest, Linn, and Hyde 2010), on average girls tend to underperform in domains related to mathematics, whereas they outperform boys in subjects related to reading (e.g. Driessen and van Langen 2013; Mullis, Martin, Foy, and Arora 2012; Mullis, Martin, Foy, and Drucker 2012; OECD 2011, 2013). For instance, in the PISA-test 2012, girls surpassed boys in reading in every participating country by an average of 38 points – the equivalent to one year of schooling – whereas in mathematics boys achieved higher levels of competency than girls in 37 of the 65 participating countries (girls scored higher than boys in five countries) and outperformed girls by an average of 11 score points. However, in only six countries is the gender gap in mathematics larger than the equivalent of half a school year (OECD 2013). These differences in domain-specific competencies are partly due to girls' overrepresentation in learning environments, which are particularly supportive of students' cognitive development. When type of school attended is accounted for, boys extend their lead in mathematics, while girls' advantage in reading diminishes (cf. Becker et al. 2006; Köller, Knigge, and Tesch 2010; Zimmer, Burba, and Rost 2004).

When compared with the variations in boys' versus girls' performances in standardised tests described above, measures of motivation yield much larger gender differences (for a review, see Hannover and Kessels 2011), with most studies focusing on STEM (science, technology, mathematics, engineering) subjects. Relative to males, females are less confident of their mathematics- and science-related capabilities (e.g. Kessels and Hannover 2008); they indicate weaker mathematics and technology related self-efficacy, but stronger language related self-efficacy (for a meta-analysis, see Huang 2013); display weaker interest in mathematics and science (e.g. Eccles 2011); are more likely to experience anxiety; and are less likely to report joy in learning with respect to mathematics (Frenzel, Pekrun, and Goetz 2007). While gender differences in these motivation-related variables are attenuated once differences in level of competence are taken into account, they still remain statistically significant.

Boys report more positive attitudes than girls towards STEM subjects. Yet the opposite is true regarding their attitudes towards school and learning in general. Many studies show that boys report they are less engaged and interested at school, enjoy it less, find coursework less meaningful and spend less time on homework than girls (Driessen and van Langen 2013; Hannover and Kessels 2011; Lam et al. 2012).

Interestingly, when gender differences in educational participation and competencies at the end of the compulsory school years are continued into older age cohorts, young women do not seem to succeed in transforming their higher level certificates into top-quality future study or well-paid, high-qualification professions: even today, women earn less and are under-represented in management and executive positions, but over-represented in service and low-paying jobs (e.g. WEF 2010). At the same time, young women seem to retreat from the domains in which they are relatively less successful (Eccles 2011). Regardless of level of qualification, males are clearly over-represented among professionals in the realm of science and technology.

To summarise, boys lag behind girls on indicators of educational success such as leaving certificates or type of school attended, but they tend to achieve higher levels of competence in subject domains related to mathematics. While differences in competencies between the genders that emerge during the school years are relatively small, they coincide with much larger differences in motivation-related variables, and thus seem to channel students into lifelong gendered pathways via gendered educational and occupational preferences. Neither males' lagging behind in educational participation and success, nor females' lower levels of interest and achievement in mathematics and science, can sufficiently be explained by gender differences in cognitive abilities or school type.

How academic engagement is related to students' identity

To expand the research into the psychological origins of gender differences in subject-specific competencies and motivation described above, we have proposed and extensively tested a model linking the development of interest and competence to the learner's self or identity. We call this the *Interests as Identity Regulation Model* (IIRM; Kessels and Hannover 2004, 2007). Long before school entrance, around the child's second birthday, a concept of the self starts to develop (e.g. Hannover and Greve 2012; Harter 2003; Ruble et al. 2004). From that point, knowledge about who one is and who one will be in the future is continually generated in everyday social interactions, as well as via the individual's reflections on feedback provided by the social environment. Our IIRM suggests that an important cognitive input for the construction and further extension of school students' self are social meanings associated with learning opportunities provided within the learning environment. For instance, school subjects differ in their social meaning, i.e. in relation to assumptions about which typical contents and scripts are associated with them (what we call *image of a school subject*; Kessels and Hannover 2007), and with respect to the characteristics that are commonly associated with students who have a strong preference for a particular subject (what we call *prototype of a school subject*; Hannover and Kessels 2004). IIRM's core assumption is that by investing interest and effort into a certain school subject, students not only acquire relevant knowledge and skills, but also adapt or expand their view of whom they are by incorporating the social meaning attached to that particular domain into their self. By preferring certain school subjects over others, students can develop and demonstrate their identity as persons with specific interests and characteristics. As an illustration, if the prototype of a school subject (i.e. the assumptions young people share about someone who is fanatical about that subject) is that such a person is typically a badly dressed and socially isolated so-called 'nerd', a student's commitment to this school subject will depend (among other things) on whether he or she would like to be associated with the specific social meaning this subject possesses.

Identity regulation not only impacts students' subject preferences or dislikes, but may also influence the extent to which they display effort, diligence and commitment to school and learning in general. Research by Boehnke (2008) has shown that students tend to associate these behaviours with predominantly negative social meanings; according to our IIRM, this may explain why many students try to hide effort investment in school from others.

How academic engagement is related to gender identity: empirical evidence

Gender is a very prominent personal characteristic, with a self-concept referring to one's biological sex emerging as early as two to three years old (Fagot and Leinbach 1985). Applied to our current topic, gendered preferences or gender differences in academic engagement should become more likely when the image or the prototype of a school subject (or learning in general) are more strongly associated with one gender rather than the other. The following section will provide evidence that the under-representation of female students in STEM subjects is related to the perceived misfit between girls' gendered self-concept and the image of science. Next, we will provide evidence that boys' generally lower engagement at school is similarly related to a perceived misfit between boys' gendered self-concept and the overall image of academic engagement.

A misfit between girls' gender identity and STEM subjects?

IIRM proposes that students are more likely to engage in domains they perceive as fitting their (actual or desired) identity and abstain from domains they consider dissimilar to themselves. To explain the lower engagement of females in STEM subjects, our approach focuses on the perceived fit or misfit between girls' feminine gender identity and the masculine stereotyping of these domains.

In what follows, we first summarise research that shows that STEM subjects are perceived as a male domain, and that students liking or excelling in STEM subjects are perceived by adolescents as being unfeminine. In a second step, we cite evidence showing that the subjectively perceived misfit between girls' identity and the masculine image of science has an effect on girls' level of interest, performance and choices in STEM subjects.

Masculine stereotyping of STEM subjects has been found in many studies, mostly focusing on the perception of mathematics as a male subject. When school students are asked whether they perceive these subjects as more appropriate for one gender rather than the other (using *explicit* measures such as self-report questionnaires), most of them endorse clear-cut math–male stereotypes (e.g. Martinot, Bagès, and Désert 2012), and ascribe more talent, ability and interest in mathematics to boys than to girls (e.g. Chatard, Guimond, and Selimbegovic 2007; Steffens and Jelenec 2011). The *implicit* stereotyping of STEM subjects has usually been measured with the Implicit Association Test (IAT; Greenwald, McGhee, and Schwartz 1998), a computer-based measure for assessing the strength of automatic associations between two pairs of concepts (e.g. maths and male, language and female). Strength of association for one concept is always assessed in relative comparison with strength of association for a second concept, with the IAT effect measuring the difference in the relative strengths (e.g. strength of association between maths and male in comparison to strength of association between language and female). On average, students clearly associate mathematics and physics more strongly with maleness than with femaleness (Cvencek, Meltzoff, and Greenwald 2011; Kessels, Rau, and Hannover 2006; Nosek, Banaji, and Greenwald 2002; Steffens, Jelenec, and Noack 2010).

The masculine stereotyping of STEM subjects is not only limited to the subject itself, but also extends to people associated with these subjects. Many decades ago, Mead and Metraux (1957) reported on perceived stereotypes of scientists, finding that they were often described as an elderly man who wears a white coat and works in a laboratory. In explaining girls' lesser academic engagement in these subjects, however, prototypes (typical examples) of students liking or excelling in those respective domains should be even more informative. IIRM suggests that a misfit between girls' own identity and descriptions of typical students who like science is not only perceived with respect to visible and physical characteristics, such as in the examples of the stereotypical 'badly dressed nerd' or the 'elderly man wearing a white coat' described above, but also on the level of identity-relevant personality traits. Kessels (2005) found that girls whose favourite subject was physics were regarded by their peers as possessing more masculine traits and fewer feminine traits than girls (and boys) whose favourite subject was music.

In summary, our studies show that adolescents perceive maths and science as something male, and that an interest in these domains is an indicator of masculinity, implying a greater misfit between girls' identity and STEM subjects when compared with boys. Not all girls, however, perceive STEM subjects as masculine to the same degree, and not all girls perceive themselves as highly feminine. Several of our studies have actually tested whether the *individually* perceived misfit between girls' gender (or gender identity) and their image of STEM is related to their liking for, performance in and choice of STEM subjects. The studies on implicit gender stereotyping of school subjects usually report that students' performance/attitudes/career aspiration can be predicted by an interaction term of participants' gender and the IAT effect, indicating that the stronger female students' implicit STEM subject-male associations are, the worse they perform and the worse their explicit attitudes are towards the respective subject (e.g. Kessels, Rau, and Hannover, 2006; Kiefer and Sekaquaptewa 2007; Lane, Goh, and Driver-Linn 2012; Nosek, Banaji, and Greenwald 2002; Steffens and Jelenec 2011; Steffens, Jelenec, and Noack 2010). Taken together, these studies provide a great deal of evidence for the importance of individually perceived gender-appropriateness with regard to liking, interest and performance in the respective domains.

The subjectively perceived fit or misfit between one's own gender-related self-concept and the ascription of masculinity and femininity to the prototype of someone who studies physics proved to be a significant predictor for girls' liking of physics in a study based on the 'self-to-prototype matching paradigm' (Niedenthal, Cantor, and Kihlstrom 1985). Applied to the school context, this theory states that when having to choose (e.g. their major subject), students compare their actual or desired (gendered) self with the defining characteristics of the different school subjects' image or prototype, and then select the option providing the best match between self and image/prototype (Hannover and Kessels 2004). Kessels (2005) found that the more similarly girls described themselves to the 'typical student liking physics best' (using scales measuring femininity and masculinity), the more they reported liking physics themselves. It therefore seems that the incompatibility of the STEM-preferring prototype to female students' self-image is crucial in explaining why female students do not wish to specialise in STEM subjects.

A misfit between boys' gender identity and engagement at school?

It is apparent that boys lag behind girls on important indicators of academic success, and report less engagement and more negative attitudes towards school in general

(Driessen and van Langen 2013; Hannover and Kessels 2011; Lam et al. 2012). In what follows, we summarise evidence substantiating IIRMs suggestion that boys' general lower academic engagement is related to their intention to demonstrate and verify their identity as masculine. Much of the previous research on the misfit between male gender identity and academic engagement has used qualitative ethnographic methods, such as observations or interviews. These studies suggest that many male students experience a fundamental conflict between putting effort into schoolwork or following rules at school and maintaining a cool and masculine image in front of their peers – so-called 'laddish behaviour' (e.g. Hadjar, Lupatsch, and Grünewald-Huber 2010; Mac an Ghaill 1994).

That masculine aspects of boys' self-concept are actually connected to an important aspect of self-regulated learning has been demonstrated in a study on academic help-seeking by Kessels and Steinmayr (2013), in which boys indicated less intention to seek help at school than girls. Psychological gender was also correlated with help-seeking attitudes, as well as with school performance: the higher boys scored on negative masculinity (a scale consisting of socially undesirable traits that are typical for males, but not females), the weaker both their help-seeking attitudes and their grades were. Taken as a whole, this study shows that specific aspects of students' masculinity are, in fact, negatively correlated with academic engagement, as suggested by the IIRM.

The often cited misfit between being a 'real boy' and engagement at school suggests that school, in general, is perceived as feminine by the majority of students. However, very few studies exist that provide evidence of gender stereotyping of school and learning in general. Heyder and Kessels (2013) developed a test for assessing the implicit gender stereotyping of school, demonstrating that, overall, students associate school more strongly with 'female' than with 'male'. The more strongly boys associated school with 'female' and the more they ascribed negative masculine traits to themselves, the lower their grades in German were. Boys' grades in mathematics, however, were unrelated to the extent to which they perceived school as feminine and themselves as masculine.

Boys' enacting masculinity in the classroom might be another important factor for understanding boys' lower academic success. Budde (2009) has argued that the more boys enact their masculinity at school, the more negatively they will be evaluated by their teachers, as the 'traditional male habitus' is increasingly seen as inadequate in Western societies today. However, empirical evidence actually supporting this statement is scarce. In a recent experimental study by Heyder and Kessels (submitted), teachers read one of four vignettes describing a male (or female) student enacting gender (or not), and rated how likely this student would be to display behaviours impeding or fostering learning. Teachers ascribed fewer behaviours fostering learning and more behaviours impeding learning to male target students and to target students enacting their gender identity. As a result, the male target student who actively demonstrated his masculinity at school received the least favourable ratings by teachers.

An additional factor that may contribute to an explanation of boys' lower educational participation and success might be the stereotype threat emanating from the negative expectations expressed in public discourse on boys as 'scholastic failures'. Stereotype threat is defined as the 'social-psychological threat that arises when one is [...] doing something for which a negative stereotype about one's group applies' (Steele 1997, 614). In four studies, Latsch and Hannover (in press) have found that male students being directly exposed to a prototypical piece of evidence from the media's portrayal of 'failing boys' underperformed on tasks that are connoted as female (reading) and focused their learning goals on tasks that are connoted as male (mathematics). The media's portrayal seems to contribute to the maintenance of gender-stereotypes by impairing boys' performance in female domains and by prompting them to align their learning goals with the gender-connotation of their own domain.

To summarise, empirical evidence supports the assumptions made in the IIRM, i.e. students seem to calibrate the direction and amount of their engagement at school in accordance with their (gender) identity. The direction of academic engagement has been addressed in studies that aim to explain the under-representation of female students in STEM subjects. The research shows a male stereotyping of mathematics and science, and illustrates how important the individually perceived gender-appropriateness of a school subject is for liking, interest and performance in particular domains. In line with the assumptions of IIRM, boys' gender identity seems to conflict with displaying effort and commitment to school and learning to the extent that they perceive school as feminine.

Our model's assumptions are also substantiated by a recent experimental study by Elmore and Oyserman (2012). According to their identity-based motivation theory (IBM), individuals prefer to act in ways that they feel are in line with important social identities, such as gender. Gender identity–congruent behaviours coincide with feelings of subjective importance and being worthwhile, so that difficulties encountered will promote investment of effort, rather than avoidance or giving up. In the school environment, gender identity–congruence or incongruence of different behaviours is deduced from social cues about how to be male or female. Elmore and Oyserman manipulated the gender identity–congruence of success by providing school students either with information on males' higher income (congruence for boys, incongruence for girls) or females' higher graduation rates (congruence for girls, incongruence for boys). As expected, compared to students in the control group or the other experimental condition, boys and girls for whom gender and success felt congruent indicated more school-related self-aspects in an open self-description, considered their academic and occupational success in the future as higher, and (only boys) tried harder on a mathematics task.

Both our IIRM and IBM theory predict that students scan the school environment for social meanings associated with different possible behaviours (e.g. which subject to choose, whether to invest effort or not) and opt for the behaviour associated with social meanings that most closely match – or are congruent with – their self. While Elmore and Oyserman (2012) investigated their model using 'success' as an important social meaning students may want to incorporate into their self, our model's assumptions were substantiated in a variety of studies (described above) addressing different social meanings and different aspects of students' identities.

Practical implications deduced from the IIRM would be to develop strategies aimed at enhancing the individually perceived fit between a student's gender identity and engagement in specific subjects or learning activities perceived as gendered. Both strategies reducing the stereotyping of STEM as male and the stereotyping of diligence and commitment at school as female would offer pathways for students to develop to their full individual potential, regardless of cultural gender stereotypes. A different approach would be to reduce the salience of gender in the classroom or during learning activities, making engagement in those subjects or activities deemed inappropriate to one's own gender more likely (Kessels and Hannover 2008).

Funding

This work was supported by two grants by the Deutsche Forschungsgemeinschaft [KE 1412-2-2], [HA 2381-11-2], allocated to the first author and the last author.

References

Becker, M., O. Lüdtke, U. Trautwein, and J. Baumert. 2006. "Leistungszuwachs in Mathematik: Evidenz für einen Schereneffekt im mehrgliedrigen Schulsystem? [Performance Growth in Mathematics: Evidence for Increasing Disparities in a Tracked Schooling System?]" *Zeitschrift für Pädagogische Psychologie* 20 (4): 233–242.

Boehnke, K. 2008. "Peer Pressure: A Cause of Scholastic Underachievement? A Cross-cultural Study of Mathematical Achievement in German, Canadian, and Israeli Middle School Students. *Social Psychology of Education* 11 (2): 149–160.

Budde, J. 2009. "Perspektiven für Jungenforschung an Schulen [Perspectives for Research on Boys in Schools]." In *Jungenforschung empirisch: Zwischen Schule, männlichem Habitus und Peerkultur*, edited by Jürgen Budde and Ingelore Mammes, 73–90. Wiesbaden: VS, Verlag für Sozialwissenschaften.

Chatard, A., S. Guimond, and L. Selimbegovic. 2007. "'How good are you in math?' The Effect of Gender Stereotypes on Students' Recollection of their School Marks." *Journal of Experimental Social Psychology* 43 (6): 1017–1024.

Cvencek, D., A. N. Meltzoff, and A. G. Greenwald. 2011. "Math-gender Stereotypes in Elementary School Children." *Child Development* 82 (3): 766–779.

Department for Education and Skills. 2007. Gender and Education: The Evidence on Pupils in England (accessed 7 October 2013). https://www.education.gov.uk/publications/eOrderingDownload/00389-2007BKT-EN.pdf.

Driessen, G., and A. van Langen. 2013. "Gender Differences in Primary and Secondary Education: Are Girls Really Outperforming Boys?" *International Review of Education* 59 (1): 67–86.

Eccles, J. S. 2011. "Gendered Educational and Occupational Choices: Applying the Eccles et al. Model of Achievement-related Choices." *International Journal of Behavioral Development* 35 (3): 195–201.

Education, Audiovisual and Culture Executive Agency (EACEA). 2010. *Gender Differences in Educational Outcomes: Study on the Measures Taken and the Current Situation in Europe*. Brussels: EACEA P9 Eurydice.

Elmore, K. C., and D. Oyserman. 2012. "If 'We' Can Succeed, 'I' Can Too: Identity-based Motivation and Gender in the Classroom." *Contemporary Educational Psychology* 37 (3): 176–185.

Else-Quest, N. M., J. S. Hyde, and M. C. Linn. 2010. "Cross-national Patterns of Gender Differences in Mathematics: A Meta-analysis." *Psychological Bulletin* 136 (1): 103–127.

Fagot, B. I., and M. D. Leinbach. 1985. "Gender Identity: Some Thoughts on an Old Concept." *Journal of the American Academy of Child Psychiatry* 24 (6): 684–688.

Frenzel, A. C., R. Pekrun, and T. Goetz. 2007. "Perceived Learning Environment and Students' Emotional Experiences: A Multilevel Analysis of Mathematics Classrooms." *Learning and Instruction* 17 (5): 478–493.

Greenwald, A. G., D. E. McGhee, and J. L. K. Schwartz. 1998. "Measuring Individual Differences in Implicit Cognition: The Implicit Association Test." *Journal of Personality and Social Psychology* 74 (6): 1464–80.

Hadjar, Andreas, ed. 2011. *Geschlechtsspezifische Bildungsungleichheiten* [Gender Disparities in Education]. Wiesbaden: VS Verlag für Sozialwissenschaften.

Hadjar, A., J. Lupatsch, and E. Grünewald-Huber. 2010. "Bildungsverlierer/-innen, Schulentfremdung und Schulerfolg [Academic Underachiever, School Alienation, and Academic Success]." In *Bildungsverlierer: Neue Ungleichheiten* [Academic Underachiever: New Disparities], edited by Gudrun Quenzel and Klaus Hurrelmann, 223–244. Wiesbaden: VS, Verlag für Sozialwissenschaften.

Hannover, B. and W. Greve. 2012. "Selbst und Persönlichkeit [Self and Personality]." In *Entwicklungspsychologie* [Developmental Psychology], 7th ed., edited by, Wolfgang Schneider and Ulman Lindenberger, 543–561. Weinheim: Beltz.

Hannover, B., and U. Kessels. 2004. "Self-to-prototype Matching as a Strategy for Making Academic Choices: Why High School Students do not Like Math and Science." *Learning and Instruction* 14 (1): 51–67.

Hannover, B., and U. Kessels. 2011. "Sind Jungen die neuen Bildungsverlierer? Empirische Evidenz für Geschlechterdisparitäten zuungunsten von Jungen und Erklärungsansätze [Are Boys Left Behind? Reviewing and Explaining Education-related Gender Disparities]." *Zeitschrift für Pädagogische Psychologie* 25 (2): 89–103.

Harter, S. 2003. "The Development of Self-representation During Childhood and Adolescence." In *Handbook of Self and Identity*, edited by Mark Leary and June Tangney, 610–642. New York: Guilford.

Heyder, A., and U. Kessels. 2013. "Is School Feminine? Implicit Gender Stereotyping of School as a Predictor of Academic Achievement." *Sex Roles* 69: 605–617.

Heyder, A., and U. Kessels 2015. "Do teachers equate male and masculine with lower academic engagement? How students' gender enactment triggers gender stereotypes at school." *Social Psychology of Education* 18: 467–485.

Huang, C. 2013. "Gender Differences in Academic Self-efficacy: A Meta-analysis." *European Journal of Psychology of Education* 28 (1): 1–35.

Kessels, U. 2005. "Fitting into the Stereotype: How Gender-stereotyped Perceptions of Prototypic Peers Relate to Liking for School Subjects." *European Journal of Psychology of Education* 20 (3): 309–323.

Kessels, U., and B. Hannover. 2004. "Entwicklung schulischer Interessen als Identitätsregulation [The Development of Academic Interests as Identity Regulation]." In *Bildungsqualität von Schule: Lehrerprofessionalisierung, Unterrichtsentwicklung und Schülerförderung als Strategien der Qualitätsentwicklung*, edited by Jörg Doll and Manfred Prenzel, 398–412. Münster: Waxmann.

Kessels, U., and B. Hannover. 2007. "How the Image of Math and Science Affects the Development of Academic Interest." In *Studies on the Educational Quality of Schools: The Final Report of the DFG Priority Programme*, edited by Manfred Prenzel, 283–297. Münster: Waxmann.

Kessels, U., and B. Hannover. 2008. "When Being a Girl Matters Less: Accessibility of Gender-related Self-knowledge in Single-sex and Coeducational Classes and its Impact on Students' Physics-related Self-concept of Ability." *British Journal of Educational Psychology* 78 (2): 273–289.

Kessels, U., M. Rau, and B. Hannover. 2006. "What Goes Well with Physics? Measuring and Altering the Image of Science." *British Journal of Educational Psychology* 76 (4): 761–780.

Kessels, U., and R. Steinmayr. 2013. "Macho-man in School: Toward the Role of Gender Role Self-concepts and Help Seeking in School Performance." *Learning and Individual Differences* 23: 234–240.

Kiefer, A. K., and D. Sekaquaptewa. 2007. "Implicit Stereotypes, Gender Identification, and Math-related Outcomes: A Prospective Study of Female College Students." *Psychological Science* 18 (1): 13–18.

Köller, Olaf, Michel Knigge, and Bernd Tesch, eds. 2010. *Sprachliche Kompetenzen im Ländervergleich. Befunde des ersten Ländervergleichs zur Überprüfung der Bildungsstandards für den Mittleren Schulabschluss in den Fächern Deutsch, Englisch und Französisch* [A Comparison of Verbal Competencies in the German Laender]. Münster: Waxmann.

Lam, S. -F., S. Jimerson, E. Kikas, C. Cefai, F. H. Veiga, B. Nelson, C. Hatzichristou, et al. 2012. "Do Girls and Boys Perceive Themselves as Equally Engaged in School? The Results of an International Study from 12 Countries." *Journal of School Psychology* 50 (1): 77–94.

Lane, K. A., J. X. Goh, and E. Driver-Linn. 2012. "Implicit Science Stereotypes Mediate the Relationship Between Gender and Academic Participation." *Sex Roles* 66 (3–4): 220–234.

Latsch, M., and B. Hannover. 2014. "Smart girls, dumb boys!? How the discourse on "failing boys" impacts performances and motivational goal orientation in German school students." *Social Psychology* 45: 112–126.

Mac an Ghaill, M. 1994. *The Making of Men*. Buckingham: Open University Press.

Martinot, D., C. Bagès, and M. Désert. 2012. "French Children's Awareness of Gender Stereotypes about Mathematics and Reading: When Girls Improve their Reputation in Math." *Sex Roles* 66(3–4): 210–219.

Mead, M., and R. Metraux. 1957." Image of the Scientist Among High-school Students: A Pilot Study." *Science* 126 (3270): 384–390.

Mullis, I., M. Martin, P. Foy, and A. Arora. 2012. *TIMSS 2011 – International Results in Mathematics*. Chestnut Hill, MA: IEA Publishing.

Mullis, I., M. Martin, P. Foy, and K. Drucker. 2012. *PIRLS 2011 – International Results in Reading*. Chestnut Hill, MA: IEA Publishing.

Niedenthal, P. M., N. Cantor, and J. F. Kihlstrom. 1985. "Prototype Matching: A Strategy for Social Decision Making." *Journal of Personality and Social Psychology* 48 (3): 575–584.

Nosek, B. A., M. R. Banaji, and A. G. Greenwald. 2002. "Math = Male, Me = Female, Therefore math ≠ me." *Journal of Personality and Social Psychology* 83 (1): 44–59.

Organization for Economic Cooperation and Development (OECD). 2011. *Education at a Glance 2011*. Paris: OECD Publishing.

Organization for Economic Cooperation and Development (OECD). 2013. *PISA 2012 Results: What Students Know and Can do. Student Performance in Mathematics, Reading and Science. Volume I*. Paris: OECD Publishing. http://dx.doi.org/10.1787/9789264201118-en.

Ruble, D. N., J. Alvarez, M. Bachman, J. Cameron, A. Fuligni, and C. Garcia Coll. 2004. "The Development of a Sense of 'we': The Emergence and Implications of Children's Collective Identity." In *The Development of the Social Self*, edited by Mark Bennett and Fabio Sani, 29–76. New York: Psychology Press.

Snyder, T. D., and S. A. Dillow. 2011. *Digest of Education Statistics 2010*. Washington, DC: National Center for Education Statistics.

Statistisches Bundesamt. 2011. *Bildungsstand der Bevölkerung* [The Population's Educational Attainment]. Wiesbaden: Statistisches Bundesamt.

Steele, C. M. 1997. "A Threat in the Air: How Stereotypes Shape Intellectual Identity and Performance." *American Psychologist* 52 (6): 613–629.

Steffens, M. C., and P. Jelenec. 2011. "Separating Implicit Gender Stereotypes Regarding Math and Language: Implicit Ability Stereotypes are Self-serving for Boys and Men, but not for Girls and Women." *Sex Roles* 64 (5–6): 324–335.

Steffens, M. C., P. Jelenec, and P. Noack. 2010. "On the Leaky Math Pipeline: Comparing Implicit Math-gender Stereotypes and Math Withdrawal in Female and Male Children and Adolescents." *Journal of Educational Psychology* 102 (4): 947–963.

World Economic Forum (WEF). 2010. The Global Gender Gap Report 2010. http://www3.weforum.org/docs/WEF_GenderGap_Report_2010.pdf. Accessed April 1, 2012.

Zimmer, K., D. Burba, and J. Rost. 2004. "Kompetenzen von Jungen und Mädchen [Competencies of Boys and Girls]. In *PISA 2003: Der Bildungsstand der Jugendlichen in Deutschland: Ergebnisse des zweiten internationalen Vergleichs*, edited by PISA-Konsortium, 211–223. Münster: Waxmann.

Gender differences in school success: what are the roles of students' intelligence, personality and motivation?

Birgit Spinath[a], Christine Eckert[a] and Ricarda Steinmayr[b]

[a]Educational Psychology, Department of Psychology, Heidelberg University, Heidelberg, Germany; [b]Educational Psychology, Institute for Psychology, Technical University Dortmund, Dortmund, Germany

Background: Education is a key variable for reaching individually and socially desired outcomes. Specifically, school grades are important admission criteria for higher education and job positions. Nowadays, in countries committed to equal opportunities, girls obtain better school grades than boys, but the reasons why girls outperform boys are not well understood. In the following, individual student characteristics (i.e. intelligence, personality, motivation) were investigated as promising candidates that may account for gender differences in school performance.

Purpose: This is a review of research findings on gender differences in performance-related individual students' characteristics. These findings may help to explain differences in boys' and girls' school achievement. It was hypothesised that girls are better adapted to today's school environment because of their intelligence (general, specific), personality (Big Five) and motivation (ability self-concept, interest or intrinsic values, goal orientations). To investigate this hypothesis, we reviewed literature with respect to five questions: (1) How strongly are intelligence, personality and motivation associated with school achievement? (2) Are there mean level differences between boys and girls in these characteristics? (3) Do these characteristics show gender differences in predicting school achievement? (4) Can gender differences in these characteristics explain the association between gender and school achievement? (5) Are gender differences in these characteristics causally related to differences in boys' and girls' school achievement?

Sources of evidence: We mainly based our review on meta-analyses and literature reviews. If no meta-analyses or reviews were available, we reported results of representative single studies, including results from our own studies. To illustrate the magnitude of gender differences, we also reported statistical parameters (correlation coefficients, effect sizes and regression coefficients).

Main argument: Concerning the five research questions, we found that, first, among the characteristics investigated here, general intelligence, ability self-concepts and self-discipline were the most important predictors of school performance. Second, gender differences in students' individual characteristics varied from non-existent (e.g. general intelligence) to strong (e.g. self-discipline). Third, there was no indication that these characteristics were differently important for boys' and girls' school performance. Fourth, gender differences in intelligence, personality and motivation partially mediated the association between gender and school achievement but cannot fully explain it. Fifth, whether differences in intelligence, personality and motivation cause performance differences between boys and girls remains unknown because there were no studies that have investigated this question with designs that could test for causal inferences.

Conclusion: Gender differences in students' individual characteristics contribute to a significant extent to gender differences in school performance. Taken together, the effects of gender differences in students' individual characteristics can partially but not fully account for gender differences in school performance. Girls are somewhat better adapted to today's school environments, especially because of their better verbal intelligence, higher Agreeableness, stronger self-discipline, as well as certain aspects of their motivation. In light of these specific differences, it is argued that changing certain aspects of school environments might help boys to better succeed in school and, thus, reduce educational inequality.

Introduction

Since the 1990s, there has been increasing evidence that, in countries committed to equal opportunities, girls outperform boys on different academic achievement criteria (e.g. USA: Epstein et al. 1998; Hong Kong: Wong, Lam, and Ho 2002; Scotland: Scottish Office 1998; Germany: Steinmayr and Spinath 2008; Austria: Freudenthaler, Spinath, and Neubauer 2008). The reasons for these gender differences are not well understood. Individual student characteristics have been shown to explain the largest portion of variance in school performance among all possible classes of variables (e.g. Baumert, Trautwein, and Artelt 2003). Therefore, from a psychological perspective, individual student characteristics such as intelligence, personality and motivation seem to be promising candidates for accounting for gender differences in school performance. We hypothesised that, in countries that are dedicated to equal opportunities, girls are better adapted to the demands of school environments because of their intelligence, personality and motivation. To investigate this hypothesis, we reviewed the literature with respect to five questions:

(1) How strongly are intelligence, personality and motivation associated with school achievement?
(2) Are there mean level differences between boys and girls in these characteristics? How large are these differences?
(3) Does the importance of these characteristics as predictors of school achievement differ for boys and girls?
(4) Can gender differences in these characteristics explain the association between gender and school achievement?
(5) Are gender differences in these characteristics causally related to differences in boys' and girls' school achievement?

To our knowledge, no previous review has summarised research findings on intelligence, personality, motivation and school success at the same time. Moreover, no previous work has simultaneously targeted the five research questions to provide a systematic review of the research findings.

When possible, we drew on meta-analyses or literature reviews. We included meta-analyses reporting gender differences in school achievement that were included in the data bases PsycINFO and ERIC in 2013. If no such comprehensive analyses were available, representative results of single studies are reported. For these single studies, we often draw on research from our own group because in many cases these are the only studies available. To highlight which results came from meta-analyses or literature reviews, we marked the corresponding references with *MA/LR*. If references are not marked, reported results stem from single studies. Our review is not fully comprehensive concerning questions for which no meta-analyses or reviews were available, because it was not possible to provide a complete overview of all single studies. Moreover, we drew on school-aged samples when they were available. If no such samples were available, results relied on adult samples. Finally, because gender differences vary according to the operationalisation of school achievement, it is important to note that we preferred studies that operationalised school achievement in terms of grades over studies that used standardised achievement test data. This choice was made because grades are the most ecologically valid measure of school success.

How strongly are intelligence, personality and motivation associated with school achievement?

In this section, first, we will briefly define the constructs that we focussed on. Second, we will answer the question of how strongly intelligence, personality and motivation are associated with school achievement by reporting the corresponding correlations. Correlations of $r < 0.30$ are considered small, correlations of $r = 0.30–0.49$ to be moderate, and correlations of $r \geq 0.50$ to be strong (based on Cohen 1988).

Intelligence

Although the word intelligence means many different things to different people (Cianciolo and Sternberg 2004; Neisser et al. 1996), a central feature of most definitions of intelligence is the ability to learn. Correlations between measures of general intelligence and measures of educational achievement are strong ($r = 0.50$; *MA/LR*: Gustafsson and Undheim 1996). This relation is even stronger when it is modelled on a latent basis (*MA/LR*: Neisser et al. 1996; e.g. Deary et al. 2007). Specific types of intelligence (e.g. verbal, numerical) typically have weaker ($r < 0.40$) associations with corresponding school achievement than general intelligence (e.g. Calvin et al. 2010; Freudenthaler, Spinath, and Neubauer 2008; Steinmayr and Spinath 2008). The results are summarised in Table 1.

Personality traits

The personality model most commonly used in recent years is the Five-Factor Model or the Big Five (Digman 1990; Goldberg 1990; McCrae and Costa 1987). In this model, personality is described by five broad factors, namely Conscientiousness, Openness, Agreeableness, Neuroticism and Extraversion. Findings on the relation between the Big Five and school achievement have been rather inconsistent. The most consistent results have been found for Conscientiousness, which has a positive association with school achievement ($r = 0.19$; *MA/LR*: Poropat 2009). The facets of Conscientiousness, such as competence, order, dutifulness, achievement striving, self-discipline and deliberation (cf. Costa, Terracciano, and McCrae 2001), represent behaviours that contribute to better school achievement (e.g. doing assigned homework; Trautwein et al. 2006). Among the facets of Conscientiousness, self-discipline is considered especially important when investigating gender differences in school (e.g. Duckworth and Seligman 2005, 2006; *MA/LR*: Silverman 2003). Self-discipline is defined as the ability to suppress prepotent responses in the service of a higher goal (Duckworth and Seligman 2006). In single studies, associations between self-discipline and grades (GPA) have been found to be strong ($r = 0.57/0.67$; Duckworth and Seligman 2005, 2006).

Table 1. Gender differences and school achievement: Overview of results for the five research questions.

	Question 1 Association (r) with grades	Question 2 Effect size (d) of gender differences in means	Question 3 Evidence of differential prediction of school achievement between genders	Question 4 Mediation effects between gender and school achievement	Question 5 Evidence of causal effects of gender differences on school achievement
Cognitive abilities					
General intelligence	0.50	0.00	—	0.00	—
Verbal intelligence	<0.40	−0.45 to −0.02	—	1/3 of variance	—
Numerical intelligence	<0.40	−0.14 to 0.16	—	1/2 of variance	—
Personality traits					
Openness	0.10	0.00	—	0.00	—
Extraversion	−0.01	0.00	—	0.00	—
Neuroticism	−0.01	−0.30	—	0.00	—
Agreeableness	0.07	−0.28	—	1/4 of variance	—
Conscientiousness	0.19	0.00	—	0.00	—
Self-discipline	0.57–0.67	−0.09 to −0.71	—	1/2 of variance	—
Motivation					
Ability self-concept					
School in general	0.40–0.61	0.11	—	0.00	—
Mathematics	0.40–0.61	0.28	—	Suppressor effect	—
Languages	0.40–0.61	−0.23	—	1/4 of variance	—
Intrinsic motivation/ interest					
School in general	0.20–0.30	−0.29 to −0.33	For boys more important?	0.00	—
Mathematics	0.20–0.30	0.15–0.69	For boys more important?	Suppressor effect	—
Languages	0.20–0.30	−0.30 to −0.62	For boys more important?	1/2 of variance	—
Learning goals	0.10–0.11	−0.24 to 0.04		—	—
Performance- approach goals	0.06–0.13	−0.04 to 0.19		—	—
Performance- avoidance goals	−0.13	0.00–0.12			—
Work-avoidance goals	−0.20 to −0.30	0.16–0.54	—	1/3 of variance	—

Negative d indicates larger means for girls.

Openness involves active imagination, aesthetic sensitivity, attentiveness to inner feelings, preference for variety and intellectual curiosity. The positive relation between Openness and achievement ($r = 0.10$; MA/LR: Poropat 2009) is partly due to the medium correlation between Openness and intelligence (MA/LR: Chamorro-Premuzic and Furnham 2005). Nevertheless, after controlling for intelligence, Openness is still associated with school achievement (MA/LR: Poropat 2009). Agreeableness, Neuroticism and Extraversion are not related or are only weakly related to school performance. Agreeableness is characterised by adjectives such as kind, sympathetic, cooperative, warm and considerate. Agreeableness has been found to be weakly associated with school achievement when it is measured as grades ($r = 0.07$; MA/LR: Poropat 2009) compared with standardised achievement tests (MA/LR: Chamorro-Premuzic and Furnham 2005). Agreeableness can facilitate learning through cooperation and compliance with teachers' instructions. Even though the meta-analysis by Poropat (2009) did not find an association between the broad trait Neuroticism and school performance ($r = -0.01$), facets of Neuroticism were negatively associated with school performance, that is, primarily test anxiety and fear of failure (MA/LR: Zeidner 1995). Moreover, monitoring one's emotional state tends to distract from achievement-related behaviour (MA/LR: Eysenck et al. 2007). Poropat (2009) also found that Extraversion was, on average, not related to grades ($r = -0.01$). However, as was the case for all other associations between the Big Five and grades, substantial heterogeneity was found among correlations. Negative associations between Extraversion and school performance, for example, have been argued to be due to students pursuing social activities instead of studying (MA/LR: De Raad and Schouwenburg 1996).

Motivation

Motivation is the force that energises and directs experience and behaviour. In contrast with the construction of intelligence and personality, there is no single leading model and many different motivational constructs have been used in this research. For this review, from the vast array of achievement motivation theories (cf. Murphy and Alexander 2000), we chose two theoretical frameworks that have been extensively investigated in school settings: expectancy-value and goal theory.

In the expectancy-value model (Eccles et al. 1983; Wigfield and Eccles 2000), ability self-concepts (i.e. beliefs about one's own ability) and the values ascribed to tasks are the most proximal determinants of achievement-related behaviour. Among different values, intrinsic or interest values (i.e. engaging in a task for reasons that lie within the task itself rather than in its consequences) are the best-investigated task values. Both ability self-concepts and intrinsic or interest values can be investigated domain-specifically or for school in general. Associations with grades do not differ according to the investigated domain. For ability self-concepts, the relations with school achievement are moderate to strong ($r = 0.40–0.61$; MA/LR: Hansford and Hattie 1982; MA/LR: Möller et al. 2009). For intrinsic or interest values, the relation to school achievement is weak to moderate ($r = 0.20–0.30$; MA/LR: Schiefele, Krapp, and Winteler 1992; e.g. Gottfried 1985, 1990; Steinmayr and Spinath 2007, 2009).

Goal theories (Dweck 1986; Elliot 1999; Nicholls 1984) hold that achievement behaviour can be explained by the pursued goals. Best investigated is the trichotomous goal framework (Elliot 1999), in which three goals are distinguished: learning goals (wanting to increase one's competence), performance-approach goals (wanting to demonstrate high competence) and performance-avoidance goals (trying not to demonstrate low competence). Moreover, work-avoidance goals (wanting to invest little effort) can be described as the opposite of achievement motivation (e.g. Nicholls 1984). Overall, the associations between goal orientations and school achievement have been weak. Recent meta-analyses (*MA/LR*: Huang 2012; *MA/LR*: Hulleman et al. 2010) have reported the following average correlations between academic achievement and goal orientations: learning goals ($r = 0.10/0.11$), performance-approach goals ($r = 0.06/0.13$) and performance-avoidance goals ($r = -0.13$). Work-avoidance goals were not included in these analyses. Single studies have reported that an orientation towards work-avoidance goals is consistently negatively associated with achievement ($r = -0.20$ to -0.30; e.g. Dupeyrat and Mariné 2005; Steinmayr and Spinath 2008).

Summary RQ 1

The first research question focussed on how strongly intelligence, personality and motivation are related to school achievement. In sum, the strongest relations have been found for intelligence, self-discipline and ability self-concepts, whereas the relations between school achievement and the other constructs have been moderate (intrinsic or interest values, work-avoidance goals) or weak (Openness, Agreeableness, Conscientiousness, Neuroticism, Extraversion, learning goals, performance-approach and performance-avoidance goals).

Are there mean level differences in these characteristics between boys and girls?

To answer this question, we will report mean level differences between boys and girls in terms of the effect size Cohen's d (Cohen 1988). Cohen's d can be interpreted as the difference between boys' and girls' mean levels in a certain characteristic in standard deviation units. Effects of $d \leq 0.35$ are considered small, d between 0.36 and 0.79 to be medium and $d > 0.80$ to be strong (based on Cohen 1988). In the following, a positive d stands for larger means in boys, whereas a negative d denotes larger means in girls.

Intelligence

Most studies have found no or only negligible gender differences in general intelligence (*MA/LR*: Halpern 2012; *MA/LR*: Hyde 2005; e.g. Johnson, Carothers, and Deary 2008; Strand, Deary, and Smith 2006). Boys show greater variability in general intelligence, that is, they are overrepresented in the extremes of the intelligence distribution (e.g. Johnson, Carothers, and Deary 2008). Similarly, there are, by and large, no or only small gender differences in most specific kinds of intelligence (*MA/LR*: Else-Quest, Hyde, and Linn 2010; *MA/LR*: Halpern 2012; *MA/LR*: Hyde 2005). Hyde's (2005) overview of meta-analyses on gender differences reported that girls have a small to moderate advantage over boys on most verbal intelligence subtests ($-0.45 \leq d \leq -0.02$), whereas boys have a small advantage over girls on some numerical ability tests but not on others ($-0.14 \leq d \leq 0.16$).

Personality traits

Gender differences in mean expressions of personality traits are small compared with the individual variation within genders (Costa, Terracciano, and McCrae 2001; Feingold 1994). On the level of the broad Big Five factors, gender differences have been found for Neuroticism and Agreeableness with women being less emotionally stable

($d = -0.30$) and more agreeable ($d = -0.28$; *MA/LR*: Costa, Terracciano, and McCrae 2001; *MA/LR*: Feingold 1994). For all other Big Five factors, gender differences should not be interpreted on the factor level but rather on the facet level because gender differences vary depending on the facet being considered (*MA/LR*: Costa, Terracciano, and McCrae 2001, for facet level). For Extraversion, adult females score higher on warmth, gregariousness, activity and positive emotions, whereas adult males score higher on assertiveness and excitement seeking. Concerning Openness, adult women score higher on four facets (aesthetics, feelings, actions, values), whereas males show higher scores on one facet (ideas). Regarding Conscientiousness, females show more dutifulness and self-discipline, whereas males show higher scores on competence. Whereas the magnitude of gender differences in self-discipline is small according to meta-analyses ($d = -0.09$; *MA/LR*: Costa, Terracciano, and McCrae 2001; $d = -0.12$; *MA/LR*: Silverman 2003), in single studies, moderate gender differences have appeared in self-discipline in favour of girls ($d = -0.71/-0.41$; Duckworth and Seligman 2005, 2006).

Motivation

With regard to gender differences in mean levels, the ability self-concept and intrinsic or interest values need to be examined domain-specifically. Boys have a more positive ability self-concept in mathematics ($d = 0.28$) and girls in languages ($d = -0.23$; *MA/LR*: Wilgenbusch and Merrell 1999). If school-related ability self-concepts are assessed in general, boys score slightly higher than girls ($d = 0.11$; *MA/LR*: Wilgenbusch and Merrell 1999). In a similar vein, intrinsic or interest values are higher for boys in mathematics ($d = 0.15–0.69$) and higher for girls in languages ($d = -0.30$ to -0.62; e.g. Spinath, Freudenthaler, and Neubauer 2010; Steinmayr and Spinath 2008, 2010; Wigfield et al. 1997). For school in general, girls show higher intrinsic motivation ($d = -0.29$ to -0.33; e.g. Freudenthaler, Spinath, and Neubauer 2008; Steinmayr and Spinath 2010).

Regarding goals, girls achieve slightly higher scores in learning goals ($d = -0.24$ to 0.04; e.g. Freudenthaler, Spinath, and Neubauer 2008; Nie and Liem 2013; Steinmayr and Spinath 2008), whereas boys have weakly to moderately higher work-avoidance scores ($d = 0.16–0.54$; e.g. Freudenthaler, Spinath, and Neubauer 2008; Steinmayr and Spinath 2008). No consistent gender differences have been found for performance-approach ($d = -0.04$ to 0.19) and performance-avoidance goals ($d = 0.00–0.12$; e.g. Freudenthaler, Spinath, and Neubauer 2008; Steinmayr and Spinath 2008).

Summary RQ 2

The second research question focussed on whether girls and boys differ in their intelligence, personality traits and motivation. In sum, there are no gender differences in general intelligence and small to moderate differences in verbal and numerical intelligence. Concerning personality traits, small to moderate gender differences have been found for Agreeableness, Neuroticism and self-discipline. With regard to motivation, there are weak gender differences for learning goals and weak to moderate gender differences for work-avoidance goals, domain-specific intrinsic motivation and ability self-concepts.

Does the importance of these characteristics as predictors of school achievement differ between boys and girls?

Next, we looked at whether intelligence, personality or motivation showed gender differences in predicting school performance. Such differences might be observed in significantly different correlations or regression weights for boys and girls when predicting school achievement with these characteristics.

Intelligence

Neither general intelligence (e.g. Calvin et al. 2010; Fischer, Schult, and Hell 2013; Freudenthaler, Spinath, and Neubauer 2008; Steinmayr and Spinath 2008) nor domain-specific intelligence (e.g. Calvin et al. 2010; Freudenthaler, Spinath, and Neubauer 2008; Steinmayr and Spinath 2008) have been found to be differently related to school success when comparing relations for boys versus relations for girls.

Personality traits

Similarly, there have been no consistent findings that the Big Five personality traits predict school success differently for boys and girls (e.g. Freudenthaler, Spinath, and Neubauer 2008; Mellon, Schmitt, and Bylenga 1980; Steinmayr and Spinath 2008).

Motivation

By and large, motivation is, like intelligence and personality traits, not differently related to school success when comparing relations for boys with relations for girls. Meta-analyses have shown no differential prediction of boys' and girls' school achievement from the ability self-concept (*MA/LR*: Hansford and Hattie 1982; *MA/LR*: Möller et al. 2009) or from goals (*MA/LR*: Huang 2012; *MA/LR*: Hulleman et al. 2010). Some studies have found that intrinsic motivation is more important for predicting boys' compared with girls' school achievement (e.g. Freudenthaler, Spinath, and Neubauer 2008), but other studies have not been able to replicate this finding (e.g. Steinmayr and Spinath 2008).

Summary RQ 3

The third research question focussed on whether students' individual characteristics differently predict gender differences in school performance. In sum, no gender differences were found in the prediction of school achievement for intelligence, personality traits or motivation.

Can gender differences in these characteristics explain differences in boys' and girls' school achievement?

Mediation analyses were needed to answer this question. Mediation analysis can show whether the association between gender and school achievement diminishes or even vanishes completely when a certain student characteristic is controlled for. An important prerequisite for mediation is a substantial correlation between the student characteristic and school achievement. Therefore, in the following, we will report only results for characteristics that have been shown to be associated with school achievement. Although mediation is an important prerequisite for causal relations, causality cannot be established by the kind of mediation analysis used in most of the extant studies.

Intelligence

The finding that girls outperform boys on most verbal intelligence subtests and that boys outperform girls on some numerical intelligence subtests (*MA/LR*: Else-Quest, Hyde, and Linn 2010; *MA/LR*: Halpern 2012; *MA/LR*: Hyde 2005) raises the question of whether these differences account for the association between gender and school achievement. Mediation analyses have shown that girls' better verbal abilities cannot (e.g. Deary et al. 2007; Freudenthaler, Spinath, and Neubauer 2008; Steinmayr and Spinath 2008) or can only partly (about 30%; Calvin et al. 2010) explain their better school performance in languages and in general. In the same vein, boys' better numerical abilities cannot (e.g. Steinmayr and Spinath 2008; Freudenthaler, Spinath, and Neubauer 2008) or can only partly (about 50%; Calvin et al. 2010) explain their better performance in mathematics.

Personality traits

Duckworth and Seligman (2006) found that gender significantly predicted grades (GPA; Study 1: $\beta = 0.31$; Study 2: $\beta = 0.26$). When self-discipline was introduced as a mediator, the association between gender and grades was reduced to non-significance (Study 1: $\beta = 0.13$; Study 2: $\beta = 0.12$). Thus, self-discipline explained almost 50% of the magnitude of the association between gender and grades. These results held after controlling for intelligence. In a similar vein, Steinmayr and Spinath (2008) showed that Agreeableness partially mediated the association between gender and general school achievement (explaining 25% of the total effect of gender on general school achievement) as well as performance in German (as a first language) (explaining 17% of the total effect of gender on achievement in German) after controlling for intelligence.

Motivation

A study by Steinmayr and Spinath (2008) investigated different motivational constructs as mediators after controlling for intelligence. These mediating effects have to be reported on a domain-specific level, separately for performance in German and mathematics. In both ability domains, intrinsic values and ability self-concept influenced the association between gender and grades but in different ways. For performance in German, intrinsic values in German explained 48% and ability self-concept in German explained 25% of the total effect of gender on performance in German (the indirect effect of gender via motivation on school performance in relation to the total gender effect on school performance). Therefore, girls' higher performance in German could be partly explained by their higher ability self-concept and task values in German. For performance in mathematics, intrinsic values and ability self-concept in mathematics (with boys having higher scores) functioned as suppressors. In contrast with a mediator effect, a suppression effect is shown when the association between gender and school achievement is enhanced when a certain student characteristic is controlled for (cf. Tabachnick and Fidell 2007). In this regard, intrinsic values and ability self-concept enhanced the direct effect of gender on performance in mathematics (after controlling for intelligence) by 12% (intrinsic values) and 19% (ability self-concept). This means that boys' higher ability self-concept and intrinsic values in mathematics prevent them from attaining even worse grades in mathematics than girls. Furthermore, work avoidance mediated the association between gender and grades in German (explaining 19% of the total effect of gender on performance in German). On the domain-general level, work-avoidance goals were shown to partially mediate the association between gender and GPA (explaining 35% of the total effect of gender on GPA) so that girls' higher grades in German and school performance in general could be attributed in part to their lower tendency to avoid work.

Summary RQ 4

The fourth research question focussed on whether gender differences in intelligence, personality and motivation can explain differences in boys' and girls' school achievement. In sum, gender differences in students' characteristics contribute to gender differences in school performance but cannot fully explain them.

Are gender differences in these characteristics causally related to differences in boys' and girls' school achievement?

Finally, the last research question refers to whether gender differences in the aforementioned variables cause performance differences between boys and girls in school. The answer to this question remains open for all characteristics considered here. To establish causality, experimental approaches must ideally be employed. For obvious reasons, this is not possible with regard to intelligence, personality and motivation. Thus, although mediation analyses can point out some promising candidates for explaining gender differences in school achievement, it remains unknown whether these effects are actually causal or whether they might be explained by other mechanisms.

Conclusion

With this article, we aimed to provide a systematic answer to the question: To what extent can gender differences in intelligence, personality and motivation account for gender differences in school performance? It was shown that intelligence, personality and motivation are important predictors of school achievement, but they can only partially explain gender differences in school success. It can be concluded that girls are somewhat better adapted to today's school environment than boys, and this can partially explain why they often outperform boys in academic contexts. In the following, we will briefly summarise our main findings and finish with a suggestion for how to change the school environment might be altered to help boys better adapt to academic demands.

First, we looked at the roles of intelligence, personality and motivation in school achievement (Question 1). To succeed in school, students benefit most from general intelligence, followed by self-discipline, the ability self-concept, intrinsic values and low work-avoidance goals. Because these variables are important predictors of school performance, we were interested in whether boys and girls differ in these characteristics (Question 2) and whether these characteristics predict the school performance of boys and girls differently (Question 3). Taken together, girls have small (higher verbal intelligence) to medium (higher self-discipline, domain-specific ability self-concept, intrinsic motivation, lower work-avoidance goals) advantages over boys in their achievement-related characteristics. None of these characteristics predicts girls' school achievement better than it predicts boys' school achievement.

The last two questions focussed on whether gender differences in these variables can explain (Question 4) and have been found to cause gender differences in school performance (Question 5). Although boys and girls differ in their verbal and numerical abilities, these differences only partly contribute to girls' higher performance in languages and in general and boys' higher performance in mathematics, respectively. Concerning personality traits, girls outperforming boys in school in general can be partly attributed to girls' higher self-discipline and higher Agreeableness. Similarly, on a domain-specific level, the ability self-concept and intrinsic motivation seem to partly explain girls' higher performance in languages and boys' higher performance in mathematics, respectively. On a domain-general level, girls' higher grades can partly be attributed to their lower work-avoidance goals. Although gender differences in intelligence, personality and motivation contribute to gender differences in school performance, these differences cannot fully explain performance differences between boys and girls in school.

Finally, regarding research question 5, it remains unresolved whether girls outperform boys both in languages and in general because they have a higher verbal intelligence, self-discipline, ability self-concept and intrinsic values. Such causal inferences cannot be drawn on the basis of correlational studies. Thus, the present review identified a research gap with respect to the question of potentially causal mechanisms behind the mediation effects. The best way to establish causality is by means of experimental approaches. However, given the specific research topic of gender differences in individual student characteristics, experimental approaches are difficult or even impossible to employ. Future research should look for alternative methodological approaches to address the question of causality. For example, cross-lagged panel longitudinal designs provide an approach that comes close to establishing causality. Promising candidates for causal influences on gender differences in school achievement are the characteristics that were shown to mediate gender effects on school achievement in this review.

Moreover, future research should take into account the finding that intelligence, personality and motivation are not independent from one another. Investigating several constructs at a time and looking at combined effects will probably result in even larger shares of explained variance in boys' and girls' school achievement.

As a limitation concerning the presented findings, it needs to be noted that our review was not fully comprehensive. For some research questions, there were no meta-analyses because only a few studies exist. Of these single studies, we included only some representative examples. Thus, our review was not fully comprehensive concerning questions for which no meta-analyses were available. Moreover, the research summarised here stems from societies in which gender equality is largely realised.

If individual differences are a means for adapting to the environment, then a better adaptation can be achieved either by changing individual characteristics or by changing the environment. Although individual characteristics are malleable to some extent, changing the environment might be easier to realise. In the school environment as it is today, boys might 'get away with' behaviour that hampers learning, such as not doing homework, showing externalising behaviour, etc. A school environment that does not tolerate noncompliance with rules could decrease differences in boys' and girls' school achievement. Arguably, the challenge for schools is to generate an environment that grants students the freedom to grow up as responsible self-determined individuals, but at the same time helps individuals to reach desired outcomes such as good grades. Thus, by changing certain aspects of the school environment, it may be possible to reduce gender differences in school success and increase educational equality.

References

Baumert, J., U. Trautwein, and C. Artelt. 2003. "Schulumwelten – institutionelle Bedingungen des Lehrens und Lernens [School Environments – Institutional Conditions of Teaching and Learning]." In *PISA 2000: Ein differenzierter Blick auf die Länder der Bundesrepublik Deutschland* [PISA 2000: A Differentiated View on the Federal States of the German Federal Republic], edited by J. Baumert, C. Artelt, E. Klieme, M. Neubrand, M. Prenzel, U. Schiefele, W. Schneider, et al., 261–331. Opladen: Leske + Budrich.

Calvin, C. M., C. Fernandes, P. Smith, P. M. Visscher, and I. J. Deary. 2010. "Sex, Intelligence and Educational Achievement in a National Cohort of Over 175,000 11-year-old School Children in England." *Intelligence* 38: 424–432.

Chamorro-Premuzic, T., and A. Furnham. 2005. *Personality and Intellectual Competence*. Mahwah, NJ: Erlbaum.

Cianciolo, A. T., and R. J. Sternberg. 2004. *Intelligence: A Brief History*. Oxford: Blackwell Publishing.

Cohen, J. 1988. *Statistical Power Analysis for the Behavioral Sciences*. 2nd ed. Mahwah, NJ: Lawrence Erlbaum Associates.

Costa, P., A. Terracciano, and R. R. McCrae. 2001. "Gender Differences in Personality Traits Across Cultures: Robust and Surprising Findings." *Journal of Personality and Social Psychology* 81: 322–331.

Deary, I. J., S. Strand, P. Smith, and C. Fernandes. 2007. "Intelligence and Educational Achievement." *Intelligence* 35: 13–21.

De Raad, B., and H. C. Schouwenburg. 1996. "Personality in Learning and Education: A Review." *European Journal of Personality* 10: 303–336.

Digman, J. M. 1990. "Personality Structure: Emergence of the Five-factor Model." *Annual Review of Psychology* 41: 417–440.

Duckworth, A. L., and M. E. P. Seligman. 2005. "Self-discipline Outdoes IQ in Predicting Academic Performance of Adolescents." *Psychological Science* 16: 939–944.

Duckworth, A. L., and M. E. P. Seligman. 2006. "Self-discipline Gives Girls the Edge: Gender in Self-discipline, Grades, and Achievement Test Scores." *Journal of Educational Psychology* 98: 198–208.

Dupeyrat, C., and C. Mariné. 2005. "Implicit Theories of Intelligence, Goal Orientations, Cognitive Engagement, and Achievement: A Test of Dwecks' Model with Returning to School Adults." *Contemporary Educational Psychology* 30: 43–59.

Dweck, C. S. 1986. "Motivational Processes Affecting Learning." *American Psychologist* 41: 1040–1048.

Eccles, J., T. F. Adler, R. Futterman, S. B. Goff, C. M. Kaczala, J. L. Meece, and C. Midgley. 1983. "Expectancies, Values, and Academic Behaviors." In *Achievement and Achievement Motives*, edited by J. T. Spence, 75–146. San Francisco, CA: Freeman.

Elliot, A. J. 1999. "Approach and Avoidance Motivation and Achievement Goals." *Educational Psychologist* 34: 169–189.

Else-Quest, N. M., J. S. Hyde, and M. C. Linn. 2010. "Cross-national Patterns of Gender Differences in Mathematics: A Meta-analysis." *Psychological Bulletin* 136: 103–127.

Epstein, D., J. Elwood, V. Jey, and J. Maw. 1998. *Failing Boys? Issues in Gender and Achievement*. Buckingham: Open University Press.

Eysenck, M. W., N. Derakshan, R. Santos, and M. G. Calvo. 2007. "Anxiety and Cognitive Performance: Attentional Control Theory." *Emotion* 7: 336–353.

Feingold, A. 1994. "Gender Differences in Personality: A Meta-analysis." *Psychological Bulletin* 116: 429–456.

Fischer, F., J. Schult, and B. Hell. 2013. "Sex Differences in Secondary School Success: Why Female Students Perform Better." *European Journal of Psychology of Education* 28: 529–543.

Freudenthaler, H., B. Spinath, and A. Neubauer. 2008. "Predicting School Achievement in Boys and Girls." *European Journal of Personality* 22: 231–245.

Goldberg, L. R. 1990. "An Alternative 'description of personality': The Big-five Factor Structure." *Journal of Personality and Social Psychology* 59: 1216–1229.

Gottfried, A. E. 1985. "Academic Intrinsic Motivation in Elementary and Junior High School Students." *Journal of Educational Psychology* 77: 631–645.

Gottfried, A. E. 1990. "Academic Intrinsic Motivation in Young Elementary School Children." *Journal of Educational Psychology* 82: 525–538.

Gustafsson, J.-E., and J. O. Undheim. 1996. "Individual Differences in Cognitive Functions." In *Handbook of Educational Psychology*, edited by D. C. Berliner and R. C. Calfee, 186–242. New York: Prentice Hall International.

Halpern, D. F. 2012. *Sex Differences in Cognitive Abilities*. 4th ed. New York: Psychology Press.

Hansford, B. C., and J. A. Hattie. 1982. "The Relationship Between Self and Achievement/Performance Measures." *Review of Educational Research* 52: 123–142.

Huang, C. 2012. "Discriminant and Criterion-related Validity of Achievement Goals in Predicting Academic Achievement: A Meta-analysis." *Journal of Educational Psychology* 104: 48–73.

Hulleman, C. S., S. M. Schrager, S. M. Bodmann, and J. M. Harackiewicz. 2010. "A Meta-analytic Review of Achievement Goal Measures: Different Labels for the Same Constructs or Different Constructs with Similar Labels?" *Psychological Bulletin* 136: 422–449.

Hyde, J. S. 2005. "The Gender Similarity Hypothesis." *American Psychologist* 60: 581–592.

Johnson, W., A. Carothers, and I. J. Deary. 2008. "Sex Differences in Variability in General Intelligence: A New Look at the Old Question." *Perspectives on Psychological Science* 3: 518–531.

McCrae, R. R., and P. T. Costa. 1987. "Validation of the Five-factor Model of Personality Across Instruments and Observers." *Journal of Personality and Social Psychology* 52: 81–90.

Mellon, P. M., N. Schmitt, and C. Bylenga. 1980. "Differential Predictability of Females and Males." *Sex Roles* 6: 173–177.

Möller, J., B. Pohlmann, O. Köller, and H. W. Marsh. 2009. "A Meta-analytic Path Analysis of the Internal/External Frame of Reference Model of Academic Achievement and Academic Self-concept." *Review of Educational Research* 79: 1129–1167.

Murphy, P. K., and P. A. Alexander. 2000. "A Motivated Exploration of Motivation Terminology." *Contemporary Educational Psychology* 25: 3–53.

Neisser, U., G. Boodoo, T. J. Bouchard, A. W. Boykin, N. Brody, S. J. Ceci, D. F. Halpern, et al. 1996. "Intelligence: Knowns and Unknowns." *American Psychologist* 51: 77–101.

Nicholls, J. G. 1984. "Achievement Motivation: Conceptions of Ability, Subjective Experience, Task Choice, and Performance." *Psychological Review* 91: 328–346.

Nie, Y., and G. A. D. Liem. 2013. "Extending Antecedents of Achievement Goals: The Double-edged Sword Effect of Social-oriented Achievement Motive and Gender Differences." *Learning and Individual Differences* 23: 249–255.

Poropat, A. E. 2009. "A Meta-analysis of the Five-factor Model of Personality and Academic Performance." *Psychological Bulletin* 135: 322–338.

Scottish Office. 1998. *Raising Standards – Setting Targets: Gender Issues in Raising Attainment*. Edinburgh: HMSO.

Schiefele, U., A. Krapp, and A. Winteler. 1992. "Interest as a Predictor of Academic Achievement: A Meta-analysis of Research." In *The Role of Interest in Learning and Development*, edited by K. A. Renninger, S. Hidi, and A. Krapp, 183–212. Hillsdale, NJ: Lawrence Erlbaum Associates.

Silverman, I. W. 2003. "Gender Differences in Delay of Gratification: A Meta-analysis." *Sex Roles* 49: 451–463.

Spinath, B., H. Freudenthaler, and A. Neubauer. 2010. "Predicting Domain-specific School Achievement in Boys and Girls by Intelligence, Personality and Motivation." *Personality and Individual Differences* 48: 481–486.

Steinmayr, R., and B. Spinath. 2007. "Predicting School Achievement from Motivation and Personality." *Zeitschrift für Pädagogische Psychologie* [German Journal of Educational Psychology] 21: 207–216.

Steinmayr, R., and B. Spinath. 2008. Sex Differences in School Achievement: What are the Roles of Personality and Achievement Motivation? *European Journal of Personality* 22: 185–209.

Steinmayr, R., and B. Spinath. 2009. "The Importance of Motivation as a Predictor of School Achievement." *Learning and Individual Differences* 19: 80–90.

Steinmayr, R., and B. Spinath. 2010. "Konstruktion und erste Validierung einer Skala zur Erfassung subjektiver schulischer Werte (SESSW) [Construction and First Validation of a Scale for Assessing Subjective School-related Values]." *Diagnostica* 56: 195–211.

Strand, S., I. J. Deary, and P. Smith. 2006. "Sex Differences in Cognitive Ability Test Scores: A UK National Picture." *British Journal of Educational Psychology* 76: 463–480.

Tabachnick, B. G., and L. S. Fidell. 2007. *Using Multivariate Statistics*. 5th ed. Boston, MA: Pearson.

Trautwein, U., O. Lüdtke, H. W. Marsh, O. Köller, and J. Baumert. 2006. "Tracking, Grading, and Student Motivation: Using Group Composition and Status to Predict Self-concept and Interest in Ninth-grade Mathematics." *Journal of Educational Psychology* 98: 788–806.

Wigfield, A., and J. S. Eccles. 2000. "Expectancy-value Theory of Achievement Motivation." *Contemporary Educational Psychology* 25: 68–81.

Wigfield, A., J. S. Eccles, K. S. Yoon, R. D. Harold, A. J. A. Arbreton, C. Freedman-Doan, and P. Blumenfeld. 1997. "Change in Children's Competence Beliefs and Subjective Task Values Across the Elementary School Years: A 3-year Study." *Journal of Educational Psychology* 89: 451–469.

Wilgenbusch, T., and K. W. Merrell. 1999. "Gender Differences in Self-concept Among Children and Adolescents: A Meta-analysis of Multidimensional Studies." *School Psychology Quarterly* 14: 1001–1120.

Wong, K.-C., Y. R. Lam, and L.-M. Ho. 2002. "The Effects of Schooling on Gender Differences." *British Educational Research Journal* 28: 827–843.

Zeidner, M., ed. 1995. *Personality Trait Correlates of Intelligence*. New York: Plenum Press.

Teacher evaluation of student ability: what roles do teacher gender, student gender, and their interaction play?

Katarina Krkovic[a], Samuel Greiff[a], Sirkku Kupiainen[b], Mari-Pauliina Vainikainen[b] and Jarkko Hautamäki[b]

[a]Research Group Computer-Based Assessment, EMACS, University of Luxembourg, Luxembourg; [b]Centre for Educational Assessment, Department of Teacher Education, University of Helsinki, Finland

Background: Recent decades have been marked by an extensive movement to analyze bias in people's thinking, especially in gender-related issues. Studies have addressed the question of gender bias in classrooms on different levels—the use of gender in books, learning opportunities determined by students' gender, or teachers' gender preferences.

Purpose: In this study, we aim to answer the question of whether and under which circumstances the interaction between teacher gender and student gender positively or negatively influences teachers' evaluations of students' performance, while controlling for objective measures of students' performance. For instance, it could be possible that a teacher with the same gender as a student evaluates the student as better than opposite-gender students, independent of their objective performance.

Sample: The sample consisted of n > 1,500 Finnish 6th grade students (*M*age= 12.67) and their respective class teachers.

Design and methods: Students completed several academic skills tests, including a mathematical thinking test, reading comprehension test, and scientific reasoning test. Furthermore, teachers provided their evaluation of each student, evaluating students' performance in different school subjects and answering questions regarding their probability of academic success. To test whether the teacher-student gender interaction had an effect on the criterion variable, i.e. teachers' evaluation of the students' performance, multilevel analyses accounting for between- and within-class effects were applied. Thereby, the effect of students' objective performance on teachers' evaluation of the students and main effects of gender were controlled for as covariates.

Results: The main results indicated that the interaction between student and teacher gender did not influence teachers' evaluation of the students. However, regardless of their gender, teachers tended to evaluate girls as better than boys in first language performance (i.e. Finnish language) and potential for success in school. Teacher gender did not influence the evaluation.

Conclusions: The results of the study suggest that the interaction between teacher and student gender is unlikely to be a source of possible bias in the evaluations of students in the Finnish educational system.

Introduction

The impact of belonging to a specific social group on the course of an individual's life has been a popular research topic for scholars across the globe for over a century. In many societies, gender is a topic of major political, social, and personal importance. Over the course of the development of society, there have always been gender stereotypes – gender-typical occupations, rituals, leisure activities, and even colors and clothes. Since the middle of the 20th century, the role of gender in society has been changing, and gender equity in education and the labor market has increasingly been perceived as a relevant topic. However, many cultures still confront gender-stereotypical ways of raising children with gender-specific toys, sports, and gender-specific behavior models. This renders it difficult for teachers and educational policy makers to structure a gender-fair educational system that provides equal learning opportunities for both genders (OECD 2007; Sadker, Sadker, and Zittleman 2009).

To this end, the aim of this study is to improve the understanding of gender effects in classrooms, by focusing on effects of the teacher-student gender interaction (i.e., same-gender interaction versus opposite-gender interaction) on teachers' subjective evaluations of students in several academic areas.

The research of gender differences in abilities and performance has a long tradition, and the findings are mostly in the same direction – males and females perform differently in some areas. Some of the most investigated differences are those in reading competencies, where, typically, females outperform males, and in mathematics, where, typically, males outperform females. The report of one of the most recognized international large-scale surveys, PISA (Programme for International Student Assessment), shows that these performance differences are significant in the half of participating jurisdictions for mathematics, and for reading, where girls outperformed boys in majority of countries in previous PISA cycles, the gender gap increased even more in the last cycle (OECD 2010; 2013).

Regarding the development of such performance differences, Dee (2006) reports in a large-scale longitudinal study from the United States of America that when children enter kindergarten, they do not show performance differences in mathematical and reading skills. However, already at the end of the 3rd grade, boys outperform girls in mathematics, and girls outperform boys in reading. By puberty, these gender performance gaps have doubled (Dee 2006). This raises the question of whether gender gaps in performance are the result of cognitive development only or whether they develop in part from peoples' different perception and treatment of male and female students. That is, do teachers, parents, and society encourage boys to be interested in the natural sciences and girls to be interested in the social sciences, leading to actual performance differences (cf. Jones and Wheatley 1990)? To answer this question, various studies have investigated gender effects in education. Mostly, such studies have focused on the main effects of student gender and teacher gender and have neglected the teacher-student gender interaction (cf. Jones and Dindia 2004).

The literature on the main effect of student gender has mostly revealed that even though there is some development toward gender equity, teachers still treat boys and girls differently (Zaher 1996). For instance, in their meta-analysis on 32 empirical studies on gender differences, Jones and Dindia (2004) found that male students have more interaction opportunities with their teachers and are more frequently called on and responded to in the classroom than females. Sadker and Zittleman (2005) also state that although teachers want to treat all students equally, boys and girls often receive different treatment. For instance, Spilt, Koomen, and Jak (2012) state that teachers of both genders report more conflictual relationships with boys than with girls. Hopf and Hatzichristou (1992) showed in a sample of Greek students that boys are generally evaluated as having lower performance in language than girls. In line with this, Siegle and Reis (1998) also showed that teachers evaluate female students higher than males in language, whereby they did not find gender bias in other subjects. Similarly, Bennett and Bennett (1990) reported that teachers evaluate girls as better in content areas and boys as more skilful in traditional male areas such as metalworking or woodworking.

Further possible main effects of gender are effects of the teacher's gender. Still, few studies have examined the effects of teacher gender in classrooms (cf. Hopf and Hatzichristou 1999). Hopf and Hatzichristou (1999) found female teachers to evaluate students' behavior more positively than male teachers. In line with this, Split, Koomen, and Jak (2012) also found female teachers to report better relationships with students than male teachers. Hopf and Hatzichristou (1999) further found effects of teacher gender on evaluations of students in history and language, whereby students of female teachers were given better grades.

Teachers' subjective evaluations seem to significantly influence students' development, making 'self-fulfilling prophecies' an important research subject in other words, if and how the expectations of teachers (i.e., the discrepancy between subjective evaluations of students by teachers and students' actual measured performance) influence students' actual academic success. Madon, Jussim, and Eccles (1997) showed that teachers' over- and underestimations of students' abilities are related to students' future performance. In their meta-study, Jussim and Harber (2005) suggested that teachers' expectations may predict students' academic outcomes because the teachers are good at estimating students' future success rather than because the expectations are self-fulfilling. As teachers' expectations seem to be significantly related to students' academic outcomes, it is essential to investigate whether these expectations are prone to gender effects of any kind. However, to understand possible biases in teachers' subjective evaluations, apart from an effect of student gender and an effect of teacher gender, the teacher-student gender interaction needs to be taken into account. Previous studies on student-teacher gender interaction effects have offered very heterogeneous results and have differed in their interpretations. Whereas Winters et al. (2013) and Neugebauer, Helbig, and Landmann (2010) showed that having a teacher of the same gender does not affect students' achievement, Dee (2006) reported strong evidence that girls' performance is generally benefitted from being taught by female teachers and boys by male teachers. Moreover, he concluded that girls find classes and their content less attractive and useful when taught by male teachers. Furthermore, female teachers have more often found boys to be disruptive in classes than male teachers. Parker-Price and Claxton (1996) found other differences in evaluations depending on teacher gender and student gender, as male teachers evaluated boys as better visual learners and girls as more helpful in the classroom. Dee (2007) further reported that the teacher-student gender interaction affects teachers' perceptions of students' performance, as teachers preferred students of the same gender. Moreover, Shepardson and Pizzini (1992) showed gender effects on student evaluations, suggesting that female teachers evaluate girls and boys differently on their scientific skills.

Thus, previous research on gender interaction effects offers ambiguous conclusions about whether or not the teacher-student gender interaction has an effect in classrooms. Apart from the questions of whether and how the interaction of student and teacher gender affects student achievement, there is also the question of whether and how this gender interaction affects teachers' subjective evaluations of students. Dee's study (2006; 2007) is one of the few that have investigated the impact of the gender interaction on the subjective evaluation of teachers and not only students' actual performance.

Nevertheless, when investigating teachers' subjective evaluation, it is important to control, as far as possible, for the students' objective[1] performance in order to draw conclusions about whether differences in subjective evaluations of girls and boys by their male and female teachers involve a gender effect and whether this effect persists after controlling for objective performance. For this reason, in the present study, we examined the influence of the teacher-student gender interaction on teachers' subjective evaluations of students in two different school subjects and in evaluations of the potential for school success, whereby we controlled for students' objective performance in the respective academic skills.

Based on gender schema theory (Bem 1981; see also gender typing, Turner, Gervai, and Hinde 1993), the notion that that students relate better to teachers of the same gender further suggests positive effects of a same-gender student-teacher interaction such that, because of the lack of male teachers in educational systems, boys are disadvantaged (for an overview, see Cushman 2007). Hitherto, the research findings on whether same-gender and opposite-gender interactions relate differently to teachers' evaluations of the students have offered ambiguous findings. Whereas some empirical findings (e.g., Neugebauer, Helbig, and Landmann 2010; Spilt, Koonen, and Jak 2012; Holmlund and Sund 2006) have disputed differences between same-gender and opposite-gender interactions, others have found them to be a determining factor for students' achievement (e.g., Dee 2006; 2007; Nixon and Robinson 1999; Robst, Keil, and Russo 1998). For this reason, we addressed this research question once again and examined whether or not there are teacher evaluation differences between same-gender interaction groups (i.e., female teacher and female student, and male teacher and male student) and opposite-gender interaction groups (i.e., female teacher and male student, and male teacher and female student).

Research questions

Since the issue of same-gender versus opposite-gender interactions remains inconclusive in the literature, the main research question in this study was whether there would be differences in teachers' subjective evaluations of the students between these two teacher-student gender interactions (i.e., same-gender interaction and opposite-gender interaction) beyond 'objective' measured performance in academic skills relevant to the academic area in question and beyond the main effects of students' and teachers' gender. In the present study, we focused on teachers' subjective evaluations in two important school subjects that have been shown to be prone to gender differences in the literature (i.e., mathematics and first language) and also teachers' expectations of students' general school success.

Specifically, we examined the influence of teacher-student gender interactions on teachers' subjective evaluations after controlling for:

- students' objective performance in the respective academic skill (i.e., mathematical thinking for mathematics; reading comprehension for first language; mathematical thinking, reading comprehension, and scientific reasoning for the potential for general school success);

- the main effect of student gender (e.g., female students may be generally evaluated as better);
- the main effect of teacher gender (e.g., male teachers may give higher evaluations overall).

Hypothesis 1

Teachers' subjective evaluations of students' performance in mathematics will differ across the two teacher-student gender interaction patterns (i.e., same-gender interaction and opposite-gender interaction) beyond objective performance in mathematical thinking and beyond the main effects of student and teacher gender.

Hypothesis 2

Teachers' subjective evaluations of students' performance in first language will differ across the two teacher-student gender interaction patterns (i.e., same-gender interaction and opposite-gender interaction) beyond objective performance in reading comprehension and beyond gender main effects.

Hypothesis 3

Teachers' subjective evaluations of students' potential for school success will differ across the two teacher-student gender interaction patterns (i.e., same-gender interaction and opposite-gender interaction) beyond objective performance in mathematical thinking, reading comprehension, and scientific reasoning, and beyond gender main effects.

Method

Participants

In this study, 6th graders in a large urban municipality in Southern Finland were selected to participate. The sample consisted of 2,113 students in 118 classes in 37 schools in Finland. Due to the exclusion criteria, the final number of assessed 6th graders was 1,979. Five students did not report their gender and were therefore eliminated from the study, leaving a total of 986 girls and 988 boys, clustered into 102 classes. The average age of the students was $M = 12.67$ years with a standard deviation of $SD = 0.43$. Majority of students had Finnish as their first language. Additionally, 188 class teachers took part in the survey.

Procedure and instruments

Teachers' evaluations of students, which served as the criterion in this study, were obtained from a questionnaire administered to teachers. Teachers were asked to evaluate each student's performance in the school subjects mathematics and first language and to evaluate students' potential for success in school. For each student, clustered into 102 classes, the same teacher made the evaluation in all three areas. The evaluation was made on a seven point likert scale, which included questions about students' behaviour, studying, and personality. The evaluation of the performance and potential were obtained by single explicit questions on each subject separately (1) "How would you grade the student's performance in mathematics?" for Hypothesis 1; (2) "How would you grade the student's performance in first language?" for Hypothesis 2; and (3) "How well do you believe the student will do at the end of the school year?" for Hypothesis 3.

Participants completed three different academic skills tests: a mathematical thinking test, reading comprehension test, and scientific reasoning test. The data obtained from these tests were used to control for objective performance in different academic areas before examining the teacher-student gender interaction.

For Hypothesis 1, mathematical thinking skills were assessed with a test containing two subtasks measuring mathematical thinking in arithmetic. The mathematical thinking test was administered to assess students' objective performance in mathematical thinking, which was a hypothesized covariate in Hypothesis 1. The first subtask was a modified group-version of Sternberg's Triarchic Test (H-version) Creative Number Scale (Sternberg et al. 2001). In this subtask, an invented arithmetical operator (e.g. x 'lag' y) is conditionally defined depending on the values of the digits the operator combines (e.g., if x < y, then the arithmetical operator stands for addition, otherwise for subtraction). The subtask consisted of eight items with four multiple-choice alternatives (e.g. What is 4 lag 7? a) -3, b) 3, c) 11, d) -11) for correct solutions coded 0 or 1. The second subtask on the mathematical thinking test was based on the quantitative-relational arithmetic operators task by Demetriou et al. (1991) and Demetriou et al. (1996). The subtask comprised eight problems with one to four unknown operators (e.g., (5 a 3) b 4 = 6). In this subtask, the operators marked by letters (e.g., a / b) stood for addition, subtraction, division, or multiplication. The student had to decide which operators needed to be inserted in order to achieve the predefined result (e.g., in (5 a 3) b 4 = 6, the correct solution is "-" for a and "+" for b). As all 16 items across the two subtasks were coded 0 or 1, a sum score ranging from 0 to 16 was calculated as the total test score.

For Hypothesis 2, reading comprehension was assessed to provide an objective indicator of students' skills in their first language. It was assessed by a reading comprehension test composed of two subtasks. The first subtask was a macro-processing task, construed within Kintsch and van Dijk's (1978) theoretical framework and calibrated on an adult's interpretation of the text (cf. Lehto et al. 2001; Lyytinen and Lehto 1998). Students were asked to read a one-page text and assess 16 statements based on the text as to whether they (a) provide a good description of the text as a whole, (b) present important information regarding the content of the text, or (c) refer to only minor details in the text. The other reading comprehension subtask was a shorter text set in a context closer to everyday life, adapted from a Finnish Vocational Guidance Office test. It assessed students' ability to understand, analyze, and interpret written information with four multiple-response items (Lyytinen and Lehto 1998). For both subtasks, each item was scored 0 or 1, and the overall score was calculated as a sum score ranging from 0 to 20 across the two subtasks.

In addition to mathematical thinking and reading comprehension, which served as covariates in Hypothesis 3 as well, we further tested for scientific reasoning skills to serve as the third covariate for cognitive competence. The scientific reasoning test consisted of one task. The task was a "control of variables" task, which is a modified version (Hautamäki 1984; Hautamäki et al. 2002) of the Scientific Reasoning Task "Pendulum" by Shayer (1979), based on one of the formal schemata identified by Inhelder and Piaget (1958). Each item consisted of four input variables (e.g. driver, car, tyres, and track) with two different manifestations (e.g. for track – Monaco, or

Hockenheim) and one additional outcome variable (e.g. time per lap to be measured). The goal was to compare the influence of manifestations of the input variable on the outcome variable. There were four items consisting of three or four Yes/No questions regarding whether it is possible to draw a conclusion about the effects of a single-variable manifestation from the given state and two comparison sets with different variable manifestations to be complemented. The items were coded 0 or 1. The test result was calculated as a sum score ranging from 0 to 6.

The student assessment as a whole consisted of a test battery on academic skills (as described above) and a self-report questionnaire lasting approximately 90 minutes. The test battery comprised the academic skills tests for reading comprehension, mathematical thinking, and scientific reasoning. Additionally, students completed a self-report questionnaire, which was not the subject of this study and will not be discussed in this paper.

In addition, teachers completed a questionnaire for each student, and the information obtained from it served as the criterion for teachers' evaluations of the students.

Statistical analyses

To test our hypotheses, we calculated multilevel regression analyses, which allows for analysing data that is nested, for instance into school classes, institutions, or geographical areas. This was done in order to adjust for possible effects of the school classes that students belonged to. In school survey analyses, this is a common approach because it is quite imaginable that the teachers who are rating the students will have different frames of reference. For instance, in classes in which the general level of mathematical skills is rather high, students will not be evaluated in comparison to the average of other classes but in comparison to the generally high average in their class. For this reason, we calculated our regression models on two levels – a student level (i.e., Level 1) and a class level (i.e., Level 2). Prior to testing our hypotheses, we followed the recommended procedure in multilevel modelling and first examined item-level intraclass correlations (ICCs), which are estimates of the amount of variance that can be attributed to the between-students' level (i.e., class level) (cf. Dyer, Hanges, and Hall 2005). Intraclass correlations indicate the amount of variance that is found on the class level (i.e., between-level variance). ICCs were .10 for evaluation in mathematics, .13 for evaluation in first language, and .18 for success prediction, indicating that the majority of the variance was found at the individual student level (i.e., within-students' level variance) and not at the class level (i.e., between-level variance). However, there was also sufficient variance across levels to warrant the application of multilevel methods (cf. Tabachnick and Fidell 2007). Thus, in all subsequently reported analyses, we used the standard procedure of random intercept multilevel models to account for the clustered structure of the data.

For each of the three multilevel procedures, the assumed predictors on the student level were students' performance on the achievement test of the respective domains (i.e., mathematical thinking for mathematics; reading comprehension for first language; mathematical thinking, reading comprehension, and scientific reasoning for school success potential) and students' gender. The predictor on the second level of class was teachers' gender in all three analyses. The predictor of main interest in this study – the student-teacher gender interaction – was classified as a cross-level interaction because it is the result of the student characteristics on the first and teacher characteristics on the second level at the same time.

Results

Descriptive Statistics

Descriptive statistics for all criteria and predictors are presented in Table 1 for all four combinations of gender interaction and on the overall level. On all three academic skills tests, there were students with very high scores and students with very low scores. The mean scores across the four combinations were similar for all gender combinations on all three tests. In all three areas of interest, teachers tended to evaluate students rather highly (cf. Table 1).

The academic skills tests employed in this study showed acceptable internal consistencies (cf. Kline 1999), with Cronbach's alphas of .72 for mathematical thinking (16 items), .63 for reading comprehension (20 items), which is on the border of acceptable internal consistency, and .69 for scientific reasoning (six items).

Table 1.   Descriptive statistics. Number, mean, standard deviation, minimum and maximum for all variables in four gender interaction combinations and on the overall level.

	Math. Eval.	First l. Eval.	Succ. Eval.	Math. Think.	Read. Comp.	Sc. Reas.
Combination 1 (female teacher – female student)						
N	719	715	720	727	739	737
Mean	4.80	5.26	5.92	5.99	8.67	2.14
Sd	1.22	1.03	1.24	2.75	3.29	1.60
Min	1	2	1	0	2	0
Max	7	7	7	14	18	6
Combination 2 (male teacher – female student)						
N	194	192	184	202	208	207
Mean	4.88	5.35	5.80	6.29	8.19	2.33
Sd	1.19	1.03	1.34	2.63	3.26	1.54
Min	2	2	2	0	2	0
Max	7	7	7	15	19	5
Combination 3 (female teacher – male student)						
N	742	735	742	730	746	759
Mean	4.84	4.65	5.53	5.85	8.33	2.12
Sd	1.24	1.08	1.43	2.92	3.30	1.64
Min	1	2	1	0	1	0
Max	7	7	7	15	19	6
Combination 4 (male teacher – male student)						
N	185	183	176	180	188	194
Mean	4.67	4.60	5.31	5.31	7.69	1.64
Sd	1.35	1.18	1.68	2.54	3.07	1.60
Min	1	1	1	0	3	0
Max	7	7	7	14	17	5
Overall						
N	1852	1836	1834	1848	1890	1907
Mean	4.81	4.96	5.70	5.90	8.38	2.11
Sd	1.24	1.11	1.40	2.79	3.28	1.61
Min	1	1	1	0	1	0
Max	7	7	7	15	19	6

Note: Math. Eval.= Evaluation in mathematics; First l. Eval.= Evaluation in first language; Succ. Eval.= Evaluation of success chances; Math. Think.= Mathematical thinking skills test; Read. Comp.= Reading comprehension skills test; Sc. Reas.= Scientific reasoning skills test.

Hypotheses 1 to 3

For Hypothesis 1, the results of the multilevel analysis indicated that 29% of the variance in teachers' evaluations was predicted by our model on the student level (R^2 = .288, SE = .019, p< .001). Thereby, only mathematical thinking skills entered on the within-students' level significantly predicted teachers' evaluations (β = −.537, SE = .018, p< .001), whereas student gender did not have a significant influence on the evaluation (β = −.013, SE = .026, n.s.). Thus, as expected, students' mathematical thinking skills significantly influenced teachers' evaluations. Teachers' gender, which was a predictor variable on the class level did not significantly predict teachers' evaluations (β = −.029, SE = .120, n.s.). Finally, the hypothesized predictor variable, the teacher-student gender interaction, was entered into the equation as a cross-level interaction. The analysis showed that the gender interaction did not influence teachers' evaluations of the students in mathematics (β = .016, SE = .026, n.s.). See Table 2 for model estimation details.

Table 2. Summary of multilevel random intercept estimates for variables predicting teachers' evaluations of students' performance in mathematics.

	β	R^2
Level 1		0.288(0.019)***
Mathematical thinking	0.537(0.018)***	
Student gender	−0.013(0.026)	
Cross-interaction		
Gender interaction	0.016(0.026)	
Level 2		0.001
Teacher gender	−0.029(0.120)	

Note: Parameter estimate standard errors listed in parentheses. ***p< .001.

As we did for Hypothesis 1, we conducted a multilevel analysis with a random intercept to address Hypothesis 2. The results indicated that reading comprehension and student gender on Level 1 together explained 20% of the variance in teachers' evaluations (R^2 = .203, SE = .018, p< .001). Thereby, both student gender and reading comprehension were significant predictors (gender: β = .315, SE = .027, p< .001; reading comprehension: β = .329, SE = .021, p< .001).

Adding teachers' gender as a Level-2 predictor did not improve the prediction of teachers' evaluations (β = −.08, SE = .116, n.s.). To summarize, students' reading comprehension skills influenced teachers' evaluations. Moreover, teachers of both genders tended to evaluate female students' performance in first language higher than male students' performance.

Adding the hypothesized predictor variable as a cross-level interaction, the teacher-student gender interaction did not influence teachers' evaluation of the students in first language (β = .36, SE = .028, n.s.). See Table 3 for model estimation details.

Finally, the results of the third multilevel analysis indicated that hypothesized predictors on the student level – students' mathematical thinking, reading comprehension, and scientific reasoning skills – as objective predictors of overall school success, as well as students' gender explained 24% of the variance in teachers' evaluations (R^2 = .203, SE = .018, p< .001). Thereby, objective predictors of overall school success, mathematical thinking

Table 3. Summary of multilevel random intercept estimates for variables predicting teachers' evaluations of students' performance in first language.

	β	R^2
Level 1		0.203(0.018)***
Reading comprehension	0.329(0.021)***	
Student gender	0.315(0.027)***	
Cross-interaction		
Gender interaction	0.036(0.028)	
Level 2		0.006(0.019)
Teacher gender	−0.080(0.116)	

Note: Parameter estimate standard errors listed in parentheses. ***$p <$ .001.

(β = .273, SE = .025, $p <$ .001), reading comprehension (β = .079, SE = .024, $p <$ .05), and scientific reasoning (β = .220, SE = .025, $p <$ .001) significantly influenced the prediction of teachers' evaluations. Moreover, students' gender also significantly predicted teachers' evaluations (β = .136, SE = .029, $p <$ .001). Teachers of both genders tended to evaluate female students' potential for school success higher than male students'. However, teachers' gender did not influence teachers' evaluations (β = .036, SE = .113, n.s.).

Finally, the teacher-student gender interaction was entered as a cross-level interaction. The teacher-student gender interaction did not influence teachers' evaluation of students' school success potential (β = −.012, SE = .029, n.s.). See Table 4 for model estimation details.

In brief, students' objective (measured) performance significantly influenced teachers' evaluations in all three analyses. Moreover, in first language and in the school success evaluation, teachers evaluated girls as better than boys after objective performance was controlled. The subjective evaluations in mathematics did not show any gender effects. Teachers' gender did not influence teachers' evaluations.

Finally, regarding the hypothesized predictor in this study, our analyses showed that the teacher-student gender interaction did not influence teachers' evaluations of the students in any of the three tested areas.

Table 4. Summary of multilevel random intercept estimates for variables predicting teachers' evaluations of students' chances of success in comprehensive school.

	β	R^2
Level 1		0.24(0.020)***
Mathematical thinking	0.273(0.025)***	
Scientific reasoning	0.220(0.025)***	
Reading comprehension	0.079(0.024)**	
Student gender	0.136(0.029)***	
Cross-interaction		
Gender interaction	−0.012(0.029)	
Level 2		0.001(0.008)
Teacher gender	0.036(0.113)	

Note: Parameter estimate standard errors listed in parentheses.
***$p <$ .001; **$p <$ .005.

Discussion

The main goal of this study was to enhance the understanding of the effect of the tea-cher-student gender interaction on teachers' evaluations, as this appears to be a neglected topic in gender research. In particular, a number of studies have investigated gender differences in classrooms, mostly finding that teachers treat male and female students differently (cf. Jones and Wheatley 1990; Jones and Dindia 2004; Sadker, Sadker, and Zittleman 2009). However, few studies have examined teacher gender effects, and even fewer studies have investigated the teacher-student gender interaction. To this end, this study focused on effects of the teacher-student gender interaction on teachers' evaluations in a large sample of Finnish 6th grade students.

Effects of the teacher-student gender interaction on teachers' evaluations were examined in mathematics, first language, and school success potential. The results of the present study suggest that neither the opposite nor the same teacher-student gender interaction influenced teachers' evaluations. Hence, male teachers do not evaluate boys as better or worse than girls, and female teachers do not evaluate girls as better or worse than boys. The relatively large sample size should have facilitated detection of even very small interaction effects. However, in contrast to the gender interaction effects found by Dee (2006; 2007) in an American student sample (e.g., teachers evaluate students of the same gender higher than students of the opposite gender), and in line with Neugebauer, Helbig, and Landmann (2010), we did not find that the teacher-student gender interaction influenced teachers' evaluations.

The reason for the discrepancy between the results of this study and Dee's (2006, 2007) may be due to the fact that we directly controlled for the objective (measured) performance of students. Hence, it may be possible that in studies that found a gender interaction effect, differences in evaluation were partly the result of objective differences in the measured performance of students and not due only to the teacher-student gender interaction (e.g., male teachers did not evaluate boys as better than girls because they were of the same gender but because boys actually performed better than girls and the other way around). Another explanation of diverging results may be found in the school system in Finland. The Finnish school system is known for its quality so that one explanation may be that Finnish teachers are more aware of gender-effects and are taught how to try to evaluate performance as objectively as possible (cf. Sahlberg 2011). However, the main effects of gender found in the current study show that Finnish teachers are not entirely resistant to gender stereotyping. For instance, we found that in first language and school success potential, teachers of both genders evaluated girls as better than boys, whereby they overestimated their actual performance. This finding is in line with previous research on gender main effects, where various studies have shown that teachers of either gender treat and evaluate boys and girls differently (cf. Jones and Wheatley 1990; Jones and Dindia 2004). One possible explanation for this finding is that girls tend to have more positive attitudes toward school and put more effort into their schoolwork, and teachers not only evaluate students' competence, but also reward effort and positive attitudes toward the school subject in question (FNBE 2004; cf. Kupiainen et al. 2011). Moreover, if we consider that girls tend to be perceived as less disruptive than boys (cf. Spilt, Koonen, and Jak 2012), this could also result in teachers overestimating girls' performance.

Study limitations

As a word of caution when interpreting the results of this study, we must consider that the operationalization of objective (measured) performance did not include all relevant academic skills – i.e. the domain assessed by the tests was not exactly the same as the domain evaluated by the teachers. For instance, in Hypothesis 2, only reading comprehension was included as the objective performance predictor for first language. However, performance in first language may also rely on other skills such as proficiency in grammar, vocabulary, or literature. Moreover, for Hypothesis 3, we must expect many additional factors that influence general school success, apart from mathematical thinking, reading comprehension, or scientific reasoning (e.g. motivation, working habits, or divers social factors). Such additional predictor variables were not available. Nevertheless, insufficient control of objective performance may confound the gender interaction effect and the effect of objective performance (e.g., male teachers did not evaluate boys as better than girls because they are of the same gender but because boys actually performed better than girls and the other way around). In that case, the analysis would show a spurious effect of gender interaction instead of hiding the genuine effect of it, and this was not the case in this study.

Another limitation is the internal consistency of the instruments used in this study. The reading comprehension test showed the lowest Cronbach's alpha (α= .63), which is the lowest border of acceptable internal consistency. For scientific reasoning it is possible that relatively low, but acceptable Cronbach's alpha of .69 was the result of a small number of items used to assess this skill (Cortina 1993).

The sample in this study was composed of 6th grade students from Finland. Hence, the results should not be generalized to other age groups or to educational systems in other countries, because the presence and construct of gender stereotypes and gender effects will not be the same across educational systems. In educational systems in which gender stereotypes are more present, researchers may find stronger gender effects.

All in all, the results of this study offer evidence that the teacher-student gender interaction should not be regarded as a source of possible effects on teachers' subjective evaluations of Finnish 6th graders. To this end, the outcome of the present study shows how important it is not only to investigate direct effects of gender, but also to examine how the interaction between different direct effects may influence the evaluation. Most importantly, being able to show that gender effects do not exist in classrooms could lead to a greater trust of students and their parents in the educational system: having students in the classroom who believe in the fairness and objectivity of their teachers is one step further toward a high quality education.

Acknowledgements

This research was funded by a grant from the Fonds National de la Recherche Luxembourg (ATTRACT "ASSKI21" and AFR "COLPASS"). The data collection for this study was funded by the Finnish municipality where the study was conducted.

Note

1. Please note that the term 'objective' is only used to differentiate from 'perceived' (e.g. test data versus (self-)evaluation). However, the test data is not necessarily objective, and may or may not be biased in any way.

References

Bem, S. 1981. "Gender Schema Theory: A Cognitive Account of Sex-typing." *Psychological Review* 88: 354–364.

Bennett, C. K., and 1. A. Bennett. 1994. April. "Teachers' Attributions and Beliefs in Relation to Gender and Success of Students." Paper presented at the Annual Meeting of the American Educational Research Association, New Orleans, LA. (ERIC Document Reproduction Service No. ED375 127).

Cortina, J. M. 1993. "What is Coefficient Alpha? An Examination of Theory and Applications." *Journal of Applied Psychology* 78 (1): 98–104.

Cushman, P. 2007. "The Male Teacher Shortage: Synthesis of Research and Worldwide Strategies for Addressing the Shortage." KEDI *Journal of Educational Policy* 4: 79–98.

Dee, T. S. 2006. "The Why Chromosome. How a Teacher's Gender Affects Boys and Girls." *Education Next* 6 (4): 69–75.

Dee, T. S. 2007. "Teachers and the Gender Gaps in Student Achievement." *Journal of Human Resources* 42 (3): 528–554.

Demetriou, A., M. Platsidou, A. Efklides, Y. Metallidou, and M. Shayer. 1991. "The Development of Quantitative-relational Abilities from Childhood to Adolescence: Structure, Scaling, and Individual Differences." *Learning and Instruction: The Journal of European Association for Research in Learning and Instruction* 1: 19–43.

Demetriou, A., A. Pachaury, Y. Metallidou, and S. Kazi. 1996. "Universals and Specificities in the Structure and Development of Quantitative-relational Thought: A Cross-cultural Study in Greece and India." *International Journal of Behavioral Development* 19 (2): 255–290.

Dyer, N. G., P. J. Hanges, and R. J. Hall. 2005. "Applying Multilevel Confirmatory Factor Analysis Techniques to the Study of Leadership." *The Leadership Quarterly* 16: 149–167.

FNBE. 2004. *National Core Curriculum for Basic Education 2004*. Finnish National Board of Education. http://www.oph.fi/english/sources_of_information/core_curricula_and_qualification_requirements/basic_education

Hautamäki, J., P. Arinen, S. Eronen, A. Hautamäki, S. Kupiainen, B. Lindblom, M. Niemivirta, L. Pakaslahti, P. Rantanen, and P. Scheinin. 2002. *Assessing Learning-to-learn: A Framework*. Helsinki: National Board of Education.

Hautamäki, J. 1984. *Peruskoululaisten loogisen ajattelun mittaamisesta ja esiintymisestä* [Measuring and the Occurrence of Logical Thinking Among Basic School Students]. Joensuun yliopiston yhteiskuntatieteellisiä julkaisuja 1. Joensuu: Joensuun yliopistopaino.

Holmlund, H., and K. Sund. 2006. "Is the Gender Gap in School Performance Affected by the Sex of the Teacher?" *Labour Economics* 15: 37–53.

Hopf, D., and C. Hatzichristou. 1999. "Teacher Gender–related Influences in Greek Schools." *Educational Psychology* 69 (1): 1–18.

Inhelder, B., and J. Piaget. 1958. *The Early Growth of Logic in the Child*. London: Routledge & Kegan Paul.

Jones, S. M., and K. Dindia. 2004. "A Meta-analytic Perspective on Sex Equity in the Classroom." *Review of Educational Research* 74 (4): 443–471.

Jones, M. G., and J. Wheatley. 1990. "Gender Differences in Student–teacher Interactions." *Journal of Research in Science Teaching* 27 (9): 861–874.

Jussim, L., and K. D. Harber. 2005. "Teacher Expectations and Self-fulfilling Prophecies: Knowns and Unknowns, Resolved and Unresolved Controversies." *Personality and Social Psychology Review* 9 (2): 131–155.

Kintsch, W., and T. A. van Dijk. 1978. "Towards a Model of Text Comprehension and Production." *Psychological Review* 8 (5): 363–394.

Kline, P. 1999. *The Handbook of Psychological Testing*. 2nd ed. London: Routledge.

Kupiainen, S., J. Marjanen, M.-P. Vainikainen, and J. Hautamäki. 2011. "Oppimaan oppiminen Vantaan peruskouluissa. Kolmas-, kuudes ja yhdeksäsluokkalaiset oppijoina keväällä 2010 [Learning to Learn in Vantaa Comprehensive Schools. 3rd, 6th and 9th Graders as Learners in Spring 2010]." City of Vantaa. http://www.vantaa.fi/instancedata/prime_product_julkaisu/vantaa/embeds/vantaawwwstructure/74425_web_kolmas_kuudes_yhdeksas.pdf.

Lehto, J. E., P. Scheinin, S. Kupiainen, and J. Hautamäki. 2001. "National Survey of Reading Comprehension in Finland." *Journal of Research in Reading* 24 (1): 99–110.

Lyytinen, S., and J. E. Lehto. 1998. "Hierarchy Rating as a Measure of Text Macroprocessing: Relationship with Working Memory and School Achievement." *Educational Psychology* 18 (2): 157–169.

Madon, S., L. Jussim, and J. Eccles. 1997. "In Search of the Powerful Self-fulfilling Prophecy." *Journal of Personality and Social Psychology* 72: 791–809.

Neugebauer, M., M. Helbig, and A. Landmann. 2011. "Unmasking the Myth of the Same-sex Teacher Advantage." *European Sociological Review* 27 (5): 669–689.

Nixon, L. A., and M. D. Robinson. 1999. "The Educational Attainment of Young Women: Role Model Effects of Female High School Faculty." *Demography* 36 (2): 185–194.

OECD. 2010. *PISA 2009 at a Glance*. Paris: OECD Publishing. http://dx.doi.org/10.1787/9789264095298-en.

OECD. 2013. *PISA 2012 Results: What Students Know and Can Do – Student Performance in Mathematics, Reading and Science*. Paris: OECD Publishing. http://dx.doi.org/10.1787/9789264201118-en.

OECD. 2007. *No More Failures: Ten Steps to Equity in Education*. Paris: OECD Publishing.

Parker-Price, S., and A. F. Claxton. 1996. "Teachers' Perceptions of Gender Differences in Students." Paper presented at the Annual Convention of the National Association of School Psychologists, Atlanta, GA. *Distributed by ERIC Clearinghouse*, http://www.eric.ed.gov/contentdelivery/servlet/ERICServlet?accno=ED397373.

Robst, J., J. Keil, and D. Russo. 1998. "The Effect of Gender Composition of Faculty on Student Retention. "*Economics of Education Review* 17 (4): 429–439. doi: http://dx.doi.org/10.1016/S0272-7757(97)00049-6.

Sadker, D., and K. R. Zittleman. 2005. "Closing the Gender Gap-again!" *Principal Magazine* 84: 18–22.

Sadker, D., M. Sadker, and K. R. Zittleman. 2009. *Still Failing at Fairness: How Gender Bias Cheats Girls and Boys and What We Can Do About it*. New York: Charles Scribner.

Sahlberg, P. 2011. "PISA in Finland: An Education Miracle or an Obstacle to Change?" *Centre for Education Policy Journal* 1 (3): 119–140.

Shayer, M. 1979. "Has Piaget's Construct of Formal Operational Thinking any Utility?" *British Journal of Educational Psychology* 49 (3): 265–276.

Shepardson, D. P., and E. L. Pizzini. 1992. "Gender Bias in Female Elementary Teachers' Perceptions of the Scientific Ability of Students." *Science Education* 76 (2): 147–153.

Siegle, D., and S. M. Reis. 1998. "Gender Differences in Teacher and Student Perceptions of Gifted Students' Ability and Effort." *Gifted Child Quarterly* 42 (1): 39–47.

Spilt, J. J., H. M. Y. Koomen, and S. Jak. 2012. "Are Boys Better Off With Male and Girls with Female Teachers? A Multilevel Investigation of Measurement Invariance and Gender Match in Teacher-student Relationship Quality." *Journal of School Psychology* 50: 363–378.

Sternberg, R., J. L. Castejon, M. D. Prieto, J. Hautamäki, and E. Grigorenko. 2001. "Confirmatory Factor Analysis of the Sternberg Triarchic Abilities Test in Three International Samples." *European Journal of Psychological Assessment* 17 (1): 1–16.

Tabachnick, B. G., and L. S. Fidell. 2012. *Using Multivariate Statistics* 6th ed. Boston: Pearson.

Turner, P. J., J. Gervai, and R. A. Hinde. 1995. "Gender-typing in Young Children: Preferences, Behaviour and Cultural Differences." *British Journal of Developmental Psychology* 11 (4): 323–342.

Winters, M. A., R. C. Haight, T. T. Swaim, and K. A. Pickering. 2013. "The Effect of Same-gender Teacher Assignment on Student Achievement in the Elementary and Secondary Grades: Evidence form Panel Data." *Economics of Education Review* 34: 69–75. http://dx.doi.org/10.1016/j.econedurev.2013.01.007.

Zaher, S.. 1996. "Gender and Curriculum in the School Room." *Education Canada* 36 (1): 26–29.

Index